New developments in foster care and adoption

edited by John Triseliotis

New developments in foster care and adoption

Routledge & Kegan Paul
London, Boston and Henley

First published in 1980
by Routledge & Kegan Paul Ltd
39 Store Street, London WC1E 7DD,
Broadway House, Newtown Road,
Henley-on-Thames, Oxon RG9 1EN and
9 Park Street,
Boston, Mass. 02108, USA

Set in Phototronic Plantin by
Saildean Ltd, Kingston
and printed in Great Britain by
Unwin Brothers Ltd,
Old Woking, Surrey

British Library Cataloguing in Publication Data

New developments in foster care and adoption.

1. Foster home care
2. Adoption
I. Triseliotis, John Paul
362.7'33 HV875 79-41295

ISBN 0 7100 0368 4
ISBN 0 7100 0461 3 Pbk

To Vivienne, Anna and Paul

Contents

Notes on contributors

Margaret Adcock is the Assistant Director of the Association of British Adoption and Fostering Agencies.

Jane Aldgate is a Lecturer in Applied Social Studies at the University of Oxford. Her contribution is based on her research into factors influencing the lenth of children's stay in care which was successfully submitted for a PhD at the University of Edinburgh in 1977.

Wendy Cann was, until recently, Senior Social Worker with the Guild of Service in Edinburgh. She is now Assistant Principal (Children) with Coventry Social Service Department.

Ralph F. Davidson is a Lecturer in Social Work at the University of Edinburgh, with wide experience in child care.

Nancy Hazel is a Senior Research Fellow at Kent University and Co-ordinator of the Special Family Placement Project in Kent.

Robert Holman was formerly Professor of Social Administration at Bath University and is now a community worker with the Church of England's Children's Society.

Mary James is the Director of the Independent Adoption Society in Peckham, London.

Carol Lindsay Smith set up and ran the Barnardo's New Families Project in Glasgow until June 1978. Previously she set up the first adoption advice service phone-in, in Yorkshire.

Christine S. Reeves is the Director of the National Foster Care Association.

Jane Rowe was, until recently, the Director of the Association of British Adoption and Fostering Agencies and is the author of a number of books on adoption.

Phillida Sawbridge is the Director of the Parents for Children Project in Camden, London. She was previously involved with the Adoption Resource Exchange and the 'Soul Kids' campaign.

Rosamund Thorpe was, until recently, a Lecturer in Social Work at Nottingham University and is now teaching at the University of Sydney, Australia. Her contribution is based on research in foster care which was successfully submitted for a PhD at the University of Nottingham in 1974.

John Triseliotis is the Director of Social Work Education in the Department of Social Administration at the University of Edinburgh. His writings include books on adoption, immigration and social welfare.

Acknowledgments

I am most grateful to the contributors who helped to make this book possible. Also to the *British Journal of Social Work* and *Adoption and Fostering* for giving me permission to reproduce Robert Holman's and Jane Rowe's articles respectively. Finally, I am greatly indebted to the secretaries who patiently and carefully typed from drafts and I owe my thanks to Valerie Chuter, Judy Adams, Margaret Thomson and Bette Henderson.

J. T.

Introduction

This book attempts to bring together those most recent developments in the field of foster care and adoption which are of direct relevance for social workers. They contain new thinking, fresh knowledge from research, and new concepts derived from special projects set up to find families for hard-to-place children. The last ten years have seen a number of changes in child welfare legislation and in child care practice. Some of the changes have come about as a result of greater awareness of children's rights and the need to develop policies and programmes that promote children's interests. The 1975 Children Act, in spite of some limitations, marks a significant shift towards safeguarding the child's interests. Put simply, these interests could be summarised as follows.

It is in the child's best interests to grow up in its own natural family where continuity of care can be maintained and biological and psychological bonding develop simultaneously. In the event of a child coming into public care, he has a right to expect the best possible services from agencies and professionals charged to safeguard his interests. Too often the question of rights is approached as being solely an issue between the child and its parents, instead of including also society itself and the obligations of those delegated to look after the child's welfare. It is in the child's best interests that, whenever possible, he and his parents are consulted and involved in any contemplated plans. The eventual aim of reception or committal into care is the restoration of the child to its family. However, restoration may not always be possible, either because of the parents' inability to have the child back or because the child has formed new meaningful attachments. In this event it is important that the position of the child and of the family who cares for him is made secure. Children require permanence and continuity of care and the avoidance of unnecessary disruptions in their lives to enable them to complete their developmental tasks. Finally, children need to know about their antecedents and to develop self-knowledge, which includes the family of origin.

Although the contributors to this book focus their attention on children who have already experienced a separation from their natural family, it is recognised that a child's first claim and right is to grow up with its parents. Social policies and social service programmes need to be geared towards supporting families to provide for their children's needs. Whilst the provision of broad social services for all families is recognised, it is important also to stress the need for improved specialised services and programmes for the more vulnerable. It is children from families exposed to economic and social pressures who predominate among those coming into public care. Social service policies and programmes could provide greater emotional and practical support at times of crisis to prevent possible breakdown and disruption in the children's lives. In addition, continuous and long-term services may be needed for a small group of families to alleviate chronic personal and social problems. The imaginative and flexible use of resources, such as day-care provision, home help services, peripatetic caretakers, the development of neighbourhood support systems and of other similar measures can immensely help to reduce the number of children coming into care. Half the children coming into care each year return to their families within a period of twelve months or less; but for some, once a disruption occurs, it signals the beginning of more to come.

Though it is in a child's best interests to grow up in its own natural family, the stage must also be recognised when continued perseverance in keeping the family together may prove disastrous for the child. Deciding on the right time to remove a child is not always easy, and it involves both experience and good judgment. Such decisions should be based on an accurate assessment of the emotional climate of the home and of the physical circumstances of the child. Inter-professional co-operation and good communication can be of the utmost importance. Reception or committal into care, when decided upon, should be accompanied by flexible plans which can be adapted in the light of developments and of new information. Preferably such plans should be submitted within a short period of time, to a panel which includes citizen participation. Furthermore, every child's case should be regularly reviewed by such a panel, and the professionals called upon to account for their activities and work so far. Citizen participation in review panels could ensure better plans and more informed decisions being made on behalf of children in care. Lay members from such panels who know the child may act as his advocates in disputed court proceedings.

Margaret Adcock (Chapter 1) outlines the kinds of consideration that need to be examined when assessing situations and making plans for children. Planning, as she points out, must take into account the child's current situation rather than focus on possible past mistakes and failures. Jane Aldgate (Chapter 2) highlights a number of factors, deduced from research, which appear to influence a child's length of stay in care. Children and their parents have a right to be involved and to participate in planning; and it is also in a child's interests to be helped to understand what has been happening to him and what the future holds, including the fact that the future may be uncertain. It is easier for a child to cope with reality, even painful reality, than with fantasies about his situation. The latter can become an emotionally draining experience.

Assessment and good planning should eventually lead to decisions about the type of care the child needs. The decision may be between residential care, fostering, or in certain circumstances adoption. It is increasingly recognised that residential care exhausts its possibilities within definable periods of time and that it may not always be in a child's best interests. Ralph F. Davidson (Chapter 3) discusses the practice issues surrounding the restoration of children to their families, and how to rebuild lost relationships between parents and children.

The decision to foster a child is usually made in the knowledge that about half of all long-term foster placements will fall through. The search to find ways in which to reduce this poor record has to continue, but in the meantime serious thought needs to be given to some factors which appear to mitigate against successful fostering in certain definable situations. Jane Rowe (Chapter 4) points out the importance of greater awareness of the distinctiveness of different forms of fostering in order to respond to the diverse needs of children. Robert Holman's article (Chapter 5) poses the useful concept of 'exclusive' and 'inclusive' fostering as a guide for examining foster-care relationships.

From early on there may be indications that the child's length of stay in care will be indefinite, and plans therefore have to be formulated to take this into account, with the child's best interests in mind. At this stage long-term foster care or adoption may be the appropriate form of care. Equally, though some children may start in short-term or intermediate fostering, the indications may be that in spite of all efforts, it is unlikely that the natural family will resume care in the near or even distant future. A decision will then have to be reached, before the child develops meaningful attachments in its current foster home, as to what will happen to it in the long term. Rosamund Thorpe (Chapter 6) demonstrates how children are able, when in short and medium forms of foster care, to retain their affection for and loyalties to their birth parents, especially when the latter visit frequently and where the foster family include the family of origin in their day-to-day care of the child.

Where the natural parents, for whatever reasons, begin to drop out of the child's life by paying fewer and fewer visits and not keeping promises, the child then begins to transfer its affection to its caretakers (see John Triseliotis, Chapter 9). If the current caretakers are willing and able to continue parenting the child on a long-term basis, then they may have to give up short and intermediate forms of foster care. Children who have experienced disruptions in their lives feel threatened by the frequent goings and comings of other children into the family (see John Triseliotis, Chapter 9). Where the current foster parents are unable or unwilling to continue fostering on a long-term basis, a new family will have to be found that is prepared to parent the child permanently or indefinitely. It may be that because of the parents' total disappearance or perhaps given consent, an adoptive home may have to be looked for.

When children settle into a long-term fostering arrangement and develop attachments and loyalties with the people who care for them, they and their caretakers will need protection and security of tenure. The child has already suffered disruptions, and the possibility of further changes such as return to the natural family with whom emotional relationships have been severed, sometimes for years, is unlikely to be in his best interests. An arrangement that offers children greater security need not prevent parental or sibling access.

Nancy Hazel (Chapter 7) provides a detailed discussion of the Kent Family Placement Project, which focuses on the fostering of adolescents. Christine S. Reeves (Chapter 8) points the way to a more symmetrical relationship between social workers and foster parents in the interests of children. A role needs to be found for foster parents to feel involved and sharing. John Triseliotis (Chapter 9) outlines the results of research into long-term fostering as seen through the eyes of former foster children and their caretakers.

Turning to adoption, a number of significant changes have taken place over the last ten years. Adoption is no longer a service for infants and mostly childless couples. The decrease in the number of children made available for adoption, due mostly to changing social attitudes towards unwed parenthood, helped to focus attention on children needing families and described as hard to place. Ten or fifteen years ago a hard-to-place child was one over the age of six to twelve months, whilst now it would usually be a teenager or a severely handicapped child. A number of studies (referred to in the book) show how older children with 'poor' histories and disruption in their lives can settle well in adoptive and foster homes and cope satisfactorily in adult life.

The previous policy of asking doctors or other professionals to declare children 'fit' for adoption has given way to the different practice whereby adoption workers believe that parents can be found for any child. The pace for this change in approach has mostly been set by parents' groups rather than professionals. The various programmes described in this part of the book by Phillida Sawbridge (Chapter 10), Mary James (Chapter 11) and Carol Lindsay Smith (Chapter 12) convincingly demonstrate that families can be found for even the hardest-to-place children. Successful home finding and placement often requires a special project or service being set up with definable responsibilities and objectives. Two of the projects described here also show how the voluntary and public sectors can work together in the interests of children. To expect hard-pressed social workers with many other tasks to find homes for such children seems unrealistic. Equally important is the need for arrangements that can ensure that children in one area or region are linked with available adoptive parents perhaps in a different locality. The 'Soul Kids' project in this country and similar projects elsewhere have also shown that, given resources, it is possible to find homes among ethnic and racial minorities such as West Indians, who can be encouraged to foster or adopt children from their own background. Only when such homes cannot be found is it justifiable to explore other possibilities. The policy of placing children within their own ethnic or racial groups reduces the possibility of difficulties in connection with identity problems.

The diagnostic approach to selection of adoptive parents which has been followed over many years is now giving way to group and individual approaches which help to reduce the element of authority and dependence generated by the former system. Adoption agencies are now dealing with atypical children who possibly require equally atypical families to adopt them. These parents' qualities may fall outside traditional and often biased views of what is a 'suitable' family to adopt. The different types of family described in the projects here brought qualities that seemed to respond to the needs of different children. The agency's responsibility was to recognise these qualities and help applicants through a process of social education to decide for themselves whether they were interested in a particular child or not. The inclusion in the discussions of families who have already adopted can prove illuminating and sometimes can help to allay anxieties in new applicants. Similar processes can be used in the selection of foster parents. The agency still retains responsibility to say 'No' where all the indications are that a particular placement may not be in the best interests of the child.

The process of finding families and placing children demands that considerable support be made available both to the workers and to the family. Wendy Cann (Chapter 13) discusses how the maintenance of the placement is crucial for its success. Informed support can help to reduce the amount of risk which is inherent in these arrangements.

Finally, there is the child's need for self-knowledge and information about its antecedents. Whether adopted, fostered or in step-parent relationships, children have a psychological need to know about their first parents and genealogy. Such knowledge is necessary to enable them to integrate it into their developing personalities. Where explanation and detailed information are given during childhood, it reduces fantasies about the family of origin and seems to diminish the desire to search, in adult life, either for information or for the first parent(s). In Scotland, adopted adults always had the right of access to their original birth records. Following research carried out in Scotland (see John Triseliotis, *In Search of Origins,* Routledge & Kegan Paul, 1973), the law in England and Wales has changed, allowing for retrospective access to birth records. However, a condition in the English legislation is that adopted adults seeking access should first see a counsellor attached to Register House or to any of the Social Service Departments in England and Wales. The concept of counselling is discussed by John Triseliotis (Chapter 14).

Margaret Adcock

1 Dilemmas in planning long-term care

In the last few years there has been increasing concern and controversy about the lack of constructive long-term planning for children in care. Many people, both lay and professional, have expressed the view that, far more often than social workers will acknowledge, children in care need to be given greater protection against parental rejection and ambivalence. Others have argued that it is the lack of proper help, rather than parental failure, that is the cause of so many children remaining in care, unvisited and without hope of rehabilitation with their parents.

Despite the arguments, most people would agree that happy outcomes for children in care and their parents are rarely achieved by social workers postponing decisions or waiting upon events. Not making a decision is in fact a decision in itself which can be detrimental to both children and their parents. Rowe and Lambert [1] in their study of children in care estimated that once a child had been in care for more than six months there was a 75 per cent chance of his remaining in care throughout childhood. On the basis of their study it was thought that about 6,000 children in Great Britain were waiting for permanent substitute homes. In *Who Cares?*, a report from the National Children's Bureau[2], a group of children themselves described the disadvantages, difficulties and unhappiness of a childhood spent in care without a home and family of their own. Thorpe [3] and Aldgate [4] have shown that parents suffer equally in situations of uncertainty and lack of effective social work intervention. They argue that many children in care could be returned to their parents if the parents were given help.

To meet children's needs effectively intervention must have an appropriate focus and purpose. Social workers trying to formulate this may find themselves in a dilemma, unable to decide which families need what kinds of help. They may find it hard to assess which children would benefit by attempts at rehabilitation, and which children need secure permanent substitute care, either with or without parental involvement.

Whilst it seems clear from the findings of Aldgate[4] and others that with good social work help, more children in care could be discharged to their parents and grow up in their natural families, there is also widespread agreement that some parents will never be able to meet their children's needs satisfactorily. These children are likely to need permanent substitute care and may be very damaged by intensive efforts towards rehabilitation which ultimately prove unsuccessful. Rowe and Lambert[1] found that three out of every ten children in their study had been in care on more than one occasion. A similar figure was obtained from a subsequent study by Adcock[5] of 240 children who had been in the care of one local authority for more than three months at the time of the study. It was also found in this study that one out of every ten children in residential care had had between two and six previous receptions into care. One boy had already been in care six times at sixteen months old. When the study was made, the child, then aged seven, was described as mentally unstable, unable to concentrate and generally unco-operative.

How then can social workers decide on a focus for their work which avoids increasing pain and damage to children and their parents? Examination of research findings and practice experience suggests that there is a considerable amount of knowledge already available which could help social workers in making long-term plans for children in care.

A framework for making decisions

There is a statutory obligation that in any decisions relating to a child in care first consideration must be given to promoting the long-term welfare of the child (1975 Children Act, Section 59). If this obligation is to be fulfilled, any decisions about the possibility of rehabilitation or the long-term care must be preceded by a careful assessment of the specific needs of the child in question, taking into account his age, the effect of past experiences, and any individual difficulties he may have, e.g., physical or emotional handicaps. It may then be helpful to consider six inter-related questions:

1 What kind of relationship did the child have with his parent before coming into care?
2 Are a child's parents likely to be willing to have him home? Research findings make it clear that there should be no automatic assumption that this will be the case.

3 Given help, are the parents likely to be able to care for this child and meet his needs adequately?
4 How long will it take for such help to be effective? What will happen to the child in the meantime?
5 What effect will separation have had on the parent-child relationship? (This must take account of the projected length of time during which rehabilitation is being attempted as well as the length of separation already experienced.)
6 How would the child be affected by a move from his present placement? Would the benefits of such a move outweigh any difficulties or disadvantages?

In the subsequent sections of this chapter each question is discussed in detail and research findings, pertinent to formulating answers, are considered. Two American studies, *Children Adrift in Foster Care*[6] and *A Second Chance for Families,*[7] are particularly relevant since both were projects specifically designed to reduce the length of time in care by the application of intensive social work help to parents. Other studies are mainly concerned with descriptions of the characteristics of children in care and their parents, the frequency of contact, and the relationship of these to the likely duration of care. Although it is clear from all the studies that the nature and quantity of social work help given to parents is a vital factor in reducing the length of time in care, other variables such as the age of the child, the length of separation and certain parental characteristics are shown to have an equally important influence on the situation.

The child's relationship with parents before reception into care

Some children have never experienced a relationship with a parent based on a strong mutual attachment developed over a period of time, either because they came into care when they were under a year old or because they have been looked after mainly by other people. Since there seems to be very little likelihood of establishing this kind of relationship for the first time once the child is in care, it is important to discover whether or not it has previously existed.

Heinecke and Westheimer[8] in their study *Brief Separation* showed that a mother's ability to respond appropriately to a young child depended very much on picking up cues from the child through actual physical contact and care. When the mother was separated and then later resumed contact with the child she no longer knew instinctively how to respond appropriately and had to relearn this, often very painfully. If a mother has never had an experience of a satisfying relationship with a particular child she is not likely to have much motivation to undertake the intensive visiting that is a necessary pre-requisite for getting to know the child and responding to his cues.

The DHSS *Guide to Fostering Practice*[9] comments that:

> In many ways the parents' view of themselves as parents predetermines their subsequent performance in the parental role. Parents separated from their children very early in the children's lives will have had little opportunity to build up the shared experience and learned competence that are necessary for establishing the parental role: these are also the parents most likely to leave the children in care. Where parents have established their role but later relinquish or hand over the day-to-day care of their children for prolonged periods of time, they may become less and less parents both in their own eyes and in the eyes of their children.

If, when a child comes into care, there appears to be little evidence of a strong mutual attachment with the parent, it is important to discover the reasons for this. Some parents may have little feeling or may actually be rejecting a particular child. Others may, because of personal difficulties, be incapable of leading a sufficiently stable life to enable them to care for him. Some, however, may be ignorant of their children's needs and, overcome by purely physical and material difficulties, may in desperation arrange for the child to be cared for by someone else. In these cases the provision of information or practical help may enable a parent with a high degree of motivation to begin the intensive visiting necessary to re-establish contact. Before embarking on this, however, it is necessary to discover what attachments the child has formed to the adults who are already caring for him. If these are very strong the child may be unwilling to transfer his affections and attempts at rehabilitation could prove unsuccessful.

Parental willingness to resume care

Obviously the chances of a child's returning home are very much influenced by the parents' willingness to resume care. The attitude of parents to reception into care needs to be considered first. Both Jenkins and Norman[10] and Aldgate[11] found that children tended to return to their parents more quickly if, at reception into care, parents expressed feelings of anger, were worried about their children, and felt sad. Parents who were preoccupied with themselves and immobilised by self-pity or loss were less likely to have their child return. This needs to be taken into account in planning work with parents immediately after reception into care. If intensive social work help does not produce a more active concern for the child within a few months, consideration should be given to providing the child with permanent long-term care to meet his needs for parenting and providing him with a family base.

Research findings on the discharge of children from care suggest that the age of the child at reception into care, and the length of separation from his parents, are two additional factors that need to be considered when decisions are being made. The younger the child is when he enters care and the longer he remains in care the less likely he is to return home. Fanshel[12], who studied a group of 624 children over a period of five years after their reception into care, found that half of those who were under two at reception into care were still there five years later. In comparison, only one in four of those aged between nine and twelve at reception were still in care. Of the 624 children, only a quarter were discharged in the first year. At the end of five years, 40 per cent of the children were still in care.

It should be stressed here that, even when help is provided, it appears difficult to counteract the effect of early or prolonged separation. In *Children Adrift in Foster Care*[6] intensive social work help resulted in one in every five of the children being discharged at the end of a year's project. Discharge, however, was very much related to the length of time in care. All twenty-one children who had been in care under three months returned home, but only three of the sixty-four who had been in care for at least three years did so.

The importance of parental visiting

One explanation of this problem is that parents often find it difficult to sustain visiting when a child is admitted to care at a very young age, or when the separation is a lengthy one. Visiting has been described as the key to discharge from care. Fanshel[12] found that frequent visiting had the strongest correlation of any variable with discharge. Other studies also confirm this association (see Aldgate, Chapter 2). Frequent parental visiting appears to be related to the age of the child at reception into care and the length of separation as well as to other factors such as the reasons for reception into care. In *Children Who Wait* Rowe and Lambert[1] found that only 14 per cent of children who entered care before they were two had frequent contact with their parents, and 57 per cent never saw their parents. The situation was reversed for children admitted over the age of eight. Fanshel[12] noted that almost six out of every ten children who were still in care after five years received no visits.

As might be expected, children are more likely to return home when the original problem was caused by external circumstances such as physical illness of the mother, or by their own behaviour. Aldgate[11] found that of the children in her study who returned home from care within two years, homelessness had been the primary reason for care in a third of all the cases. When, on the other hand, the problem arises from the mother's ambivalent or negative attitudes, care is often more prolonged. Both American and British studies show a link between desertion or abandonment by the mother and a greater likelihood of remaining in care.

The effect of separation on the parent-child relationship

As separation lengthens it clearly becomes a chronic and therefore more intractable problem to resolve. In considering how far social work help can be used to resolve this, it is important to examine the effect separation has already had both on the parents' willingness to resume care and on the child himself. Jenkins and Norman[10] describe three stages of reaction to separation experienced by parents as well as children. An initial feeling of loss is followed by despair, which in turn is succeeded by a feeling of detachment. At this point parents may concentrate their energies on other children, start a new cohabitation, or conceive another baby. The child in care is then excluded from the new pattern of family life; and if he does return home it is to a new situation with consequent difficulties in adjustment for everyone in the family. The Maria Colwell case was a glaring example of the effect of mutual rejection between child and a new step-parent.

This case also highlighted the reactions of the child to separation. The child in care is likely to form new attachments to the adults caring for him. The younger the child is, the more quickly he will forget his first parents. Goldstein, Freud and Solnit[13] estimated that after two weeks' separation a two-year-old finds it hard to sustain the memory of his natural parents. The work of James and Joyce Robertson[14] showed that even conscientious attempts by foster parents to keep alive the memory of the absent parent through play, photographs and discussion were not sufficient for a young child. Children aged two years or less came to regard the foster parents as their 'real' parents within two or three weeks.

As the child grows older, his memory increases and the relationship with the parents can be sustained during separation for a much longer period; and parental visiting obviously reinforces these ties. However, Goldstein, Freud and Solnit[13] showed that even for an eight-year-old child the relationship with a parent can be very damaged after more than nine months' separation. If these attachments are in turn disrupted the child will have a further experience of loss to contend with. This may make readjustment to his own family extremely difficult, especially if the parents cannot understand or cope adequately with the child's reactions. It is, therefore, important to assess the effect that separation has already had on the child and to look at the nature and the quality of his current relationship with his parents and the duration of any new attachments he has formed. In *Children Adrift in Foster Care*[6] it was found that the more emotionally attached the child was to his mother the greater was the likelihood of his return home. Conversely, only a small proportion of children with very strong attachments to foster parents returned to their natural families. The child's attitudes and expectations were also important. Significantly, fewer of the children described as reluctant to return home did so, whereas more children who expected to return home did so.

The effects of moving a child

It is clear from what has already been said that attention must be given to the effects of moving a child. The benefits of returning home or changing placements should be at least as great as, if not greater than, maintaining the *status quo.*

Tizard,[15] comparing a group of children moved from an institution to adoptive homes with a group returned from the same institution to their mothers, found that the adopted children did well subsequently. The children returned to their mother, however, made much less satisfactory progress. They did less well at school and had more emotional problems.

Rutter[16] in his own research on deprivation and separation has provided some evidence on situations in which children can be moved without undue long-term damage. This evidence very much confirms other research findings. The important factors seem to be:

1 The child has not already experienced several previous separations.
2 The child has not been unduly damaged before separation.
3 The child has had a good experience in the foster home, where the foster parents have had a clear understanding of their role.
4 The transition back home is made as easily as possible.
5 The child is not subsequently exposed to recurrent unhappy situations.
7 The child is not returned to a home where there are many other stresses.

This evidence seems to provide some explanation for Tizard's[15] findings, since the last four criteria appeared to be fulfilled in the case of the adoptive children but not for the children returned to natural parents.

Close examination will show that a great deal of information must be obtained and assessed before these apparently simple criteria can be satisfied. Moreover, it is clear that the suitability of the new home is not the first issue that has to be considered. Initially there must be an analysis of the effects of past and present experiences on the child's development, taking into account the questions and considerations discussed in this chapter. If the child has had many previous separations or been very damaged, his need for stability and continuity may outweigh all other considerations. If he has spent a lengthy period in a foster home and has come to regard the foster parents as his 'real' parents he may be overwhelmed by losing them. He may then be so difficult in his new home that he will provoke anger and rejection. If stability and continuity are not the paramount consideration, the next issue is the parent's capacity to meet the needs of this particular child, including understanding and dealing with his reactions to change. As the Colwell case and others have shown, parents may be very adequate in their care of other children but unable to cope with a difficult or hostile addition to the existing family.

Finally, it is important to make an accurate assessment of the problems within the family. Some parents may be highly motivated to resume care of their children and yet clearly have many problems to contend with. Rutter[16] suggests that a child can develop satisfactorily in a home despite one chronic stress, such as the mental illness of a parent. However, if there are two chronic problems the chances of the child's developing a subsequent psychiatric disorder are quadrupled rather than doubled. Where there are more than two stress factors, e.g., marital problems, bad housing, physical ill health, alcoholism, etc., the risks are even greater. Adcock[5] found from her study that children who had been received into care more than once had mothers who were said by their social workers to be more limited in their parenting capacity than the mothers of children with only one reception into care. The impaired development of such children emphasises the importance of not separating the past, present and future. The child's development is a continuous process and should be viewed as such when decisions are being taken.

The effectiveness of social work help in relation to discharge from care

It is clear from all the research findings that the provision of skilled and intensive social work help increases the likelihood of children's being able to return home. In *A Second Chance for Families,*[7] where social workers provided intensive help to a group of families which had been selected because rehabilitation was thought to be a possibility, significantly more children returned home by the end of the project compared with the control group where such intensive or skilled service had not been provided. Since children are unlikely to return home if their parents do not keep in touch, and since contact tends to diminish as separation becomes more prolonged, one obvious and vital social work task is to encourage visiting with a view to returning children home as soon as possible. Foster parents and residential staff may also need help in accepting and encouraging parents to visit. It does not follow, however, that parental visiting of children in care automatically leads to rehabilitation or, in view of the number of children who experience multiple receptions into care, that discharge is always in the best interest of all children. The evidence suggests that problems of recent origin, albeit severe ones, and practical material difficulties are the easiest to resolve. It is important, therefore, that social workers are clear about the problems that need to be resolved and have made some evaluation of the likelihood of achieving this before separation itself becomes the major problem.

The relationship between reasons for admission to care and subsequent discharge has already been mentioned. Fanshel[12] reported that children with mentally ill mothers were often visited frequently, but a large proportion of them nevertheless remained in care for more than five years. Adcock[5] found that while a third of children in residential care had frequent contact with a parent – a similar figure to that reported by Rowe and Lambert[1] – only one-fifth of these were expected to leave care before they were eighteen. Many of those visited frequently had mentally ill mothers. The conclusions of the project *A Second Chance for Families*[7] were that successful outcomes (when the children returned home and were also thought to be progressing satisfactorily) were associated with the following factors:

1. The parent's personal functioning was not a factor in the original need for placement.
2. The emotional climate of the home was good: the child was loved and valued and the mother was thought to have a reasonable degree of emotional maturity.
3. The most important problem was in the area of housing, financial need, or a marital one.
4. The worker's predominant role was the arrangement of other services of an immediate practical nature which would relieve personal-relationship problems.

Cases likely to be resolved were thought to be young families coping with problems of recent origin and including an adult with some motivation to deal with the situation. Families with a severe pathology, a history of long-entrenched problems or acceptance of the *status quo* were seen as less promosing.

Social work with parents and children who will remain in care

When a decision has been taken that a child should remain in care, there is still a great need for social work with the parents. The uncertainty and stress for children involved in 'tug-of-love' cases and contested adoption applications are clear evidence of the need to work with parents and substitute parents to reduce the anger and bitterness.

If parents can be involved to some degree in the decision-making and can be helped to accept the need for the child to remain in care in a particular placement, both parents and children will benefit; the parents are less likely to feel de-valued and therefore less likely to be disruptive; the children will feel more secure in a situation free of conflict.

Direct work with children is as important as help for the parents. There seems to be almost universal agreement among experienced child practitioners and writers that children need to come to terms with the feelings of uncertainty, anxiety, anger, rejection and loss engendered by reception into care and living away from their own families. If the child does not understand his situation and is torn by violent internal conflicts he is neither free to re-establish trust and confidence in his parents nor, if his own parents cannot resume care, to develop secure relationships in a new placement.

Placement in care

If the plan for a child is that he should remain in care either indefinitely or permanently, a decision then has to be made as to whether he should be placed in residential care or a foster home. Aldgate[4] found that for some parents the stigma of an institution reinforced their feelings of failure. In cases where foster parents had managed to dispel parents' fears and had established good relationships, parents said that this alternative offered a family life which was infinitely preferable to care in a children's home. Since children who come into care may remain there for lengthy periods it seems very important to consider first how far a particular placement meets their needs. Most experts would agree that children who have already suffered separation from their parents should not be exposed to further unnecessary moves. There needs to be continuity both of environment and of important relationships. Studies make it clear, however, that many children do not have this continuity, and this is harmful to their satisfactory development. Children in residential care are much more at risk of multiple placements than children in foster care. The longer the child remains in residential care the greater the risk of further moves. Fanshel[12] reported that children who were placed in residential care at reception had more placements than children placed immediately in foster homes. Adcock[5] found that half the children in residential care who had been in care for more than five years had had three or more placements compared with only one in four of the children in foster care who had been in care for the same period. Overall the foster children in her study, as well as in Aldgate's[4], had much less parental contact than the children in residential care.

In view of the number of moves experienced by some children it is not surprising that Rowe and Lambert[1] found that almost half of the children who had had four moves were said to have behaviour problems compared with almost a quarter of children who had had only one move. Most of these children were in residential care. One of the most sobering findings in Adcock's study[5] was that just under half of the children in residential care were said to need foster homes, but over half of them had behaviour problems which were thought to be an obstacle to fostering. Over half the children needing foster homes had been in care for five years or more. Foster homes had been sought unsuccessfully for some of the children in the past. In many cases a belief that a child needed to be with siblings had made earlier placement impossible. It seemed that only as children grew older and more disturbed did social workers place less stress on keeping siblings together and attach more importance to the need for substitute parents.

Separation of siblings should not be regarded as a last resort when all attempts to keep them together have failed. In some cases placements of brothers and sisters together in a substitute family may well lead to subsequent breakdown. This is usually because the new parents cannot respond equally to each child, or because the presence of a sibling impedes the healthy development of an individual child. Forbes[17] has suggested the following criteria for separation of siblings:

1 A history of having been reared in separate foster homes or having received unequal nurturing in their natural homes.
2 Marked intellectual difference.
3 Marked personality differences.
4 Situations in which an older sibling parents a younger one.
5 Cases in which one sibling may be able to separate the parents by appealing to one more than the other.

When siblings are placed apart, the separation need not be complete. Both adoptive and foster families are often very willing to help the child to keep in touch with a brother or sister in another family. It is important, however, that this is discussed from the outset with a prospective family, so that it is an integral part of their understanding of the child and his needs. The placing agency needs to demonstrate its own recognition of the importance of maintaining links by providing help with practical arrangements such as the payment of fares.

Adoption

If a child is to remain in long-term care and has not had a consistent and affectionate relationship with his parents before he came into care, or if he came into care when he was very young, and/or he then remains in care with only sporadic or no parental contact, serious consideration should be given to the possibility of adoption. This should, of course, be discussed with the parents and, if he is old enough, with the child. Raynor's study [18] on adult adoptees and their parents, and Kadushin's [19] of older children placed for adoption, suggest that a high proportion of adoptions are satisfactory for children and parents. The National Foundation for Educational Research showed [20] that the development of adopted children compares very favourably with that of non-adopted. In contrast, the fostering breakdown is estimated to be as high as 50 per cent in some areas. Foster children appear to be more at risk in terms of stability and continuity. The foster child may well have no meaningful attachment to his own family, no sense of legally belonging to his foster family, and no certainty about his future, particularly when he has to leave care. Anxiety and uncertainty are not conducive to a child's security. Neither does it seem right that a child should be deprived of an opportunity to grow up either in his own family or in a new family which he can legally call his own, unless there are very strong reasons to justify this. Rowe and Lambert [1] found that for almost 40 per cent of the children in their study neither parent was said to be opposed to adoption. Adcock [5] also found that for a similar percentage of the foster children in her study neither parent was said to be opposed to adoption.

In New York State the Family Court now reviews all cases of children who are in care for more than eighteen months and determines whether they shall be discharged to biological parents, continue in long-term agency care, be freed for adoptive placement or placed in an adoptive home. If the child is not discharged or adopted the Court reviews the case at periodic intervals. Festinger[21] studied the impact of the Court review over a period of four years. She found that of 235 children admitted to care in 1970 and first reviewed in 1973 only 21.3 per cent were still there in 1975. Half had been placed or were about to be placed for adoption, and almost three out of every ten had been or were about to be discharged to parents. Festinger concluded that the effect of the review with its requirement that the agency should make firm plans for children was that more children were discharged to natural parents, more children were placed for adoption, and fewer children remained in the limbo of long-term agency care.

Using research findings in making decisions

Social workers are often afraid that the application of research findings may lead to stereotyping and unfair decisions. If research findings are simplified into ideologies to be pursued without regard to new evidence as it becomes available, or to all the circumstances which must be considered in each individual case, this fear may well be justified.

A different approach would allay this anxiety. The circumstances of each case should be considered and compared with the relevant research findings. The parents should then be given an opportunity to discuss their child's needs and how these can best be met. Provided that the social worker maintains the focus on the welfare of the child and does not collude with parental ambivalence, it should then be possible to utilise the concern for their child that most parents feel at some level and to involve them in making realistic long-term plans.

Research findings provide a yardstick against which patterns of behaviour, actions and relationships can be measured, as opposed to being assessed in a vacuum or on a purely value basis. If a social worker has to provide good evidence to justify a decision which does not accord with conclusions derived from studies of other similar cases, there is likely to be a much closer examination of the individual case. This approach should help to extend our knowledge and provide a firmer basis for planning and decision making. All the evidence suggests that at present too many children in care suffer from a lack of planning or hasty decisions made to resolve an immediate crisis. A more careful and scientific appraisal of all the factors in each situation will surely result in greater security and happiness for many more children and their parents.

References

1 J. Rowe and L. Lambert, *Children Who Wait,* ABAFA, 1973

2 R. Page and G.A. Clark, *Who Cares?* National Children's Bureau, 1977.

3 R. Thorpe, 'Mum and Mrs So and So', *Social Work Today,* vol. 4, no. 22, 1974 ('See also Chapter 6'); 'The Natural Parent Group', *Social Work Today,* vol. 6, no. 13, 1975.

4 J. Aldgate, 'Returning Home - Working with Parents and Children', paper given at BASW conference, 1976. (See also Chapter 2 in this book.)

5 M. Adcock, 'Children in Long-Term Care', unpublished study of the children in the long-term care of one local authority, 1976.

6 E. Sherman, R. Neuman and A. Shyne, *Children Adrift in Foster Care: A study of Alternative Approaches,* Child Welfare League of America, 1973.

7 M. Jones, R. Neuman and A. Shyne, *A Second Chance for Families: Evaluation of a Programme to Reduce Foster Care,* Child Welfare League of America, 1976.

8 C. Heinecke and I. Westheimer, *Brief Separation,* Longmans, 1965.

9 Department of Health and Social Security, *Guide to Fostering Practice,* HMSO, 1976.

10 S. Jenkins and E. Norman, *Filial Deprivation and Foster Care,* Columbia University Press, New York, 1972.

11 J. Aldgate, see Chapter 2 in this book.

12 D. Fanshel, 'Status Changes of Children in Foster Care', *Child Welfare,* vol. 55, no. 3, 1976.

13 J. Goldstein, A. Freud and A.J. Solnit, *Beyond the Best Interests of the Child,* The Free Press, New York, 1973.

14 J. Robertson and J. Robertson, 'The Psychological Parent,' *Adoption and Fostering,* 87, no. 1, 1977.

15 B. Tizard, *Adoption - a Second Chance,* Open Books, London, 1977.

16 M. Rutter, 'Are Mothers Necessary?' *Listener,* 8 October 1976.

17 L. Forbes, 'Obstacles to Placement', *Adoption and Fostering,* 90, no. 4, 1977.

18 L. Raynor, 'Twenty-One Plus and Adopted', *Adoption and Fostering,* 87, no. 1, 1977.

19 A. Kadushin, *Adopting Older Children,* Columbia University Press, New York, 1970.

20 J. Seglow, M. L. Kellmer-Pringle and P. Wedge, *Growing up Adopted,* National Foundation for Educational Research in England and Wales, 1972.

21 T. B. Festinger, 'The Impact of the New York Court Review of Children in Foster Care', *Child Welfare,* vol. 55, no. 8, 1976.

Jane Aldgate

2 Identification of factors influencing children's length of stay in care

The timing of the exit from voluntary authority care has assumed particular importance since the implementation of the 1975 Children Act. With precedence given to the welfare of the child over the needs of significant adults in his life, the reception of children into care has new implications. Stevenson[1] and Jehu[2] would argue that this event was always important, but its status in legislation has never been so explicit. Since a child's length of stay in care may be a factor to be considered in deciding his future, the onus will lie heavily on social workers to be very sure of both the advisability and the purpose of reception into care. The new Act may have the desirable effect of encouraging social workers into assertive activity to ensure that children are returned to their parents as soon as possible or that, where they do remain in care, this is by design and not default.

Much of this chapter is based on the findings of a research study into factors influencing the length of children's stay in local authority care which was undertaken in the early 1970s in Scotland.[3] Briefly, the aim of the study was to look at factors which contributed to the length of time the children of around 200 families remained in long-term care (defined as at least three months) in two local authorities. The sample of families was confined to those who had been received into care voluntarily, with the exception of some situations where parents had been prosecuted for neglect. The study attempted to compare retrospectively two groups of families, one where children were in care at the time of the study and a second where families had been reunited.

Parents, foster parents, house parents and social workers were asked to give their views. Unfortunately, only sixty parents could be traced to participate in the study, but sixty-seven foster homes and thirty-five children's Homes were visited, and twenty-eight social workers filled in written questionnaires. Several major factors emerged as significant in influencing the return of children from care.

Children seemed to have most chance of return when they were received into care from two-parent families who were living in stable accommodation, or from one-parent families headed by their mother following marital breakdown. Most at risk to long-term care were young single-parent families and one-parent families headed by fathers following the desertion of the mother. The reason for care itself influenced the outcome. There was widespread poverty among the study families, so it was hardly surprising that eviction accounted for over one third of the receptions into care. Where the main cause of eviction was financial hardship, with practical support parents were able to find new accommodation and reunite the family. Children who had been received into care because of their mother's death, desertion or long-term psychiatric illness were far more vulnerable to a lengthy separation.

It was clear that reception into care was a time of abnormality, and parents' involvement at this stage did not contribute significantly to return from care. By contrast, parents' involvement with their children during the placement was a very significant factor in influencing return. This contact was in itself dependent on several other factors like the attitude of caretakers, the distance between the parental and substitute home, the reactions of children, and the encouragement given to parents by social workers early in the placement. Social work activity, whether in the form of general encouragement, practical support or more intensive problem-solving help with emotional difficulties had a significant effect on return from care. Perhaps not surprisingly in view of the widespread poverty, practical support in terms of cash or in kind was seen as the most useful form of intervention by both social workers and parents. A common feature among children in long-term care was the passive attitude of their social workers towards any plans for either rehabilitation or alternatives.

Finally, the length of time children were in care affected contact with their parents and their social workers, and influenced their chances of return. Contact declined substantially after two years in care: social workers became less enthusiastic about encouraging parents to maintain contact, while caretakers grew increasingly anxious to assimilate children into their own family. The result of this was that the longer children remained in care the less likely they were to return home.

The experience of reception into care

Apart from the identification of factors influencing children's length of stay in care, much of the study material came from recording the experiences of parents, caretakers and social workers.

The sixty parents who were interviewed were individuals who brought a wide range of opinions on their experiences. On one major point, however, they were unanimous: that reception into care, keeping in touch with their children and getting them back home, was a traumatic and painful process. There are several explanations for this.

Despite changing patterns of family life and the often underestimated fragility of the nuclear family, our society still places considerable value on successful child rearing. In asking for help outside the family, even the most able parents are seen as failures in their own eyes and in the eyes of the community at large, because other families, similarly incapacitated, manage to contain the problem within their ranks. Parents in these families are in danger of being labelled 'irresponsible' or 'inadequate', and most of them will feel stigmatised as failed parents.

Reception into care brings other losses of status and power. Parents hand over to those who are looking after him the day-to-day decisions about what a child eats, where he plays and sleeps. Inevitably, this change of environment changes the relationship between the child and his natural family. As Stevenson suggested, at reception into care, 'we are breaking prematurely the life-line of the developing child'.[4] Most parents whose children come into care hope that this will be a temporary break and that their children will return home quickly, but sometimes reception into care may mark a more serious rift caused by deep-seated parental rejection. In these cases, all concerned may have to accept that an alternative life-line is the only way to promote the child's well-being.

The way in which parents and children react to initial separation may be the first significant factor which influences the outcome of care. We know that a child's reaction to reception into care is influenced by his stage of development and his previous life experiences. Children will express a range of emotions at separation but generally these will include elements of protest, despair and detachment. It is well documented that children need help to express and come to terms with the loss of their family in order to preserve their sense of well-being.[5] We are also aware that even the most secure child experiences some trauma on being separated from his parents, but that this trauma can be lessened if continuity between past, present and future is preserved. It is only recently that there has been any suggestion that parents go through similar experiences on separation from their chhildren. They too need to come to terms with this filial deprivation. If they do not, then there is a danger that, in the rehabilitation process, a child will return to a situation of unresolved parental conflicts which can only do him harm.

Without exception, reception into care was a very painful event for the sixty study parents. Even after several years, parents were able to recall clearly the details of the day their children went away. Reactions varied. Some felt relieved that a solution had been found to their child care problems; some were very distressed, while others blamed social workers, relatives or themselves for their children's departure. For many, feelings were ambivalent: relief tinged with guilt, or anger muted by an acute sense of loss. Although no parent's total experience of filial deprivation was identical with that of another, all the study parents had one major preoccupation: concern about their children's welfare. They were very anxious to know where their children would be eating, sleeping and living. Sometimes parents were able to translate their anxiety into action by going with their children to reassure themselves that all was well, but it was more common for them to be overwhelmed by an acute sense of anxiety which inhibited their participation.

> *A father:* Nobody knows how you feel until the bairns go away. You realise then what a mess you have made of everything. I felt that bad I could not go and see them – the shame of seeing my bairns in a home.

Preparation for care

For a fortunate minority of families, the trauma of reception into care had been significantly eased by pre-placement visits to caretakers' homes. These were valuable in different ways. They provided reassurance for parents that children's physical needs were being adequately met, and for children that they had not been rejected by their parents. The giving of information on children's habits made parents feel valued and wanted. Meeting caretakers dispelled any fantasies that children's affections were likely to be stolen away. It was easier to prepare children for separation if parents could describe where they were going to stay, and it was easier for parents to prepare themselves for separation and reduce their anxiety about a first meeting after the placement had been made.

> *A father who had been deserted:* I think going with the children to see the home beforehand made them feel they weren't just being dumped and left. They knew where they were going and that I would come back and see them.

Some time ago, an American writer said 'to prepare parent and child for their separation is not only a humane procedure but is also a sound one'.[6] It is obviously humane because it is likely to reduce separation anxieties for both parents and children; but pre-placement work with families is also a sound investment for several reasons. It allows social workers and families to get to know each other, so that everyone can be quite certain of the purpose of reception into care. Indeed, it is difficult to know how an appropriate placement can be found for a child without such knowledge. It is imperative to know at this stage how parents have coped in the past with a similar crisis, how complex are the problems they are facing at present, what are their plans for the child's return, whether or not these plans are realistic and what support parents will need during the time their children are in care. Time before reception into care also gives social workers the opportunity to record as much detailed information as possible about the child's extended family and social network which will help him build a clear self-image if the placement becomes long-term. Above all, preparation for care maximises the chances of parental involvement from the very start. If parents are excluded from plans at this stage, as Mapstone warns,[7] they may well drop out of the placement altogether or persist in adopting a negative attitude which causes a lot of trouble for all concerned.

These reasons provide cogent arguments why work towards rehabilitation should begin before reception into care. Careful preparation of parents and children for separation is often the first significant step in bringing about their eventual reunion. Sometimes it is argued that preparation for care is impossible because reception into care is used only as a last resort when all attempts to prevent family breakdown have failed. It seems very appropriate that such a strong emphasis should be placed on prevention, but this process can only be enhanced by discussions with the family about just what reception into care will mean for them. It may also be a fallacy that reception into care always occurs in a crisis for, in the study, almost three-quarters of the families had been known to social workers as current clients for over a month before reception into care took place. Even if reception into care is unexpected, it is only common sense that families be given the opportunity to make some preparations for separation.

Sometimes social workers may shy away from planned receptions into care because of their own feelings about this event. Dealing with children's distress is no less painful for social workers than for anyone else. Some workers may blame themselves for the separation of parents and children, and may feel angry that they had been unable to keep families together. Such feelings are very understandable, but they must be acknowledged and accepted before help can be offered to families. As one publication has suggested, it may be necessary to realise that pain, guilt and uncertainty are an inevitable part of work in child care.[8]

Acceptance of parents' limitations

There is another problem. Faced with parents whose child care standards leave much to be desired or those who have placed their children at risk, it is very easy to identify only with the needs of the children and give little thought to the problems which parents may be facing. As with children, there is no such thing as a typical parent. Social workers are dealing with parents at every level of development, so before work can begin the question has to be asked, what kind of parent: mature, immature, aggressive, depressed, anxious, articulate or inarticulate? Acceptance of parental limitations from the outset is the only foundation from which to work towards rehabilitation. Parents in the study were well aware of what social workers thought of them and saw through any mask of superficial acceptance.

Acceptance of parental limitations also involves recognition that, at reception into care, most parents will be functioning well below their normal capacity. Despite this, some will be able to summon up enough strength to take their children into care, but others will feel unable to hand them over personally to foster parents or residential staff. It should not be assumed that this lack of parental involvement at reception into care automatically signifies lack of concern. Certainly the evidence from the study would point to the contrary; those who were unable to participate were just as concerned as others but needed acceptance of their limitations and reassurance from social workers that their role, however small, was valued. If parents think that, from the start, social workers truly understand them, they will be more willing to establish a positive working alliance, as the following examples show. One study mother described how her social worker had accepted she could not face the parting from her children but had maximised her sense of involvement by getting her to write a list of the children's favourite foods and other idiosyncrasies. A second example came from a father who had also been unable to face separation, but who had received praise from the social worker in the way he had prepared his children for departure.

Further evidence of how reception into care can distort parental functioning came from the fact that there was no statistical relationship in the study between parental participation at reception into care and return from care. This suggests that parents' involvement at reception into care is an unsound basis from which to make any prediction about the outcome of the placement. It would seem to be far more important to rest evidence of parental capabilities on knowledge of individual personality and family functioning prior to reception into care and over a longer period of time. Recognition should be given to the fact that even where the prognosis for rehabilitation seems poor, parents may have the potential for change during the placement and, if offered appropriate social work activity, may use the time away from their children as a period of growth.

Although it is clearly wrong to label parents on the basis of their behaviour at reception into care, the degree to which they are able to participate at this time may give social workers valuable clues about the type of social work help parents will need. Those parents who have enough strength to face involvement at reception into care may also be those who can keep in contact with their children with the minimum of social work activity. By contrast, parents who seem very depressed and passive at reception into care are sometimes those whose self-esteem is so low that they need active encouragement from the professionals before they can recognise their own worth. Research evidence to support this conclusion comes from the present study and from the filial deprivation research by Jenkins and Norman,[9] who found that parents who were able to externalise emotions at reception into care were more able to effect rehabilitation than those who internalised emotions.

Contact between parents and children and its relationship to return

Reception into care is only the beginning. Once the placement has been made, patterns of contact between parents and children need to be established. This must be done as soon as possible, as the maintenance of contact by parents seems to be a very significant factor in influencing the return of children from care. In the study, where children returned there had been some contact between at least one parent and child in 90 per cent of cases, and contact monthly or more frequently in just under half the cases. A similar finding with a much larger sample came from Fanshel's longitudinal study at Columbia University, which demonstrated conclusively 'the centrality of parental visiting in the outcome of care'. [10]

Although contact seems so important, it may be completely unrealistic to expect parents to maintain frequent contact over long periods of time. Both the American and the Scottish studies found a serious decline in contact after the first two years in care. This was also matched in both studies by a significant drop in return after the two-year period. In the Scottish study, over 90 per cent of families who were reunited were reunited within two years of the children's admission to care. The decline in contact over time may well be accounted for by a natural loosening of filial bonds between parent and child, hastened on in some cases by the deterrents to contact which will be discussed later in the chapter. There will, of course, be exceptions to the rule; but, in general, it seems that if children are to return home they must do so fairly quickly, and during the period they are in care must retain meaningful contact with their parents.

The reason why contact has such a significant effect on rehabilitation is related directly to the many benefits it brings for parents and children in care. Contact reassures the child that he has not been rejected at separation and helps him to feel secure within the placement. If a child sees his parents regularly, he will have an increased understanding of why he cannot live at home; this helps to minimise fears of rejection. Being able to face reality may also prevent a child's idealisation of his parents and his retreat into a fantasy world. Writers like McIntyre [11] have emphasised how contact with parents can help to build up a child's realistic self-image. Research evidence from Weinstein and others,[12] although on a small scale, confirms the association between the well-being of children in care and frequent contact from parents. Finally, through increased understanding of the placement and the recognition that his parents have not deserted him, when the time comes for a child to return home he will be able to look forward to this without fear of further rejection.

Contact may also be a positive experience for parents. Seeing children frequently helps caretakers distinguish between parenting the child and wishing to become the child's parents, thereby reinforcing the role of the natural parents. Such role clarity allows the child to adjust to the placement and prevents his exposure to a potential conflict of loyalties between two rival sets of 'parents'.

Difficulties in maintaining contact

Recognition of the value of parental contact also acknowledges potential difficulties. Some parents fail to keep appointments to visit their children, or visit on impulse. Some act aggressively towards caretakers, criticising what they do. Others may over-indulge children with unrealistic promises and excessive gifts. In extreme cases, parents may go all out to destroy the placement.

Writers have used a dysfunctional and sociological approach to explain this behaviour. Kline and Overstreet[13] believe that the person who does not have sufficiently good parenting in his own childhood to enable him to achieve adequate parenthood himself may find it particularly hard to accept his children's reception into care. It could be argued that any parent who experiences guilt and a sense of failure on reception into care could react in the same way. By contrast, Haggstrom[14] argues that the cause of disruptive behaviour by natural parents may be poverty rather than emotional deprivation in early childhood. Poverty cannot be understood simply in economic terms. It changes the relationship of the affected person to society and can also – although not inevitably – adversely influence their personalities. Above all, it places persons in a position of dependency which may dampen initiative or may provoke release from humiliation through aggression. Both of these approaches may be valid but, as Holman suggests, the skill of the social worker lies in being able to 'distinguish between behaviour related to early psychological disturbances and that related to a position of enforced dependency. Clearly, a wrong analysis in an attempt to treat the latter as psychological only serves to reinforce the client's sense of dependency and humiliation.'[15]

The parents of children in care are often prone to feelings of dependency. These may be assuaged if parents retain contact with their children and are reassured of their continuing importance in their children's lives. Social workers can do much to encourage parents, but their skill lies in distinguishing between those parents who will visit their children in care, no matter what, and would see the offer of encouragement and other supplementary support services as a further erosion of their responsibilities, and those whose life experiences have not equipped them to take this type of initiative. An early appraisal of parental capabilities is essential to the success of the placement. The potential for detachment in a family of four children was recognised by the social worker and it was dealt with by a more directive approach. The father described the process: 'If Mrs Gordon hadn't pushed us a bit, I don't think we would have got the bairns back so soon but I'm glad we did, they were beginning to be like strangers.'

Caretakers' attitude to contact

Besides recognising the effect which previous life experiences and reception into care itself may have on families, social workers must also be sensitive to other dangers likely to cause a decline in contact between children in care and their parents. One of the most significant factors which influenced the study parents was the attitude of caretakers towards them. First impressions counted for a great deal. Parents' sense of self-esteem was often so low at the beginning of a placement that an unwelcome atmosphere or small gestures of thoughtlessness were interpreted as rejection. One father described how on the evening of his children's departure he had washed, ironed and sorted out his children's clothes. On arrival at the children's Home, his carefully prepared bundles were all tipped into one box, a gesture which so incensed him that he was unable to return to the Home for some time. Other parents made remarks like 'You've go to know your place with foster parents or else they take it out on the bairns.' By contrast, a friendly welcoming atmosphere and respect for the individuality of children meant a great deal to parents as did the discovery that caretakers were ordinary folk.

> *A father:* I wasna' worried so much about the place, but the people. It's terrible to have others looking after your bairns. . . . The big thing is not to make you feel ashamed.

Parents gained considerable confidence from being allowed to participate in the placement, particularly in the early stages. Some parents were encouraged to stay for meals, while a minority were allowed to put their children to bed. These were not children's Homes with special facilities. The Home staff were simply using their existing resources in an imaginative way. There is obviously scope for the extension of such schemes. Nowadays, the parents of young children in hospital are often given the opportunity to spend extensive periods of time in the wards. Similar participating by the parents of children who are in care could do much to reduce separation, anxieties, increase parental confidence and establish frequent contact as a norm of the placement.

Although the introduction of such a scheme into foster homes would represent a more obvious intrusion into personal privacy, there is no reason why it could not be successful, as one or two examples from the study showed. In one foster home a mother was encouraged to spend every Saturday in the foster home with her child, a venture which owed its success to the attitude of the foster parents who saw the inclusion of the mother as an essential part of the rehabilitation programme. Unfortunately, this sort of working relationship between foster homes and parents was unusual: for the most part both foster parents and parents alike felt uncomfortable about parental visits. Discomfort stemmed from parents being placed in direct competition with foster parents, having nowhere to see their children alone, and being made to feel their parental skills were being scrutinised.

Some foster parents contributed to the confusion because they seemed uncertain about their role, a confusion reflected in both research and literature.[16] Wishing to see themselves as exclusively the children's parents, these foster parents had difficulty in coming face to face with natural parents whom they compared unfavourably with themselves. It was significant that the placements which were mutually acceptable for both foster and natural families were those where foster parents gained their satisfaction from a job well done rather than from seeing the child become part of their own family. This finding has implications for the continuing development of more 'professional' foster care. Foster parents likely to contribute most to any rehabilitation programme are those who see themselves as professionals, a role which will be explicit if they receive adequate remuneration for their activities.

The reactions of children

Apart from the facilities and attitudes presented by caretakers, a second pressure contributed significantly to the alienation of parents from their children. This was children's reactions to parental visits early in the placement. The danger point often occurred around the third or fourth visit. Children could not win: if they displayed indifference to the parent this was interpreted as strong rejection, or if they showed continuing distress this increased parents' sense of guilt. Sometimes caretakers seemed to have little understanding of children's normal reactions to separation and colluded with parents' anguish by telling them, 'He only cries when you come to see him'. Faced with such an unwelcome burden of responsibility it was little wonder that parents agreed to stop visiting in order to allow the child to 'settle'. This philosophy affected all children negatively but was especially dangerous for the very young. Deprived of frequent contact the under-fives became detached from their parents remarkably quickly.

Parental contact and the social worker

The key factor in establishing and maintaining successful contact between natural families and children in care is undoubtedly the social worker. He has a dual role: to increase understanding of children's reactions to separation in both parents and caretakers, and to encourage and support them to deal with any difficulties. The cases in the study where successful contact was maintained were those where social workers, parents and caretakers are working as a team; those which failed were where parents seemed to be alone against all the professionals.

Sometimes social workers argue that they know what their role should be in the rehabilitation process but that they do not have time or resources to translate their ideals into reality. One answer to the problem might be to make more use of community-based resources to supplement social work activity. Many of the study parents had to make long, arduous and expensive journeys to visit their children. The negotiation of complex travel again demands an initiative which some natural parents may not possess, while dependency on public transport may in itself be an inhibiting factor. Some parents would have welcomed the offer of transport from social workers but others thought social worker involvement only exacerbated the erosion of their independency. Parents were, however, willing to accept help from friends and might well have been willing to accept transport from volunteers. This would not have had the stigma of statutory services and would have been an effective way of supplementing scarce social work resources. It is vital that all resources are used to prevent parents drifting out of their children's lives at an early stage, because once contact has lapsed, the problems of its renewal become extremely difficult.

The renewal of contact

In some cases it was easy enough for social workers to see that the renewal of contact was in the interest of both children and parents; but dilemmas occurred where social workers were faced with cases where parents had been absent for a considerable time. Here, the benefits may not seem so clear. At best, a child will shows some signs of disturbance or at worst parents may snatch him back from what has become the child's primary home. The positive extension of authority under the 1975 Children Act has legislated against potential 'tugs-of-love'. Furthermore, if the evidence from the study is at all representative, it may be very wrong to assume that the majority of parents will be destructive. In cases where study parents had been traced by social workers after an absence of several years, parents displayed an impressive ability to distinguish between their own desire for some links with the children and their awareness that children had transferred their primary affection to foster families. None of the study parents would have considered reclaiming their children in these circumstances.

It was clear that the study natural parents whose contact with children had lapsed did not experience filial detachment to the extent that they either wanted or were able to sever emotional links with their children. It could be argued that they are not representative of natural parents who lose contact with their children in care. As Meir suggests, there may be some individuals who have 'an irreversible incapacity to love'[17] and can only be parents in a biological sense. Adoption would seem to be appropriate legal acknowledgment that a child's substitute home has become his real home in these cases. But, additionally, there is surely a place for the type of custodianship proposed by the 1975 Act, or even an open adoption which provides security for the child but does not sever all bonds with his natural family. Creating situations in which children feel free to relate both to their natural and psychological parents is obviously more complex than the tidy sense of possession which comes from an 'exclusive' model of foster or adoptive care in which there is no place for the natural parent. There is, however, no empirical evidence to disprove the intrinsic merit of an 'inclusive' model. It would be argued that reluctance to promote inclusive alternative care may stem from the inability of adults to tolerate its complexity rather than from evidence that multiple relationships necessarily are harmful to the children.

Some parents will see themselves as full partners in the placement and will need the minimum of services and support. Others, whose own needs and problems prevent them from looking to those of their children, may need considerable help in resolving problems that caused reception into care. These parents may also be the ones who need constant help in maintaining contact with their children. Apart from the choice of appropriate activity, the social worker also has an overall responsibility to act as co-ordinator for all the services a child and his family needs and to ensure that adequate communication is maintained between the natural family, the child, the caretaker and other professionals. This range of tasks demands from social workers multiple skills. As Rowe and Lambert suggest, 'decisions about the future of children are among the most difficult confronting social workers',[18] and call for considerable support from colleagues. Sometimes when problems seem legion, it may be unrealistic and uneconomic to expect all the tasks to be accomplished successfully by one person, for if the worker feels overwhelmed by conflicting pressures he may well retreat into inactivity. In complex cases, therefore, the use of two or more workers plus a variety of supplementary resources may prove far more effective in the long erm than allowing one worker to struggle on alone.

In all circumstances, the essence of the social work task will be purposeful activity based on sound planning and decision-making. A fundamental part of the plan will be to assess the extent to which parents are capable of establishing and maintaining their parental role.

In order to put plans into action social workers need time and commitment to the task. As Parker pointed out, time for planning must be seen as an essential part of social work acitivity, even if this means an altering of priorities. [19]

There are at least three ways in which the scarce resources of social workers can be used most effectively. The first of these is effective caseload management. Brown [20] describes a successful experiment to increase efficiency in one local authority, which resulted in a reduction of the numbers of children remaining in long-term care. A second way in which existing services could be used more constructively is by improving statutory reviews of children in care. These could act as good mechanisms for forward planning, with the strengths of children and parents being stressed rather than their weaknesses. Reviews could also be more effective if they included the natural family, children and the caretakers. After all, they are the very people for whom plans are being made.

A third way in which social workers may increase their efficiency is to adopt a task-centred approach towards natural parents. Adcock [21] suggests a range of realistic ways in which such an approach could be used. It could involve the setting up of a programme of intensive contact and activity between child and parent and worker and parent, especially in the early stages. One important finding from the study was that the frequency of contact between parents and social workers contributed significantly to the rehabilitation process. [22] Over half the families in the study whose children had returned home had seen social workers at least once a month, compared with just over one sixth of those whose children were currently in care. Furthermore, home visits were very important, being viewed as an expression of social worker concern. Parental desire to have the right to make decisions went hand-in-hand with their need to see themselves as partners in the placement. Resentment arose in cases where children were moved from one Home to another without parents having been consulted, and where social workers seemed to be exclusively child-centred and were insensitive to the needs of parents. Such insensitivity only served to reinforce parents' feeling of worthlessness. By contrast, parents who were most open to help from social workers were those who felt recognised as individuals and had a sense of being truly understood.

Social workers may sometimes feel that clients do not understand the finite nature of agency resources, but there was little evidence to this effect in the study. Parents were well aware that agency resources set a limit on the help social workers could offer. These limitations were acceptable, provided social workers were honest with them. What did anger clients was the worker who made promises of help he could not keep.

Identifiable factors influencing return

It can be seen that there are several important factors which influence children's length of stay in care. The circumstances which have led to care may in themselves indicate the outcome. The maintenance of frequent contact between parents and children is an essential part of successful rehabilitation. In turn, this contact will be influenced by the attitude of caretakers, the reactions of children, and the degree to which parents are able to overcome any stigmatisation which may result from children being received into care. But perhaps the most influential factor which inter-relates with all the others is the role of the social worker. Of paramount importance is the social worker's recognition of the impact reception into care can have upon families, and of the need to offer parents encouragement to maintain contact with children early in the placement. Such an approach demands assertive activity based on accurate empathy and perception of parental capabilities. In the majority of cases this will bring positive responses and, for many families, will contribute significantly to the process of rehabilitation.

It would, however, be very wrong to assume that efforts should be concentrated solely on families for whom rehabilitation seems likely. There are considerable dangers in such an approach, because it denies the substantial effect that social work activity may have on a child's well-being by increasing the participation of parents who are unable to take initiatives themselves. The wish to protect children from distress or the fear that increasing parental contact may disrupt a long-term placement cannot be condoned as excuses for inactivity. Nor can it be assumed that all parents who have lost contact with their children are too detached or deprived to participate constructively in the placement. It is natural to hope that most children will return to their parents, but the social work task must involve consideration of constructive alternatives so that children do not drift into unplanned long-term care. This does not mean that options have to be rigid or limited. Plans should be made along a continuum which includes at the one end adoption and at the other rehabilitation, but also embraces imaginative part-time parenting or permanent inclusive long-term care.

Alternatives to rehabilitation do not preclude continuing contact between the child and his natural family where this is acceptable to all concerned; but any plans for return or otherwise must acknowledge there is a finite time scale for decision-making, caused by children's continuous development and need to put down roots.

For families who have the good fortune to be reunited, there is a great temptation for social workers to heave a sigh of relief and press on to the next case, without realising that the return home can be as traumatic as the separation which led to reception into care. Preparation and assessment of the situation when a child returns after a long absence is vital because both child and parent will have undergone changes. Inevitably, the child will have assimilated some of the values of his substitute home and, in the meantime, his parents may well have separated and re-established themselves with different partners, so that a child returns to a totally new family. Furthermore, to return home means loss and change no less than reception into care, and it is the social worker's task to help both the child and the parent come to terms with their feelings if rehabilitation is to be completely satisfactory.

Both children and parents may express considerable ambivalence and anxiety about the impending change. Kline and Overstreet believe that the further separation a child experiences on returning to his parents confronts him with 'the reawakening of early separation anxieties superimposed on current stress'.[23] Although a child's first reaction on hearing that he is to return is generally one of delight, this may be followed by strong feelings of anger towards parents who have placed him in care, and depression from guilt about the anger. A child may also regret leaving the substitute family to whom he has become attached.

Parents are no more immune to painful emotions. For many, the prospect of reunion with their children may awaken old feelings of guilt and inadequacy. At the point of return, some of the study parents feared their children would be like strangers, while others expressed resentment in giving up new-found freedom. 'We weren't really looking forward to their return. Well, that's not really true – but we knew it would be hard for us having them back after just the two of us'. Other parents found it hurtful that children might wish to retain links with their substitute homes. Some had magical expectations that children would return home to live happily ever after with their time in care seen only as a bad dream, best forgotten.

Conclusion: the social work task

In conclusion, three main factors stand out as being influential on children's length of stay in care: the circumstances which led to care, the maintenance of frequent contact between parents and children, and purposeful social work activity. Of these three, social work activity is the one which can affect the others most to bring about successful rehabilitation. The task facing social workers is difficult but not insuperable and may be well defined. There is a need for planning and decision-making which takes account of the inevitable detachment between parent and child which will result over time. Acceptance of parental limitations, accurate empathy and assertive encouragement seem to be vital components of successful contact between parents and children, along with appropriate support to caretakers. To complete the task, resources will have to be maximised to the limit and priorities altered; but the social worker's primary tool will continue to be the use of himself in providing support and services. Although plans and decisions based on accurate, detailed and relevant information are essential, workers must continue to be sensitive to the needs of individuals. In working towards rehabilitation with the families of children in care, social workers might like to think of the words of Leo Tolstoy: 'All happy families are alike, but an unhappy family is unhappy after its own fashion.'

References

1 O. Stevenson, 'Reception Into Care: Its Meaning for all Concerned', *Case Conference,* vol. 10, no. 4, 1963; also in R. J. N. Tod (ed.), *Children in Care,* Longmans, 1968.

2 D. Jehu, *Casework Before Admission to Care,* Tavistock Publications, 1963.

3 Full details of the study can be found in 'Identification of Factors Influencing Children's Length of Stay in Care' unpublished PhD thesis, University of Edinburgh, 1977. (See Chapter 2 in this book.)

4 Stevenson, op. cit., p. 12.

5 See for example N. Littner, *Some Traumatic Effects of Separation and*

Placement, Child Welfare League of America, 1965. Also J. Parfit, *The Community's Children,* Longmans, 1967, pp. 36-40.

6 E. Glickman, *Child Placement Through Clinically Oriented Casework,* Columbia University Press, 1957, p. 102.

7 E. Mapstone, 'Social Work with the Parents of Children in Foster Care', in R. J. N. Tod, *Social Work in Foster Care,* Longmans, 1971, p. 99.

8 Association of British Adoption Agencies, 'Ending the Waiting - Which Children and What Plan?' ABAA, 1975, p. 2

9 S. Jenkins and E. Norman, *Filial Deprivation and Foster Care,* Columbia University Press, New York, 1972, p. 339.

10 D. Fanshel, 'Parental Visiting of Children in Foster Care: Key to Discharge?', *Social Services Review,* vol. 49, no. 4, 1975, p. 502.

11 J. M. McIntyre, 'Adolescence Identity and Foster Family Care,' *Children,* vol. 17, no. 6, 1970, p. 215. See also E. Cowan and E. Stout, (1939) 'A Comparative Study of the Adjustment made by Foster Children after Complete and Partial Breaks in Continuity of Home Environment', *American Journal of Orthopsychiatry,* vol. 9, no. 2, 1970, pp. 338.

12 E. Weinstein, *The Self Image of the Foster Child,* Russell Sage Foundation, 1960. See also R. Thorpe, 'The Social and Psychological Situation of the Long Term Foster Child with Regard to His Natural Parents', PhD thesis, University of Nottingham, 1974.

13 D. Kline and H. M. F. Overstreet, *Foster Care of Children - Nurture and Treatment,* Columbia University Press, New York, 1972, p. 179.

14 W. Haggstrom, 'The Power of the Poor' in F. Riesman (ed.), *Mental Health of the Poor,* Collier-MacMillan, 1964

15 R. Holman, 'Poverty and Social Work' in N. Drucker (ed.), *In Cash or In Kind,* Department of Social Administration, Edinburgh, 1974.

16 See, for example, R. Holman, Chapter 5 in this book; J. Rowe, 'Fostering in the 1970s and Beyond', Chapter 4 in this book.

17 E. T. Meir, 'Reciprocities in Parent-Child and Foster Parent Relationships', *Child Welfare,* vol. 38, no. 10, 1959, p. 4.

18 J. Rowe and L. Lambert, *Children Who Wait,* 1973, p. 107.

19 R. A. Parker, 'Planning for Deprived Children', National Children's Home, 1971.

20 P. A. D. Brown, 'Caseload Management, a key to Prevention', *Adoption and Fostering,* vol. 84, no. 1, 1976, pp. 45-6.

21 M. Adcock, 'Implications of the Children Act 1975', *Adoption and Fostering,* vol. 85, no. 3, 1976, p. 87.

22 A similar finding comes from a small piece of American research. See D. Shapiro, 'Agency Investment in Foster Care, A Study', *Social Work,* vol. 17, no. 3, 1972, pp. 20-8.

23 Kline and Overstreet, op.cit., p. 288.

Ralph F. Davidson

3 Restoring children to their families

A great deal has been written about children in care and the tasks involved for a social worker in attempting to help them, their families and their substitute carers. Studies such as those by the Newsons[1] have helped us to understand the nature and importance to a young child of his experiences in his own family. Similarly Bowlby[2], the Robertsons[3] and others have helped us to understand the trauma for a young child when he is separated from his family, and the kind of substitute care that can best support and sustain him at such a time. The work of many writers such as Beedell[4] and George[5] enables us to think about the nature of the residential or foster care which the child may enter, and the opportunities and difficulties involved in such substitute care for the child, his family, the carers and the social worker. Much of this material is well known to practitioners and available to inform and sensitise our practice in receiving children into care and providing good substitute care for them. Far less attention seems to have been given, however, to the question of restoring children in care to their families.

There are so many variables involved in any discussion of working with children in care and their families that I find it difficult to know where to begin. The whole situation is considerably affected by the age of the child, the quality of his previous life experiences, particularly his family relationships, and whether the admission to care is known to be for a defined or undefined period. Some admissions to care will have been anticipated and well planned for. In other situations there may have been no preparatory work whether because of emergency factors, or because of inadequacies in professional resources, or because of a pattern of denial in the child's parental figures who are finding the prospect of the impending separation impossibly painful. Since it is not possible in a short paper to address all these variables I have chosen to concentrate on three main situations. The first of these is where admission to care has been undertaken as an essential part of the long-term maintenance of the family situation, and therefore has the eventual restoration of the child to his family planned from the start. The second situation is where the admission to care is for an indefinite period, though there are hopes that the family will come together again at a future date. The third is where one is asked to become involved with a child already in care who has little or no contact with his natural parents.

Reception into care for a defined period

In the first of these situations, though children may be coming into care for very diverse reasons, they are known to be coming for a limited period only, and the clearly recognised goal of all concerned is to ensure adequate substitute care for the children and to restore them to their family at the agreed time. It is sometimes hard for us as social workers to remember that in such situations, where we may feel no criticism of the parents, they themselves may well be feeling bereft, inadequate and guilty for failing to fulfil their parental role. Indeed, the very survival of the family unit may be much more at risk than we realise. Stevenson[6] has described the suffering involved for all concerned when a child is received into care. Bowlby[2] and the Robertsons[3] have shown how the young child will react to such suffering. Westheimer[7] has shown how similar the reaction may be for the mothers of young children, and my experience suggests that it is similar for many parents of older children too. Jenkins and Norman[8] in their study of filial loss have developed considerably our knowledge of how parents react when separated from their children, giving us a detailed picture of the complex pattern of parents' feelings during and after the reception of their children into care. In these situations the danger is that the pain and isolation of the separation become so great that the sufferer may have to withdraw from them and shut off that area of feeling. Yet if the family unit is really to continue to exist and to survive this crisis then relationships must remain alive at a feeling level.

We as social workers may have to be very active in enabling this to happen. This activity should be evident in our behaviour with the parents from the moment they approach us to request reception into care, and should take the form of encouraging them to participate as fully as is possible in the three stages of planning, reception and care itself. Exclusion from these processes will only compound their feelings of guilt and inadequacy which we have already mentioned. It is only through this active participation that we can convey to the parents our conviction about their central importance, firstly as sources of information about the needs of their child, and his likely responses to reception into care, and secondly as crucial figures of continuity and security for their child. It is only in this way that we shall communicate to the child our sensitivity to what he is undergoing, our respect for his family unit, and our commitment to its maintenance. And in this way we shall convey to the substitute carers the central role which the parents must continue to be allowed to play in their child's life.

If parental participation is to serve this essential purpose, however, it must be real participation in all three stages mentioned above. Participation does, of course, not mean the right to control decisions and actions but it does mean the right to contribute one's knowledge and skills in ways which may affect which decisions are taken, and may influence the outcome of actions. So parents must be allowed to share fully in planning into which substitute care their child should be placed. For example, a social worker might well feel that a particular foster parent, though slightly more distant, would have more to offer this child than a nearer foster parent who is also available. Yet placement with the more distant foster parent would necessitate a change of school. Only the parent can help those involved to appreciate how crucial continuity of school experiences would or would not be for this particular child at this time of stress, and to plan accordingly. And such participation by the parents in planning, though it may at times mean their facing the inadequacies of resources and lack of choice, can both help them to manage their own distress and can enable them to continue caring for their child actively, thus preparing him sensitively for what is going to happen. In this way too the child can find some security by continuing to experience his parents as being to some extent in charge, and their relationship remains alive.

We already know how important it is that a child coming into care should be carefully introduced to his substitute home. Yet research by George[5] and by Aldgate[9] suggests that very little pre-placement preparation work is actually done. Time should be found for initial visits by the child from the safety of his home base to his substitute home and, if possible, by his new carers to his home base to experience something of the reality from which he is coming. Again the participation of parents at this stage is vital in affording the child some security during this transitional period, in identifying relevant transitional objects for him, and in giving to the substitute parents the kind of information which they, as parents, know it is important that anyone trying to care for their child should have. But perhaps the most important reason to my mind for this kind of active role for the parents in this transition is that it enables them to cope with their own separation anxieties, and at the same time conveys to the child, as nothing else can, that he has not been actively removed from passive, indifferent parents who have not seen where he now is and indeed may neither know nor care, but that his parents know where he is, have planned that he should be there, and know how to find their way back to him. So even at this point of physical separation, with all its inevitable distress, this emotional relationship continues to bind them together.

Finally, this participation of the parents must be actively encouraged by us during the time of care itself. The exchange of photographs, letters, gifts and so on, between parents and child, is a useful way to keep memories alive for them, but what is much more important is to find a way of keeping them in a more real relationship with each other. George's study[5] of foster care showed how in the local authorities he studied only 3.8 per cent of natural parents received any active encouragement to maintain contact with their children. In contrast, those who were generally discouraged from contact with their children (40.6 per cent), and those who met a completely passive attitude, allowing contact but not seeking to find reasons when this contact became irregular (44.3 per cent) total a massive 84.9 per cent.

Those of us who have worked in this field know only too well the kind of pressures which can lead to this situation, despite our knowledge about the importance of this continuing parent-child relationship. So we must face the kind of feelings which make it difficult for parents to visit: their angers, their concern that they may be regarded by the substitute carers as inferior and inadequate, their anxiety that they may be overwhelmed by their own distress or by their child's distress, their fear that their child may turn on them and blame them for what is happening, and so on. As one mother said, 'How can you ask me to keep going to see her? All she does is cry and ask when she will be coming home. Haven't I hurt her enough already?' Similarly we must acknowledge the kind of feelings which will naturally tend to be true for the carers: feelings about the natural parents, feelings of rivalry with them, concerns about the 'disturbing' effects of parents on their children, feelings about caring for other people's children, the kind of feelings described by writers such as Anthony[10]. And in the middle of this emotional turbulence there is the child with his feelings about both groups and their claims on his affections and loyalties.

The conflicting pulls on the social worker in this intricate situation can be immense, but it may be his job to hold on to the necessity for parents to continue to play an active role in their child's daily life. Too often one sees parents being asked to visit their child and doing so, but feeling very helpless and hopeless and subservient in the process. 'I went to see him on Sunday but *they* (the foster family) were all there too. They just sat and watched the two of us – as if we were inside the TV. And I couldn't think of a thing to say to him. It was terrible! The furthest they ever went was next door into the kitchen, leaving the door open.' This is not the kind of participation we want. In each situation the attempt must be made to discover in what ways it is possible and realistic for the parent to maintan parts of their present parental roles with their children. In some situations that I know of, this has taken the form of continuing to go together to football matches, or continuing to provide some pocket money or clothing, or supplying a favourite comic, but it could be whatever the parent felt was realistically manageable and had a specific emotional importance in their relationship. Whatever the activity is in any given situation, it is crucial that whenever possible some activity be found which enables the parents to continue fulfilling aspects of their role in interaction with their child.

I fully realise that such interaction with parents may very easily be felt to be disruptive to the child's attempts to settle into his new surroundings. We all have in varying degrees routines and organisation in our daily living, and need these to help us to feel secure and relaxed. But we must not let a pressure to 'settle in' diminish the links of child and parent. It is not sufficient to hope that the past relationship will be strong enough to withstand the strain of the present separation. I have seen too often how the absence of continuing contact, coupled with the feelings of guilt and anger, have let the latent paranoia present in all of us develop in parents of children in care into increasingly destructive fantasy relationships with their child and his present carers. Also we know how in a family which loses a member a reallocation of roles is liable to occur to deal with the aspects of the family's functioning previously carried by the now absent member, and that after such a reallocation has become the established norm there may be very little space left for that member were he to return to resume his participation in the family. So if the parent-child relationship is to continue to be alive and real, with both its strengths and its weaknesses, then it must continue to exist through the continuing interaction of parent and child, and the enabling of this parental participation in the child's period of care is of prime importance in ensuring the maintenance of that family unit and the possibility of successful restoration of the child to his place within it.

What I have said so far may make it sound as if I think that all parents of children in care will be well adjusted competent people eager and able to co-operate constructively in the kind of participation I am demanding. I realise that this is not so, and that for various reasons of personality or circumstance parental participation may at times be hard to achieve. Both Mapstone [11] and Berry [12] have written on this topic. But the work of Aldgate [9] in this country and Fanshel [13] in America shows a direct correlation between the amount of parental visiting and involvement and the child's eventual return home. Fanshell found that 'factors significantly predictive of discharge include frequency of parental visiting, investment of casework service and caseworker assessment of overall parental performance of the mothers'. I believe strongly that the process which parents encounter when requesting reception into care for their children often creates little real opportunity for them to maintain a central role, and that it is our task to try, despite the real difficulties, to ensure that in each situation we encounter we enable each individual parent to retain as much of this role as is realistically possible for them, the child and the substitute carer.

Reception into care for an undefined period

The second situation which I want to consider briefly is where the child is being received into care for an indefinite period, but where hope remains that he can be restored to his family unit at a future date. In such situations all that we have just said about parental participation as the key to keeping the parent-child relationship alive in a way which allows restoration to be possible, still applies. However, there are several other points that we must acknowledge are also important in this type of situation. One is that it may be crucial to put a concentrated effort into working with the parents to enable them to resolve as soon as possible, if indeed it is possible, the difficulties which have led to their child coming into care. For the longer this task takes the more difficult the process of restoration becomes. This may seem very obvious, but it has interested me (from work I have seen) how often social work attention, in the period just following reception into care, moves with the child away from the parents to the substitute carers and the building and maintenance of this new relationship. This may be understandable, both in the light of some aspects of child care history and the 'rescuing' of children from their parents, or maybe as the need to turn one's back on a 'failure' of preventive work, or indeed in relation to the social worker's wish to avoid, both for the sake of the child and because of his own very pressured work situation, any breakdown in these new care arrangements. Whatever the reasons, it does seem to occur and can often leave the parents very unsupported at a time of crisis, in which some really concentrated supportive work might achieve a great deal.

I realise that sometimes the family situation from which a child is admitted to care for an indefinite period may be fraught with chronic difficulties. Standards of parental care may well be poor, whether because of acute environmental pressures such as bad housing, social isolation, subsistence level income and debts, or because of personal pressures such as illness, difficulties in marital relationships, alcoholism, poor parent-child relationships and so on. Indeed there may often be a combination of these factors. In such situations a great deal of intensive supportive work needs to be done, and done promptly, if the family unit is to survive and the child to return home. Studies by Rowe and Lambert [14] indicate that only an insignificant number of children return home after eighteen months in foster care. This certainly suggests that the first twelve to eighteen months after reception into care is a crucially important period for such supportive work towards restoration to occur. Obviously intensive help in such situations requires a good deal of social work time and the recent study by Goldberg *et al.* [15] leaves many doubts as to how far Social Service Departments are able to offer long-term supportive help. But there are also studies such as the work of Lagnese and Green [16] which show that even in very difficult family situations (e.g., mother a drug addict whereabouts unknown, father receiving in-patient treatment for drug addiction), detailed prompt work by the agency can lead to the successful restoration of the child to one or both of his parents.

It is also important to bear in mind that in situations where the length of stay in care is somewhat uncertain, there is far greater insecurity for all concerned as time passes. Marital relationships and parent-child relationships may well have been strained or inadequate already, making it the more difficult for an individual member of the family to retain during this period of separation a confidence in the love and affection of the others for him. So the child may begin to doubt whether he will ever return to his family and whether his parents really wish him to. As these doubts grow and as relationships with the carers develop, so the child finds himself confused and guilty about where his prime loyalties and affections lie.

Similarly, parents may find themselves doubting as time drags on whether it will ever be possible to re-establish their family unit and indeed whether their child will want to return to them. And given these doubts, it becomes increasingly hard for them to maintain contact with him in a positive spirit and face his questions about his future with them, without resorting to unrealistic promises and reassurances which then lead on to further disappointments and increasing lack of trust. For the carers the uncertainty about just how long the child will remain with them, and their emotional involvement with him will continue, leads to fears about their own potential hurts and an anxiety about just how close emotionally it is safe for them and the child to become. In this discomfort it becomes ever more difficult for them to remain positive and encouraging to the parents' visits when these may be seen as disappointing the child's hopes and prolonging everyone's difficulties. For the social worker there is the enormously difficult problem of deciding in such situations, as the length of stay in care develops, how destructive these insecurities are for all those involved, and can and should they be ended. If so there remains the often much more difficult assessment to determine in whose care the child should remain and where his needs will best be met and his healthy development ensured.

So while it may indeed be possible that with careful work and mutual consideration the relationship between child, parent, carer and social worker can be managed over a protracted and defined period in care in a way which keeps feelings alive enough to permit a successful restoration of the child to his family, my experience suggests quite clearly that the longer the period the greater the toll on everyone concerned. For the parents the task becomes increasingly depressing; for the carers parting with the child becomes increasingly painful; for the social worker feelings for the child and against his parents for 'letting him down' seem to accrue; and the whole task of restoring the family unit becomes increasingly daunting. It, therefore, seems essential that if the restoration of the family is to be achieved in such situations, some intensive social work help should be given to the parents, and given quickly, to try to resolve their situation, and that particular attention should be paid to the increasingly high anxiety and depression that will develop for all concerned as this undefined period in care progresses.

Rebuilding lost relationships between parents and children

The final situation which I would like to examine when considering the question of restoring children in care to their families is where one is involved or is asked to become involved with a child in care who no longer has any contact with his natural parents. Some years ago I was asked to become involved with a child who was in this situation. Mark was nine and lived in a residential school for physically handicapped children. He was paralysed from the waist down and used a wheel chair though he could also walk with crutches and calipers. He had a pleasant temperament and good verbal ability, and was an attractive-looking boy of average height. He was of at least average intelligence but his school performance was well below his potential, and in the classroom he was inattentive and unhappy. He seemed to me to have few close friendships within the school and to be an introverted and unhappy boy. Mark was born handicapped and was rejected by his parents at birth. His life so far had been spent almost entirely in institutions, partly in hospitals, partly in Homes, and finally in a residential school. He went on each of his school holidays to a foster home in which he seemed to be reasonably settled and was accepted by the other foster children who lived there.

From the start I found that my visits to Mark left me feeling depressed, and soon I began to learn how isolated and forlorn he felt. My concern about his total lack of contact with his parents, or indeed with any relative, increased because of the way that he compensated for this by resorting to fantasy. He would tell me of various things that he had done with his family and these activities became increasingly bizarre and unrealistic. Having started with visits to the zoo or the cinema, they developed into trips to Canada and America. Although they were such obvious fantasy Mark's accounts went into great detail and it became clear as we talked about them that he expected me to accept them as real or at least not to question them. All of this concerned me so much that I decided I must try to re-establish contact with Mark's parents and hope to re-introduce Mark to them.

The file showed that there had been some contacts between Mark and his parents when he was younger, but little effort seemed to have been made to build on these. Nor had there been contact maintained by previous social workers with the parents. So I expected that finding them might well be, as it often is, a long process involving requests to various bodies such as the Department of Health and Social Security, Inland Revenue, registrar, police etc., for any recent addresses, and might also necessitate advertising in the press. In this case, however, I was lucky and found that by following up the last-known addresses we had I was quite soon able to locate the present addresses of Mark's parents. Their marriage had broken down and they had now set up separate homes. Having found the addresses, I realised how ambivalent I was feeling about contacting them. I was anxious on Mark's behalf about what I would find. What would these parents who had abandoned Mark be like, and would they be prepared to consider renewed contact with him? If they did, might they reject him again? How would they measure up to the idealised filmstar-like figures of his fantasies, and how would he react to the reality?

In fact, I found that, after their initial surprise at being contacted by me, both parents were welcoming and interested to have news of Mark. It was also clear that, although they had very different ways of dealing with them, both had strong unexpressed guilt feelings about Mark and about their lack of contact with him, and these feelings had to be examined in some detail over time. I also found as I talked with them about Mark that they thought of him not as a nine-year-old but as a much younger child. They had retained a picture of him as he had been when they last saw him. So my first task was to bring them up to date, using photographs and accounts of Mark as he now was and of his current activities. Mark's parents were clearly beginning to wonder why I had sought them out and getting apprehensive about what I was going to be asking of them. I therefore made it quite clear that I was at present hoping only that they would be prepared to renew contact with Mark, so that he could know of his own family rather than live in his present solitary way in the school.

As it gradually became clear that his parents were prepared to re-establish contact with Mark and try to maintain it, I had the confidence to tell him that I had traced them and to bring him up to date with their current situations. It was clear as he looked at photographs of them that he had only a hazy recollection of their appearances and at first seemed just curious about them rather than having any closer feelings. However, he was soon as keen to meet them as they were to see him again. At first I had thought of arranging this first meeting at the school where Mark lived; but I realised as I suggested this how fearful his parents were of this reunion taking place in front of all the care staff who they feared might have very strong feelings against them because of their neglect of Mark. Also Mark, though by now quite anxious about the whole situation, was genuinely curious to see their homes. So it was arranged that I would take him to visit his parents in their separate homes.

The events of these visits are in themselves fascinating, but this is not the place to describe them in detail. What was interesting, however, was that although I had delayed the visits, which both Mark and his parents would have rushed into much sooner, until I felt that everyone had prepared themselves to handle the situation realistically and avoid rushing into plans and promises for the future which could then not be kept, much of their adjustment to the present situation had to occur in the reality of their meeting. It was fascinating to see, as family members reminisced about the past, how memories resurfaced in Mark's mind and were connected with the real people whom he was now facing. So he realised that his grandfather, who was in the room, was the man who long ago had slid down the chute in hospital to show him it was safe for him to do. As Mark recalled these events one could see him taking a long look at the adults involved, and one could almost see him fitting together the faces which were stored in his memories with the faces now confronting him.

Over a period of time Mark and his family got to know each other again. As they began to grow more secure in their relationship and their fears of recriminations and further rejections receded, so they seemed to need to rush at each other emotionally, as if to make up for all the time that had been lost in recent years. And I found that my main roles during this time were to reassure them all that their relationship was building well, but, more importantly, to help both sides to avoid asking or promising too much too soon. Gradually the regular visits extended to overnight stays, weekends and then school holidays. Eventually Mark returned to live with his mother, her second husband and their son, and attended a local school which was designed to allow for handicapped pupils. The changes in Mark were substantial improvements socially, emotionally, intellectually and physically. His parents may not have been the wealthy fantasy figures who carried him off to exciting foreign countries, but they were real and they were his, and he was very genuinely happy with them. He now had an individual sense of belonging and a personal identity in a family context. So there were the pleasures of being part of a family, of suddenly realising one day that because his married sister had a child that made him an uncle.

The work which is necessary to restore children to their parents is demanding and time-consuming. With Mark I was lucky. It might well have taken much longer to find his parents and the results might not have been nearly so positive. But I believe it would still have been well worth trying. For, whether in cases like Mark's, or in situations like those we considered earlier where children are coming into care for either defined or indefinite periods, a great deal can be done to try to ensure that children in care retain or rebuild a relationship with their parents which remains alive at a feeling level. And this work will ensure that, in those situations where it is possible, restoration of the child to his parents will be much more certain to occur because it will be the carefully planned culmination of our work.

References

1 J. Newson and E. Newson, *Patterns of Infant Care in an Urban Community,* Allen & Unwin, London, 1963; Penguin, Harmondsworth, 1968. *Four Years Old in an Urban Community*, Allen & Unwin, London, 1968.

2 J. Bowlby, *Child Care and the Growth of Love,* (2nd edition) Penguin, Harmondsworth, 1969; *Attachment and Loss, vol. 1: Attachment,* Hogarth Press, London/Penguin, Harmondsworth, 1971.

3 J. Robertson and J. Robertson, *Young Children in Brief Separation,* a series of films, Tavistock Institute of Human Relations, London.

4 C. Beedell, *Residential Life with Children,* Routledge & Kegan Paul, London, 1970.

5 V. George, *Foster Care: Theory and Practice,* Routledge & Kegan Paul, London, 1970.

6 O. Stevenson, 'Reception into Care, Its Meaning for all Concerned' in *Children in Care,* R. J. N. Tod (ed.), Longmans, London, 1968.

7 J. Westheimer, 'Changes in Response of Mother to Child During Periods of Separation', *Social Work*, vol. 27, no. 1, 1970.

8 S. Jenkins and E. Norman, *Filial Deprivation and Foster Care,* Columbia University Press, New York, 1972.

9 J. Aldgate, 'Identification of Factors Influencing Children's Length of Stay in Care', unpublished PhD Thesis, University of Edinburgh, 1977. (See Chapter 2 in this book.)

10 E. J. Anthony, 'Other People's Children' in *Children in Care,* R. J. N. Tod (ed.), Longmans, London, 1968.

11 E. Mapstone, 'Social Work with the Parents of Children in Foster Care' in *Social Work in Foster Care,* R. J. N. Tod (ed.), Longmans, London, 1971.

12 J. Berry, *Social Work with Children,* Routledge & Kegan Paul, London, 1972.

13 D. Fanshel, 'Parental Visiting of Children in Foster Care: Key to Discharge?' *Social Services Review,* vol. 49, no. 4, 1975; 'Status Changes of Children in Foster Care: Final Results of the Columbia University Longitudinal Study', *Child Welfare,* vol., 55, no. 3, 1976.

14 J. Rowe and L. Lambert, *Children Who Wait,* ABAFA, 1973.

15 M. Goldberg, W. Warburton, B. McGuinness and J. Rowlands, 'Towards Accountability in Social Work: One Year's Intake to an Area Office', *British Journal of Social Work,* vol. 7, 1977.

16 A. Lagnese, and S. Green, 'Discharge Planning in Foster Care Cases Where the Father is the Significant Parent', *Child Welfare,* vol. 55, no. 9, 1976.

Jane Rowe

4 Fostering in the 1970s and beyond

When the Association of British Adoption and Fostering Agencies published its first training pack, *Planning for Children in Long-Term Care* (1976), the association had only recently extended its area of work to cover fostering as well as adoption. As a result, the introduction to the pack included background briefing notes, research and book reviews on adoption but nothing equivalent on foster home care.

This chapter is intended to go some way toward redressing the balance, though it does not attempt a full view of recent literature on fostering. The National Children's Bureau is currently updating its *Foster Home Care: Facts and Fallacies,* and this will provide a much more comprehensive survey than is possible in the confines of a brief article.

During the latter part of the 1960s and first part of the 1970s, fostering services were in the doldrums. The enthusiasm for foster home care which had been high in the 1950s and early 1960s wilted in face of a high breakdown rate and the difficulties of recruiting suitable foster parents.

In the past few years, there has been a remarkable change, and it now looks as though fostering will be in the forefront of child care thinking for some time to come. Early signs of renewed interest were the setting up of specialist fostering sections in some London boroughs,[1] the Croydon conferences on fostering in 1973 and 1974[2] which attracted social workers from all over the country, and the DHSS Working Party on practice[3,4] All sorts of new fostering schemes are now springing up, with particular emphasis on services for children with physical or mental handicaps and for difficult and disturbed adolescents. Specialist fostering officers are being appointed in many departments, there is an upsurge of interest in training for foster parents, and group methods of selection and support are also being tried. The growth of the National Foster Care Association is both a reflection of current interest and a source of new initiatives.

Well publicised 'tug-of-love' cases and the 1975 Children Act, which increased the legal rights of foster parents, have led to renewed professional interest in fostering standards and in the whole question of decision-making for children in care.

Some facts and figures

Fostering is experienced by a large number of children. The official figures for 1976[4] show that 41 per cent of the 100,600 children in local authority care in England and Wales are boarded out. At least another 11,000 are estimated to be in private foster homes.[5] However, the proportion of children in care who are boarded out has declined. In 1966 it was 51 per cent. Only a part of this decline can be attributed to the inclusion of the former Approved School children in the general 'in care' statistics. In Scotland the decline in fostering is even more marked.

Statistical information on foster homes and foster children on a national basis is extremely scanty. For instance, we do not know what proportion of foster children are in short-stay homes or how long the long-stay children have been with their foster families or what proportion stay on after reaching their eighteenth birthday.

We do know that the proportion of children boarded out has always varied greatly from one authority to another, but that there is a general scarcity of foster homes especially for long-stay older children. The study *Children Who Wait*[6] estimated that in 1972 there were probably about 6,000 children under eleven years old who social workers felt should be placed in foster homes. There is no evidence that this figure has declined. A later study by Shaw and Lebens[7] showed that the five authorities in one region needed long-term foster homes for 280 children under fourteen years old, and foster homes that might become adoption homes for a further seventy children.

Although there are no national figures, a number of studies[8] done in different parts of the country show a consistently high breakdown rate for long-term fostering of about 50 per cent. This appalling figure can be coupled with evidence that a large proportion (40 per cent in one study)[9] of all approved foster parents give up fostering in less than a year. The causes of breakdown are still far from clear, but the amount and quality of social work support is probably a very significant factor.

Since fostering can evidently be so difficult and risky, it would not be too surprising if it had gone completely out of favour. That the opposite has happened is due to the enormous benefits that successful family placement can offer many deprived children. Though it will never be the right solution for every child, no other form of care except adoption can so nearly approximate to normal home life and provide the individualised care and affection so essential to a child's proper development.

Current emphasis on fostering is also due to a general swing toward seeking community-based solutions to social problems. This is intensified by the spiralling costs of residential provision. Between 1975 and 1976 the average cost of keeping a child in residential care for one week rose from £46.80 to £65, while the cost of foster care rose from £7 to £8.80. These figures give a slightly false picture because those for fostering do not allow for social work or administrative costs, and current boarding-out rates are in some areas so inadequate that they do not even cover the foster parents' out-of-pocket expenses in maintaining the child. When realistically costed, good foster care services are not particularly cheap. However, they are virtually always less expensive than residential care.

The theoretical background

The Curtis Committee Report which led to the Children Act 1948 and the establishment of Children's Departments can be said to be the beginning of modern fostering practice in Britain, though its roots go back into the early nineteenth century and the boarding out of children from the workhouse. From 1948 onward fostering took its place in British social work textbooks, and a number of important and helpful studies were undertaken. Nevertheless, fostering practice in children's departments basically relied on shared experience and 'practice wisdom' and, as Jean Packman described in *The Child's Generation*,[10] expectations of fostering changed as child care policy changed.

The Seebohm reorganisation of the social services and subsequent local authority reorganisation inevitably deflected social work attention away from time-consuming services such as recruitment and support of foster homes. Specialist skills were diluted or even lost in the re-shuffle and the wholesale promotion of practitioners to management. This laid bare the inadequate theoretical underpinning of fostering services. Practice wisdom is a useful, indeed an essential aid; but it is insufficient unless allied to a firmly based coherent body of knowledge. This, fostering has conpicuously lacked.

Considering the number of children and adults involved and its central place in child care provision, comparatively little has been written about foster home care in its total context. Fostering has never attracted researchers in the way adoption has done, and the studies which have been undertaken have usually been small-scale or have looked at only certain aspects or particular groups of foster children. Psychologists and psychiatrists have shown little interest, and lawyers are rarely involved since, unlike adoption, fostering has no legal status. As a result, our understanding of fostering is patchy and lacks the depth which a better integrated approach and more interdisciplinary collaboration could provide.

Definitions of fostering

Fostering is a generalised concept. The word is used to cover a wide variety of situations in which a child is cared for in a family other than his own. It ranges from day fostering, which is virtually synonymous with daily minding, to permanent placements which are the equivalent of adoption in everything but the legal sense. *The Guide to Fostering Practice,*[3] published by the DHSS, says: 'Fostering is not in itself a single identifiable method of care. It offers a range of placements which have in common only the fact that they provide care in a family setting.' No wonder, therefore, that confusion about aims and methods of practice is widespread, and that a group of people discussing fostering may unwittingly be talking about almost totally dissimilar situations requiring very different approaches. A further confusion arises from the American use of the phrase 'foster care' to include residential care too, i.e., all children 'in care' and outside their own homes.

Much of the social work writing about fostering has stressed the foster parents' difficulties in understanding their role, and their tendency to think of themselves as substitute parents when the agency wishes them to assume the role of caretaker or therapist. In reality a foster parent's role – like that of a residential worker – is always a combination of caretaker, therapist, compensatory parent and substitute parent, though the mix will vary according to the type of placement and age of the child, and may change from time to time during the child's stay in the foster home.

No one can reach an adequate understanding of fostering without first undertaking an analysis of the parental role and linking this with the needs of children at various stages of development. The concepts of biological and psychological parenting are also basic to any study of fostering relationships. Social workers are often more confused than foster parents about the appropriate division of role within the triangular fostering situation in which natural parents, foster parents and agency all carry some responsibility for the child. A foster parent's role must always depend on which aspects of the parental role are still being exercised by the natural parents and which are being undertaken by the agency. The foster parent's difficult task is to fill in the gaps, so that the child's needs are met without unnecessary overlapping of function.

The purpose of placement and the likely length of stay are crucial to role definition. If social workers are unclear about these factors, they cannot expect foster parents to know how to adapt themselves to the appropriate role. It is also rather easy for professional workers to talk about the importance of the adults concerned being willing to share the child, and to forget that it is the child who has to live with the uncomfortable experience of being 'shared' and with the gaps and overlapping which may occur. Divisions of responsibility which are satisfactory in the short term may become intolerable in the long term and, with young children in particular, caretakers quickly slip into a substitute parenting role unless natural parents remain closely involved.

For purposes of discussion, foster homes can be categorised roughly by the expected length of the child's stay, or they can be designated as professional or ordinary, or as inclusive or exclusive. An examination of each of these methods of classification in turn may be helpful.

Length of stay

The Boarding Out Regulations for England and Wales consider short stay as a period of up to eight weeks, so this is generally accepted as the dividing line, though three or even six months may be used.

Short-stay foster homes provide alternatives to using residential nurseries, short-stay children's Homes, reception and assessment centres or Remand Homes (though their use for this purpose has only just been started). In addition to individualised family care which can be adapted to each child's needs, they offer an opportunity to assess the child in a relatively familiar setting. Some of the specific purposes of short-stay fostering are:

1 Care of children during parental illness, mother's confinement or family crisis.
2 Assessment and opportunity to make long-term plans. This may include emergency placement on place-of-safety orders.
3 Pre-adoption care and preparation.
4 Relief of parents or other foster parents who are looking after a severely handicapped child
6 Weekly or weekend fostering for children with school problems or those from one-parent families whose working hours make weekday care of the child impossible. (This kind of fostering is as yet relatively unexplored.)
7 As an alternative to remand centres for children who have committed offences and where the court needs a further report before making a decision.

Except in some pre-adoption or holiday foster homes for children in long-term care, the child in a short-stay foster home usually has close links with his natural family. Problems of identity do not arise, and there is relatively little confusion over role or purpose. The review after three months, which is required by Regulations, can provide a crucial boundary to prevent drift from short-stay to long-stay.

Indefinite or medium-length foster homes are the textbook homes used as part of the plan to rehabilitate families, though a great deal of private fostering also falls into this indefinite-length category. The placement may last a few months or a few years, but it is not intended to be permanent. In agency placements, the plan is usually to keep parents in touch. The therapeutic role of foster parents may be much to the fore. Some children and adolescents are consciously placed in a foster home as a means of solving their problems of behaviour and/or relationships. In other cases the main problem may lie in the parents' health or behaviour, homelessness or marital difficulties. Under these circumstances, foster parents may be expected to play an active part in work with natural parents and to help to re-establish the family. They are certainly not intended to take over the full parental role.

In social work literature there is a generally held assumption that most foster homes nowadays are of this type, and discussion about the foster parents' role are based on the expectation that the child will be going back to his family of origin. The fact is, however, that except for the fostering of teenagers, there are comparatively few medium-length fostering placements. *Children Who Wait*[6] and subsequent studies have shown that if children do not return home within a few months, they are likely to remain in care for a very long time; and it is now only too clear that rehabilitation to parents is frequently difficult to achieve. Major findings from *Children Who Wait* were that 72 per cent of the children needing foster home placements were thought to need a 'permanent home', and only half of those for whom a foster home for an indeterminate period was being sought were actually thought likely to return to their parents.

A detailed study of the foster children in one local authority by Shaw and Lebens[11] showed that 88 per cent were expected to remain in care until their eighteenth birthday; 54 per cent of the children had already been in their foster homes for more than five years, and a further 22 per cent for between two and five years.

The discrepancy between social work theory and the fostering realities which these figures demonstrate is a serious threat to good practice. It goes a long way towards explaining the gap between social work emphasis on the need for foster parents to avoid possessiveness and not become too emotionally involved with the child and foster parents' persistence in considering themselves as substitute parents. It is clearly very difficult for foster parents to maintain a somewhat detached professional role for an extended period; but social workers often continue to apply expectations and policies that are out of keeping with the facts and with the psychological realities. It seems probable that this is due in part to social workers' very real difficulties over changing goals and plans. In part it may be due to reliance on imperfectly understood concepts of parent-child relationships, bonding and separation, and in part to failure to link knowledge of child development and the effects of the passage of time with departmental policies and plans for individual children.

Long-stay or permanent foster homes still remain much the largest group, although we tend to hear least about them. The hope has been that improved social work would mean that a high proportion of foster children would return to their families of origin. But, in fact, 70 per cent of the foster children in *Children Who Wait*[6] were expected to remain in care until eighteen; and the Shaw and Lebens study [11] showed that maintaining the child in his present foster home would be rated as top priority by social workers in 92 per cent of cases, while in only 3.4 per cent was rehabilitation to parents the top priority.

There is no general agreement as to which children should be placed for permanent fostering as the plan of choice, but the purpose of long-term fostering is clearly to give the child the benefits of family life and to provide him with as normal an experience as possible. The permanent nature of the placement may be made explicit from the start. More often what is asked for is an open-ended agreement to care for the child 'as long as necessary'. The parenting aspects of the foster parent role are inevitably highlighted in these placements and the problem of two separate sets of parents cannot be avoided. If natural parents do not keep in close touch – for whatever reason – their role inevitably diminishes and foster parents can take it over.

Virtually all recent studies of foster care have looked at the question of parental contact. With monotonous regularity, these studies show that only about 10 per cent of foster children are visited by their parents even once a month, and the majority seldom or never see them. Work with the natural parents of children in care is evidently a crucial issue as yet inadequately explored on a theoretical level, and often even less adequately carried out in practice. Our failures in this regard are highlighted by fostering breakdowns, particularly during adolescence, when the identity crises of teenage foster children, and anxiety about their origins and relationships with natural parents, so often compound and confuse the normal rebellion and developmental problems of this age group.

Professional and ordinary fostering

Writing in *Adoption and Fostering* Pugh [12] described the use of the word 'professional' as being like Humpty Dumpty in *Alice Through the Looking Glass,* who said, 'When I use a word, it means just what I choose it to mean, neither more nor less.' She points out that professional fostering has been interpreted in almost as many ways as there are professional foster parents.

The term professional can refer to the qualifications of the foster parent either through previous training and work experience (teachers, nurses, social workers) or through special preparation and in-service training or both. It almost always means 'paid for the job' over and above reimbursement of the cost of maintaining the child. In some instances, professional foster parents are considered as staff members entitled to pensions and vacations. Others are regarded as free-lance workers in their own homes. Often professional fostering is linked with the type of child to be placed and limited to children with severe handicaps or very difficult teenagers. Or it may refer to foster parents who take a number of children at once and thus become virtually a voluntary family group home.

Others would say that most short- and medium-term foster parents are professional, in that they have the professional attitude of offering their skill and their home as a resource for children in need and that they do so in a defined and disciplined manner. Since most foster parents are taking on children who display considerable problems, the difference between professional and ordinary might be thought to be mainly financial, but it seems more complicated than this.

Various studies have shown that although virtually all foster parents want the boarding-out allowance to reflect the real cost of maintaining a child at current prices, many do not want to be paid for their services. This is almost certainly because being paid is at variance with the concept of parenting. It comes back again to ideas about role. The professionals stress therapeutic and caretaking aspects, see themselves as colleagues of social workers, and expect special training. The ordinary foster parent concentrates on parenting, minimises differences, seeks to integrate the child into the family, and is often not much interested in joining a group or receiving training.

George, Adamson and others [13] have stressed the need for foster parents to take a professional stance and have pointed out the potential problems of considering them as parents. The need for new thinking about payment and new types of foster home is not in doubt. Schemes such as Kent's Special Family Placement Project or Somerset's or Leeds' special short-stay homes for handicapped children are of enormous potential importance. But it may be that some of the current social work enthusiasm for professional foster parents schemes is due to a wish to solve the dilemmas over the nature of the long-term plans for the child, as well as over the foster parents' role and their relationship with social workers. There may even be some element of hope that salaried foster parents will be more 'co-operative' and not become 'involved' in ways which lead to differences of opinion over planning and policies. If Social Services Departments merely jump on a bandwagon and produce inadequately thought-out schemes, breakdown and disillusionment are inevitable; and this could have serious backlash effects on the fostering service as a whole.

The National Foster Care Association is helping to establish and upgrade the image of fostering as a social service, and they lay stress on the importance of a close working partnership between social workers and foster parents. Nevertheless, at present the majority of foster parents are long-term non-professionals. Their attitudes and experiences are probably accurately summed up thus:

> Foster parents view fostering in terms of natural parenthood: natural parents may visit or not (preferably not); social workers are in varying degrees helpful, occasional visitors; the Department a source (also variable) of funds and of irritation. But, in general, foster parents are, in their own eyes, engaged in the task of bringing up children as they would a child of their own (precisely as the boarding-out agreement demands!) without reference to anyone else (Shaw and Lebens).[14]

There is an uncomfortably wide gap between this and the recommended concept of shared care in which each party to the arrangement works with the others in a closely integrated team.

Inclusive and exclusive fostering

Holman (see Chapter 5) has defined and described fostering as being essentially either inclusive (i.e., including the natural parents, the social worker, the child's past, etc.) or exclusive (i.e., taking the child completely into the family and trying to keep the past and the 'other' parents out). The inclusive pattern stresses honesty and openness, the exclusive commitment and continuity. It is helpful to have these essential differences spelled out. The dilemma is that the attributes of both concepts are needed, but in differing mixtures according to the particular child's situation. Recipes for successful mixtures have not yet been developed in a practical and useful form. They will be difficult to achieve because of the number of variables which must be taken into account. We do not yet know how many parents would be able to resume care of their children or at least retain more of their parental role, if they were given adequate support. The balance between economic and psychological factors in admissions to care is still unclear.

Holman declares that the evidence points to the inclusive model as being the most conducive to the child's well-being. Shaw [11] states flatly that this issue is still open to question. Holman rests his case largely on an American study, Weinstein's *Self-Image of the Foster Child* [15], and on his own, Jenkins's [16] and Thorpe's [17] work here in England. Shaw points out that all these studies were on a small scale, often methodologically suspect or even frankly impressionistic, and that they provide too shaky a foundation for a wholesale acceptance of inclusive as the best style of foster care. Tizard, [18] too, questions the benefit of parental visits in some circumstances.

Nevertheless, there is supporting evidence from a lot of other sources that all children being brought up by people other than their birth parents do need knowledge of and sometimes access to their origins if they are to have a comfortable sense of their own identity. Jolowicz, Littner, Stone and Triseliotis [19] have all written of the hidden parent that the child takes with him into placement.

Identity has been studied much more fully in relation to adoption than in relation to fostering. The same principles undoubtedly hold true for all children who are cut off from their roots. But whereas the adopted child can grapple with this problem from the security of a legally established and permanent family base, the foster child has to try and find his place in the scheme of things amid the inevitable insecurity of a fostering relationship which can be terminated at any time. Moreover, knowledge of origins and understanding of one's personal and family situation are not necessarily the same as continued contact.

Visiting

The question of natural parents visiting in foster homes lies at the heart of foster care. There is much more to it than a legal right of access, which is in any case an inappropriate concept in relation to a child's welfare. Visiting is a complicated and painful subject, and there are no easy solutions either in day-to-day practice or in theoretical understanding. Without frequent and regular visiting, close parent-child relationships cannot be maintained. Although these relationships may be rebuilt later, the process is difficult and chancy. We know from research on both sides of the Atlantic (Jenkins, [20] Tizard [18]) that visiting is closely linked to the prospect of rehabilitation; but it is impossible to know which causes which since the parents most interested in their children are likely to be those who visit most frequently anyway. We also know that natural parents find visiting very painful and difficult, that foster parents tend to discourage it, and that few parents do in fact visit their children in foster homes at all regularly (Aldgate [21], Thorpe [17], George [8], Adamson [13], Rowe and Lambert [6]).

Social workers appear confused and ambivalent about parents' visits. The theoretical stance is that visiting must and should be encouraged; but it is noticeable that advertisements for foster homes often stress that parental contact is infrequent or limited. Shaw [11] found that social workers in the county he studied thought that the amount of parental visiting was satisfactory for 60 per cent of the foster children they supervised, although only 9 per cent saw their parents as often as once a month. There are exceptions, of course, but the evidence seems to point to a general lack of sustained effort by social workers to make fostering plans with natural parents, or to provide the practical help or psychological support which might enable them to keep in touch. Whether this is colluding with foster parents who prefer not to have the bother and upset of parents' visits, or whether social workers' attitudes are based on an accurate and realistic assessment of the child's current needs and the parents' capacity to meet them, it is impossible to say without further data. It seems likely, however, that the main factors at work may be uncertainty about long-term goals linked with discomfort over the inadequacies of past and present services to parents, doubt about priorities, and a general unwillingness to provoke difficulties or 'rock the boat'.

To sum up

There seems little doubt that there are two essentially different styles of fostering. There is a basic similarity between Holman's inclusive foster parent (see Chapter 5), George's [8] recommended foster care worker, and the professional foster parent. The idea of contracts, time-limited placements, and payments for service all fit into a coherent pattern. Most short-term and medium-term placements are (or could be) of this nature and can be used successfully for the relief of families under stress and for the treatment of many child or family problems. There are great and as yet untapped potentialities in this kind of fostering as part of community social services.

By contrast, the more traditional, exclusive or ordinary fostering is unsuited to short-term placements and much more akin to adoption, though without adoption's security and legal safeguards. These foster parents seek to assume the role of parent and in doing so may be fulfilling the child's urgent need. Where problems most often arise is that natural parents or social workers – who also have responsibility for the child – differ from the foster parents in their view of the situation, of the purpose of placement and of plans for the future.

Foster homes of various types need to be seen as elements in an interlocking series of options for children whose own parents cannot care for them or can do so only partially. Sound decisions about fostering placement are based on proper diagnosis and good planning. They must also depend to a considerable extent on knowledge about alternatives. It is not enough to know the pros and cons of fostering. One needs to know about day care resources, about which children do and do not benefit from residential care of various kinds, and about adoption as an appropriate resource for some children. Studies of the outcome of different forms of care are urgently needed, and results of current work by Triseliotis[22] should be of great value. At present, research studies have so often emphasised the danger of institutionalisation, foster home breakdown and adoption problems that they have contributed to our insecurity over long-term planning in the face of limited resources. We need to know more about what works, why, and for whom. Knowledge from a range of studies needs to be brought together in order to provide a solid basis for decisions about policy and practice.

The 1975 Children Act envisages an integrated service for children in which adoption will take its place alongside fostering and residential care. There will be a new provision of custodianship, which is not yet implemented, but is intended to provide a legal relationship, more secure than fostering, but without the total 'forever' commitment of adoption. Local authorities will be able to pay allowances to custodians. Whether custodianship will offer a really satisfactory alternative to long-term fostering remains to be seen. It could offer the worst of all worlds or, to mix the metaphor, it could fall between all the stools. Better services to children in their own homes and subsidised adoption may well offer more appropriate alternatives.

Certainly, the right balance will be found only if understanding of child development, and of the needs of children and the essential role of parents in meeting these needs, is translated into foster care practice. Knowledge about bonding, separation and identification is also essential to achieving placement goals. We need to know more about the effect on children of shared parenting. More rigorous analysis, acknowledgment of reality, a new vocabulary for differentiating foster care of various kinds, more inter-disciplinary co-operation and much better assessment of present and future potentialities will all be important if we are to ensure that the current emphasis on fostering does not peter out in disappointment and frustration.

Note

This chapter is reprinted from *Adoption and Fostering*, vol. 90, no. 4, 1977.

References

1 M. Adcock and L. Lawrence 'Lack of Planning - Lack of Care', *Concern*, no. 16, 1975.

2 London Borough of Croydon, *Fostering Today and Tomorrow*, London Borough of Croydon, 1974.

3 Department of Health and Social Security, *Guide to Fostering Practice* (Monkton Report), HMSO, 1976.

4 Department of Health and Social Security, *Children in Care in England and Wales 1976*, HMSO, 1977; *Scottish Social Work Statistics 1976*, (unpublished).

5 R. Holman, *Trading in Children*, Routledge & Kegan Paul, 1973.

6 J. Rowe and L. Lambert, *Children Who Wait*, ABAFA, 1973.

7 M. Shaw and K. Lebens, *Regional Planning for 'Children Who Wait'*, University of Leicester (unpublished), 1977.

8 P. Gray, and E. Parr, *Children in Care and the Recruitment of Foster Parents*, Government Social Survey, 1957; R. Parker, *Decision in Child Care*, Allen & Unwin, 1966; V. George, *Foster Care: Theory and Practice*, Routledge & Kegan Paul, 1970; H. Napier, 'Success and Failure in Foster Care', *British Journal of Social Work*, vol. 2, no. 2, 1972.

9 E. Jones, 'A Study of Those Who Cease to Foster', *British Journal of Social Work*, vol. 5, No. 1, 1975.

10 J. Packman, *The Child's Generation*, Blackwell, 1975.

11 M. Shaw and K. Lebens, 'Children Between Families', *Adoption and Fostering*, no. 84, 1976.

12 G. Pugh, 'Professional Fostering - Defining Objectives', *Adoption and Fostering*, no. 88, 1977.

13 George, op.cit.; G. Adamson, *The Caretakers,* Bookstall Publications, 1973; R. Holman 'The Place of Fostering in Social Work', *British Journal of Social Work,* vol. 5, no. 1, 1975.

14 M. Shaw and K. Lebens, 'Foster Parents Talking', *Adoption and Fostering,* no. 88, 1977.

15 E. Weinstein, *The Self-Image of the Foster Child,* Russell Sage Foundation, 1960.

16 R. Jenkins, 'Long Term Fostering', *Case Conference,* vol. 15, no. 9, 1969.

17 R. Thorpe, 'Mum and Mrs So and So' *Social Work Today,* vol. 4, no. 22, 1974.

18 B. Tizard, *Adoption – a Second Chance,* Open Books, 1977.

19 A. Jolowicz, *The Hidden Parent,* Dept. of Public Affairs, New York, 1973; N. Littner, 'The Importance of the Natural Parent to the Child in Placement', *Child Welfare,* vol. 54, no. 3, 1975; F. H. Stone 'Adoption and Identity', in *Child Adoption,* ABAFA, 1977; J. Triseliotis, 'Identity and Adoption', *Child Adoption,* ABAFA, 1977; also *In Search of Origins,* Routledge & Kegan Paul, 1977.

20 S. Jenkins and E. Norman, *Filial Deprivation and Foster Care,* Columbia University Press, New York, 1972.

21 J. Aldgate, 'The Child in Care and his Parents', *Adoption and Fostering,* no. 84, 1976. (See also Chapter 2 in this book.)

22 J. Triseliotis, 'Research', *Adoption and Fostering,* no. 87, 1977.

Robert Holman

5 Exclusive and inclusive concepts of fostering

Jean Heywood's classic history of Children's Departments up to the late 1950s accords great prominence to fostering[1]. Interestingly, in her subsequent review of child care developments since the early 1960s, fostering rates hardly a paragraph[2]. Today fostering is reappearing as a topic of major interest not only to social workers but also to the press and parliament.

The two major antecedents of the Children Act 1948 both identified fostering (or boarding out, as it was then officially termed) as central to the care of deprived children. The Monkton Report, investigating the tragic death of a foster child, called not for less but for better fostering[3]. The Curtis Committee stressed the limitations of institutional care and warmly advocated the advantages of foster homes.[4] Not surprisingly, the seminal Children Act 1948 laid a duty upon the newly created Children's Departments to board children out 'unless it was not practicable or desirable' for the time being (paragraph 13).

As it ensued, the earliest years of the new local authority departments were taken up with finding residential places for the large numbers of children immediately received into care. Thereafter, the popularisation of Bowlby's thesis that children required above all a close relationship with a parent figure, along with the realisation that fostering was cheaper than institutional care, resulted in a decade of boarding out. Child care officers viewed with satisfaction the Home Office statistics which revealed an increase of several thousand in the numbers of foster homes in the 1950s. Children's Officers tended to regard success according to their authority's position in the boarding-out league table.

Contemporary child care literature and research both reflected and stimulated the interest in fostering. The major textbooks were expositions of child care placement practice by the Americans, Charnley, Glickman, Gordon and Hutchinson[5]. Child care casework held a prominent place on professional training courses, where it was nurtured by such outstanding teachers as Clare annd Donald

Winnicott. British research interest in fostering after the Second World War was stimulated by a government survey entitled *Children in Care and the Recruitment of Foster Parents*[6]. Subsequent research focused on the factors promoting success and failure in fostering. The influential work of Trasler and Parker established the importance of such factors as the age of the foster child, age at placement, the presence of a sibling, the ages of the foster mother and her children, and the previous experiences of the foster child[7].

During the 1960s foster care lost its leading position. A contributory factor involved some disillusionment with what was considered a high breakdown rate amongst fosterings. It is worth interjecting that a concentration of studies on long-term fosterings tended to exaggerate the extent of failure.* The failures, combined with difficulties in finding foster parents, prompted a welcome reassessment of policy, leading to fostering being regarded as only one possible form of care of deprived children along with adoption, various kinds of residential placements, and home 'on trial'.

Even more significantly, fostering's place in the centre of child care thought was displaced by new ideas and events. A series of government papers and reports focused attention on the relationship between child care and prevention, delinquency, and integration with other forms of social work. The Children and Young Persons Acts of 1963 and 1969 widened the scope of the work of Children's Departments, while the Local Authority Social Services Act 1970 absorbed them into the new Social Service Departments. Noticeably, the relevant legislation for Scotland, the Social Work (Scotland) Act of 1968, in re-enacting certain provisions, did not accord fostering the position of priority enjoyed before.

Fostering is still a major means of caring for children. Over 36,000 children were in local authority foster homes in England, Wales and Scotland on one date in 1971. To these must be added several thousands in foster homes of voluntary societies and private foster homes. As mentioned, a revival of interest in fostering has occurred.

* For instance, Napier's more recent study repeats this concentration. In order to assess long-term fosterings he excludes from his sample 402 foster children who had been rehabilitated. The step is quite legitimate as the researcher is interested only in long-term cases. But the result is that shorter-term but successful fosterings are not counted. M. Napier 'Success and Failure in Foster Care', *British Journal of Social Work*, Vol. 2, No. 2, Summer 1972.

However, it is not to be expected that the aspects which gained attention in the 1950s will do so today. The purpose of this paper is to identify the major contemporary issues and to offer some comments. The first half will concentrate on the demands to expand fostering, the conflicting positions held about the nature and desirability of fostering, and the contribution being made by child care social work. In the second half, these factors will be used in order to discuss how fostering may develop in the future.

New fostering needs

Although by the 1960s social workers had recognised the limitations of fostering, it was still accepted as a humane and desirable form of child care. Subsequent years have witnessed not a decline but an increase in the demand for foster homes. The demands have sprung less from a growth in the numbers of children in public care and more from a realisation of the fostering needs of children who previously received less attention from professional social workers. Four examples stand out.

Handicapped children

The former Children's Departments always had some physically and mentally handicapped children in their care. The government survey of 1957 stated that 13.5 per cent of children in care were handicapped.[6] Apart from the physically handicapped, most were placed in children's Homes or special boarding schools. Comprehensive data are not available, but it can be tentatively suggested that there followed a slight increase in the numbers placed with foster parents. In 1969, Walton and Heywood's sample of children in the care of six Children's Departments in north-west England revealed that some 16.7 per cent had a mental or physical handicap. Amongst these, 80 per cent of the educationally sub-normal – the largest group – were fostered. Of the physically handicapped some 50 per cent were in foster homes. Significantly, no maladjusted children were with foster parents[8]. The authors considered that, since Gray and Parr's research,[9] growth had occurred in boarding out the handicapped (and they also observed that an even larger growth concerned the number 'home on trial'). At the same time, Holman's study of two local authorities in the Midlands found that 17.5 per cent of a sample of local authority foster children were handicapped[10]. The trend has since received a two-fold stimulus. The reorganisation of the social services has placed the needs of physically and mentally handicapped children firmly in the laps of Social Service Departments. Further, reports have been received of successful projects in the USA to foster such children, while in Britain, Dr Barnardo's has initiated a scheme to do the same. Thus, whereas previously the fostering of handicapped children appeared to occur in a haphazard manner, it is now becoming an accepted objective of child care policy.

Coloured children

Government sources do not publish figures of the number of coloured children in care. Indeed, there is no agreed definition in child care circles of the meaning of 'coloured' or 'immigrant'. However, studies of individual reports from local authorities make clear the increase in care of children whose parents were born in the West Indies [11]. At one time, doubts were expressed as to whether such children could be successfully fostered. The published experiences of Dr Barnardo's and the National Children's Home suggested otherwise [12]. Interestingly, Walton and Heywood's study found that a third of coloured children in care were in foster homes, while the proportion of half-caste children - over 50 per cent - was the same as for all children. Both the principle of equality of treatment and the observed successful experiences make a case for fostering these children. The consequence is that yet further demand for foster homes is created.

Children who wait

The existence of children in residential institutions who could benefit from substitute homes was highlighted by a graphic investigation, *Children Who Wait.* By a projection of their sample, the authors estimate that over 6,000 children need a foster or adoptive home [13]. The present writer believes this study tends to overstate its conclusions but accepts the main point [14]. Whatever the number, the fact that some children in care could be fostered constitutes an additional pressure to find foster homes.

Private fostering

The final, and perhaps numerically largest, demand concerns not so much expansion of fostering but more active social work involvement in present fostering. The reference is to the recent identification of the needs of private foster homes; and, as it stemmed from the present writer's own research, it will be dealt with in a little more detail.

Private foster children are defined by the Children Act 1958 as those 'below the upper limit of compulsory school age whose care and maintenance are undertaken for reward for a period exceeding one month by a person who is not a relative or guardian'. The Children and Young Persons Act 1969 has now amended the definition to include those for whom no reward is taken and who are kept for under one month.* Local authorities have loose responsibilities and limited powers over private fosterings, but until recently little generalised knowledge existed save that the numbers of known private foster children in England and Wales numbered over 11,000 (with many more undoubtedly unknown).

Holman's research examined every private fostering in two local authorities, comparing them with a matched sample of local authority foster children[15]. Here mention can be made only of the suitability of the foster parents, the treatment of the children, and the services provided by the social workers. Suitability was assessed according to factors which official regulations and child care texts defined as being necessary in foster parents, by asking social workers to assess suitablity, and by identifying how many foster mothers had gone on to take private children after having their applications to foster for the local authority rejected. In all, 63 per cent had some major element of unsuitability. They included people whose own children were in public care, who had been convicted of neglect and even of child assault. Of course, many private foster parents were of an acceptable standard. The point is that there exists an area of fostering - largely untouched by social workers - where abuse is likely.

The actual treatment of the private foster children gave some cause for concern. Over two-thirds were placed with their foster mothers without any prior meeting. Occasionally, the parties met by accident at a bus stop or shop and a child changed hands. Despite their freedom

* The definition is restricted by a number of qualifications. See R. Holman, *Trading in Children*, Routledge & Kegan Paul, 1973, p. 268.

to take children, the private foster mothers were not in an enviable position. They were frequently coping with very difficult children. Two-thirds of the private foster children (as against one-third of the local authority children) displayed extreme and consistent aggression, anxiety or withdrawal. Again, they were significantly more likely to suffer from bronchitis, to be retarded in speech or motor development, or to have behavioural problems at school.

It might have been expected that the foster children most in need would have received extra attention from the local social workers. The opposite was true. In twelve months, 14.7 per cent of the private fosterings had not been visited at all, while 66.4 per cent were seen under five times. It was a comparatively rare occurrence for the private foster father to be contacted, for the private foster child to be talked to alone, or for the natural parents to be visited. Although the local authority fosterings were not given a comprehensive service, they were seen far more regularly and offered a far wider range of help.

Local authorities' duties to supervise and powers to offer resources to private fosterings are small compared to those towards children in care. Consequently, busy social workers tended to give the former little priority and concentrated on the latter. This occurred although the research revealed many examples of how welcome and effective social work intervention could have been. Private fostering, the report explains, is too extensive to be abolished. It therefore closes by arguing for comparatively minor legislative reforms and resource additions to enable social workers to offer private fosterings a service approaching that given to local authority ones. It is claimed that social workers could render an effective service in preventing needless placements and removals, helping foster parents cope with difficult situations and giving direct casework aid to the children.

Expansion constraints

It can be concluded that even if fostering no longer occupies the centre of the child care stage, strong demands are being made to expand both the numbers of foster homes and the quality of service given to the fostering participants. It might be interjected that the demands should be met from the increased budgets received by Social Service Departments since 1971. This argument overlooks the many additional duties already placed by new legislation on the departments: the inflationary salary and running costs which may entail, as Judge points out, a larger budget for a smaller output; and now the prospect of cutback rather than growth for the social services[16]. It is ironic that the need for fostering expansion has become most pressing at a time when social work expansion seems most in jeopardy.

Exclusive and inclusive concepts of fostering

That more foster homes are required is not in dispute. But what kind of foster homes? How can foster homes be differentiated? Building on earlier American studies and the impressionistic observations of British writers, research has identified two contrasting concepts of fostering. (It is worth noting that the concepts mainly stem from studies of long-term fosterings which exclude short-term and placements with relatives.)

Exclusive fostering

Exclusive fostering may be so termed in that it attempts to contain the foster child within the foster family while excluding other connections. Thus Holman's study revealed that 63 per cent of local authority foster parents regarded the children 'as their own' and would like to have adopted[17]. Similarly, Adamson found that over half did not think of themselves as foster mothers[18]. George records that 62.1 per cent considered 'own parent' as the best description of their position[19]. Seeing themselves as the parents, such foster parents want to exclude the natural parents. George established that 56 per cent did not think the real parents had even a conditional right to visit[20]. Of Holman's local authority foster mothers 35 per cent thought natural parents should not be encouraged to visit while, in addition, a slightly smaller proportion thought it conditional upon suitable attitudes and intentions.[21] Adamson confirmed that 46 per cent thought it best if foster children did not see their own families.[22] This negative attitude, Holman shows, is encapsulated in hostile opinions of the natural parents (such as 'She's disgusting', 'She doesn't deserve to have children') and is revealed in an unwillingness to accept or talk to the foster children about their background. It follows that if the children are regarded as natural ones then the social workers too cannot be fully accepted as having an official interest in them. Accordingly, George discovered that 48.6 per cent of foster parents described their social workers only as 'friends', while 64.6 per cent would not think it necessary to inform the social workers even if the foster children stole.[23] Adamson also noted that a considerable number of foster parents felt unease about social workers' visits, while 34 per cent would not have initiated contact with them even concerning a serious problem.[24]

The exclusive fostering concept appears to stem from a two-fold premise. Foster children need to be sheltered from the influence of, even knowledge about, natural parents. Further, the foster children and foster parents' greatest need is freedom from any fear that the fostering will be disturbed or even that the fact of fostering will be brought to their attention. In many ways, it is strikingly similar to the 'fresh start' which dominated much boarding out under the nineteenth-century Poor Law.[25]

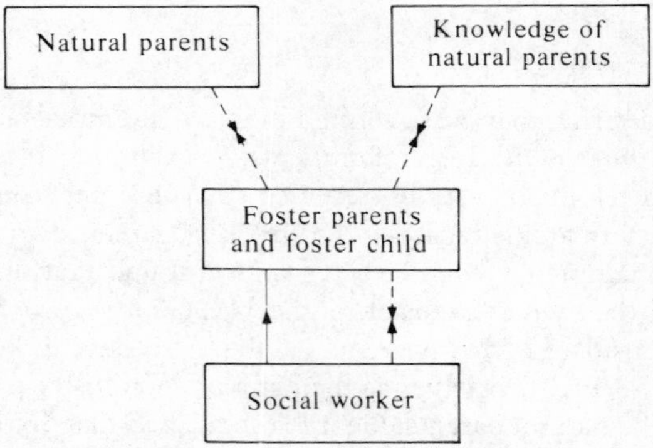

Figure 5.1

So the exclusive concept minimises the fostering aspect. The natural parents, knowledge of them, and contact with social workers are excluded in order to promote security and continuity. It can be diagrammatically expressed in the simple model in Figure 5.1. The foster parents may be able to exclude completely the natural parents and knowledge about them, while contact with social workers depends on the workers' initiative.

Inclusive fostering

By contrast, the inclusive concept is based on a readiness to draw the various components into the fostering situation. The foster parents can offer love without having to regard themselves as the real parents. Their attitude is that of the 36 per cent identified by Holman who said 'I know he's not mine but I treat him the same'.[26] A significant number did not wish to adopt, but this did not mean they lacked affection. The willingness to include others is further seen in the 31 per cent of Holman's[27] sample and 54 per cent in Adamson's[28] who considered that natural parents should see their children. Natural parents are regarded more positively, with a greater willingness that the children should possess full knowledge about them. The social workers are also included. Adamson records that over 50 per cent of the foster mothers looked forward to visits from the social workers, and would immediately contact them if difficulties rose.[29] Such foster parents, George pointed out, defined the social workers as official colleagues rather than informal friends. They were also more likely to regard themselves as possessing special skills which merited payment.[30]

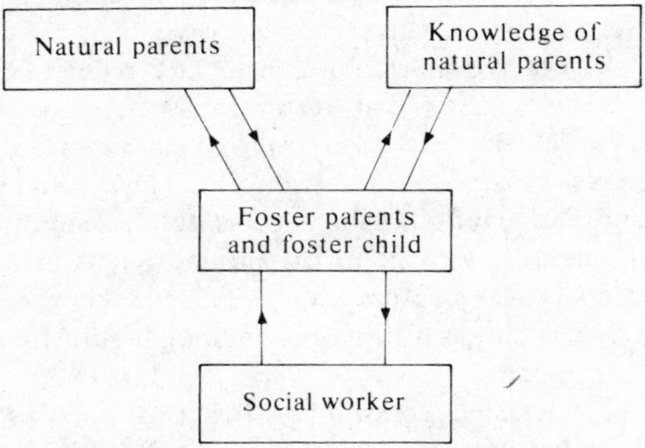

Figure 5.2

Within the inclusive concept, emphasis is placed on the children's need to obtain a true sense of their present identity and past history within a framework of affection. It accords with Ruddock's model of a role tree in which realistic grasp of personal identity is necessary so that the person can integrate various parts into a coherent pattern which will both satisfy him internally and allow him to find satisfactory external roles.[31] Moreover, it accepts that the inclusion of all the fostering participants – foster parents, children, natural parents and social workers – are needed in order to facilitate rehabilitation of the children if that is possible.

The inclusive concept can also be presented in diagrammatic form. (see Figure 5.2). It stresses not only the inclusive aspects but also the two-way nature of this form of fostering. Thus social workers visit not only because it is their statutory right but because the foster parents encourage them. Again, the foster parents are not only ready to answer the children's questions about their background but are ready to create situations in which the children feel free to ask them.

Implications

The two conceptions of fostering express polar positions within which will be many variations. None the less, contemporary research has established the existence of two types of fostering approximating to these positions. Certain important implications then follow.

No doubt foster parents acting according to either concept have much to offer. One kind gives a possessive love akin to natural parenthood, the other enables children to face reality. Significantly, recent studies do suggest that features associated with inclusive fostering are particularly related to fostering success. Here, it must be noticed, success is being defined in two ways. The method popularised by Trasler and Parker of equating success with a lack of breakdown has been continued by George in Britain and Kraus in Australia. In addition, success is also measured (by Weinstein, Thorpe, Jenkins) in terms of the foster children's present emotional adjustment, adaptation or lack of problems.

Clearly, the inclusive concept of fostering favours continued contact with natural parents and imparting background knowledge to the children. Exclusive fostering tends towards the opposite. A number of studies agree that foster children do benefit from contact and knowledge. Consider the following findings concerning parental contact.

1 Weinstein established that regular natural parent contact was associated with the foster children achieving high scores on present and future 'well-being' scales.[32]
2 Jenkins found that 57 per cent of foster children aged over one and a half years at placement with no parental contact were 'disturbed' as against only 35 per cent with regular contact.

Similar findings were reported for those under one and a half years.[33]

3 Holman observed that in general the less the contact the higher the incidence of certain emotional and physical symptoms such as soiling and ill-health.[34]

4 Thorpe's recent work revealed a trend suggesting a relationship between satisfactory adjustment and contact (although it was not statistically significant except for 11- to 13-year-olds).[35]

These findings serve to confirm the earlier view of Trasler which refuted the claim that 'children who maintain some kind of contact with their natural parents will fail in placement more frequently than those for whom contact would be impossible'.[36] The only differences concern how much contact is required. Holman actually found that although regular visits were beneficial, infrequent contact was associated with more fostering difficulties than no contact at all.[37] Jenkins had similar results,[38] but Thorpe did not find that irregular or infrequent contact was harmful.[39]

Turning to the foster children's knowledge of their own parents and of their fostering situation, Weinstein concluded that 'adequate conceptions of the meaning of foster status and of the role of the agency are important for the child's well-being'.[40] Thorpe observed that 'there is a tendency for children with good knowledge and understanding to be better adjusted in terms both of the social worker's assessment and the Rutter Behaviour Questionnaire'.[41] Not surprisingly, a relationship also exists between parental contact and the children's understanding of their situation, and between the children's adjustment and their knowledge of the social work agency.[42] In addition, factors which appear to stress the fact of fostering as opposed to natural parenthood are associated with foster homes not breaking down. Thus Kraus in an interesting study finds that older foster mothers with more than one foster child, fostering for reasons other than as a preliminary to adoption, are the most successful.[43]

There are exceptions to the above results.* But most of the evidence is in the same direction. In general, fostering success bears a closer relationship with the inclusive than with the exclusive type of fostering. The explanation, Holman suggests, is that foster parents of

* For instance, George found that the amount of parental visiting made no difference to success or failure. V. George, *Foster Care: Theory and Practice*, Routledge & Kegan Paul, 1970, p. 186.

the exclusive kind in regarding themselves as natural parents create situations of role conflict or confusion. For at times their conception must be challenged by the reality of social workers' visits, natural parent contact, or questions from the children. The resultant anxiety and confusion can be conveyed to the whole family.[44] Trasler stresses the effects on the children, arguing that a lack of knowledge creates 'severe anxiety', which is then reflected in their behaviour.[45] But perhaps the explanation has been best expressed by a foster mother herself:

> All children have a very strong basic need of their own parents, but fortunately children from normal homes do not have to keep thinking about this or proving it. . . a foster mother would be heading for much unhappiness if she ever imagined she took the place of the real mother, either through deliberate cruelty or total inadequacy to cope with motherhood. . . .[46]

The association between fostering success and inclusive fosterings would be less noteworthy if they constituted the typical foster home. But a further implication is that a substantial number of long-term foster homes operate on the exclusive concept. Putting various factors together as a 'role understanding scale', Adamson calculated that only 48 per cent possessed a 'very good' or 'good' conception.[47] Although other researchers do not compile such scales, the writer's impression is that their studies reveal an even lower proportion acting on the inclusive concept. Whatever the exact amount, it still serves to underline a major dilemma of contemporary fostering. Research findings would encourage social workers to find foster parents of the inclusive kind. Many people, however, are drawn into fostering by motivations associated with the exclusive concept. They really want to act as natural or adoptive parents. If they act accordingly they may well shut off the foster children from contact with and knowledge about their natural families. Yet, if they attempt to act against their 'natural instincts' they may feel that their own pain is intensified and the prospect of losing the children increased. As one foster mother put it so graphically:

> From their years of experience they [social workers] feel it is right for the children to grow up in touch with both worlds so that the final choice of way of life shall be their own. . . . I do really agree but it is agony to see your children being hurt by this constant reminder of the past.[48]

One result of the tension has been strong pressure to legitimise and legalise the exclusive concept of fostering. Some foster parents have actively supported legislative proposals ro reduce the rights of natural parents, to give foster parents more legal security, and to facilitate the adoption of foster children.

The intensity of foster parent feeling has meant that social workers are also drawn into the fostering dilemma. The research suggests that most social workers hold the inclusive concept of fostering.[49] They frequently work with foster parents who possess the opposite view, at a time of foster parent shortage. The social workers thus find themselves believing that foster children should be encouraged to know or know about their natural parents yet aware that to do so would endanger the fostering. The advent of aggressive natural parents or the foster children's immediate distress could precipitate the foster parents' withdrawal or even a 'tug-of-love'. What happens? George's work suggests that generally the social workers collude with the foster parents. He found that only 3.8 per cent of natural parents were encouraged to see their children,[50] while Holman calculated that in over half his cases neither natural mother nor natural father had been contacted by the social workers in the period studied.[51] Thorpe, in commenting that the mutual desire of foster children and natural parents to see each other is greater than realised, adds that, 'Many of the parents interviewed felt that from the time the children entered care they were tacitly, if not directly, excluded from involvement in their lives'.[52] George concludes his study even more strongly by saying that social workers and foster parents 'by their active hostility or passive inaction towards natural parents have forced or have merely allowed natural parents to alienate themselves from their children. This alienation has in turn been used as evidence for the natural parents' lack of interest in their children and for their inability to care for them adequately.[53] These findings are surprising in view of the emphasis which training courses and textbooks place on the social workers' role of maintaining links between children and parents. The explanation may be related to the proportion of untrained staff in the local authorities studied. As will be mentioned later, the evidence suggests that untrained workers do differ from the trained in some aspects of practice. Whatever the explanation, the fact is that the studies concur in finding some workers so caught by the need not to disturb foster homes that they find themselves reinforcing the very concept of fostering with which they disagree.

The implications of the fostering situation become even more serious when it is appreciated that the increased demand for foster parents particularly reflects a need for those of the inclusive type. The physically and mentally handicapped and those with behavioural problems described in *Children Who Wait* will require not only affection but skilled foster parents willing to co-operate with social workers. If these in-built dilemmas are disheartening then it is timely to be reminded that the same researchers have also identified what Adamson calls 'model' foster parents who are prepared to invest emotions and skills into children who will never be fully theirs. [54]

Summary

To foster children is no longer regarded as the main objective of the child care services. However, fostering is once again a matter of social work and public debate. The paper has explained that more types of children are now being assessed as requiring fostering at a time when Social Service Departments are finding it difficult to expand their number of foster homes. This greater demand for foster homes coincides with recent researches which help to clarify the nature of fostering. Accordingly, a distinction can be made between 'exclusive' and 'inclusive' fosterings. It is considered that a conflict exists between the popularity of exclusive fostering and research findings which stress the value of inclusive fostering.

Note

This chapter is a part-reprint from the *British Journal of Social Work*, vol. 5, no. 1, 1975.

References

1 J. Heywood, *Children in Care*, Routledge & Kegan Paul, 3rd edition, 1978.

2 J. Heywood, 'Recent Developments in the Structure and Practice of Child Care', *Social and Economic Administration*, vol. 4, no. 3, 1970.

3 Monkton Report, *Report on the Circumstances which led to the Boarding-Out of Dennis and Terence O'Neill at Bank Farm, Minsterly, and the Steps taken to Supervise their Welfare*, HMSO, 1945.

4 Home Office, *Report of the Committee on the Care of Children*, HMSO, 1946.

5 J. Charnley, *The Art of Child Placement,* University of Minneapolis Press, 1955:E. Glickman, *Child Placement Through Clinically Orientated Casework,* Columbia University Press, 1957: H. Gordon, *Casework Services for Children,* Houghton Mifflin, Boston, 1956: D. Hutchinson, *In Quest of Foster Parents,* Columbia University Press, New York, 3rd printing, 1943.

6 P. Gray and E. Parr, *Children in Care and the Recruitment of Foster Parents,* Government Social Survey, 1957

7 G. Trasler, *In Place of Parents,* Routledge & Kegan Paul, 1960: R. Parker, *Decision in Child Care,* Allen & Unwin, 1966.

8 R. Walton and M. Heywood, *The Forgotten Children,* University of Manchester, 1971, pp. 19-20.

9 Gray and Parr, op. cit., p. 18

10 R. Holman, *Trading in Children,* Routledge & Kegan Paul, 1973.

11 Holman, op. cit., pp. 31-3.

12 Dr. Barnardo's Homes, *Racial Integration and Barnardo's,* 1966; J. Gale, 'Non-European Children in Care', *Child Care,* vol. 17, no.4, 1963.

13 J. Rowe and L. Lambert, *Children Who Wait,* ABAFA, 1973.

14 R. Holman, 'Which Way for Child Care?' *Community Care,* no.28 1974.

15 Holman, op. cit., 1973.

16 K. Judge, 'Social Service Spending', *New Society,* vol. 29, no. 618, 1974

17 Holman, op. cit., 1973, pp. 73-5.

18 G. Adamson, *The Caretakers,* Bookstall Publication, Bristol 1973, p.161.

19 V. George, *Foster Care: Theory and Practice,* Routledge & Kegan Paul, London, 1970, p.54.

20 Ibid., p. 58.

21 R. Holman, 'Private Foster Homes,' PhD Thesis, University of Birmingham, 1971, p. 427.

22 Adamson, op. cit., p. 142.

23 George, op. cit., p. 49

24 Adamson, op. cit., p. 156.

25 George, op. cit., p. 14.

26 Holman, op. cit., 1973, p. 73

27 Holman, op. cit. 1971, p. 73.

28 Adamson, op. cit., p. 142.

29 Ibid., pp. 154-6.

30 George, op. cit., pp. 45, 46.

31 R. Ruddock (ed.), *Six Approaches to the Person,* Routledge & Kegan Paul, 1972, London, ch. 5.

32 E. Weinstein, *The Self Image of the Foster Child,* Russell Sage Foundation, 1960, p. 17.

33 R. Jenkins, 'Long Term Fostering', *Case Conference,* vol. 15, no. 9, 1969.

34 Holman, op. cit., 1973, p. 192.

35 R. Thorpe, 'Mum and Mrs So and So', *Social Work Today,* vol. 4, no. 22, 1974.
36 Trasler, op. cit., p. 233.
37 Holman, op. cit., 1973, p. 201.
38 Jenkins, op. cit.
39 Thorpe, op. cit.
40 Weinstein, op. cit., p. 18
41 Thorpe, op. cit.
42 Ibid.
43 J. Kraus, 'Predicting Success of Foster Placements for School-Age Children', *Social Work (USA),* vol. 16, no. 1, 1971.
44 Holman, op. cit., 1973, pp.78-80.
45 Trasler, op. cit., p. 107.
46 N. Timms, *The Receiving End,* Routledge & Kegan Paul, 1973, p. 58.
47 Adamson, op. cit., pp. 194-5.
48 Timms, op. cit., p. 99.
49 George, op. cit., ch. 2.
50 George, op. cit., p. 174.
51 Holman, op. cit., 1973, p. 236.
52 Thorpe, op. cit.
53 George, op. cit., p.220.
54 Adamson, op. cit., p. 193.

Rosamund Thorpe

6 The experiences of children and parents living apart: implications and guidelines for practice

Introduction

Central to the values underlying social work with children separated from their parents is the notion of acting in the 'best interests' of the child in care. However, what constitutes the child's best interests is by no means clear; the controversy which surrounded the passage of the 1975 Children Act through Parliament persists, and is symbolised by continuing conflict over the 'blood-tie' issue. On the one hand, social workers are cast in the role of misguided do-gooders, intent on returning children to the care of their natural parents, regardless of the risk of deprivation, neglect or physical abuse. On the other, there are those who favour the adoption of children who are in long-term care, with all that that invariably implies about the severance of the child's ties with his natural parents and/or other significant people from his past.

Clearly it is not helpful to polarise opinion so simply. Working in foster care is a complex and painful business and there are no easy answers. It is therefore vital that attempts are made to clarify the issues involved, and as part of this process it is important to consider what children and natural parents think and feel about 'being in care' and possible plans for their future. Accordingly, the aim of this chapter is to focus on the experiences of children and parents living apart, and to draw attention to some of the implications for social work practice. The information used will be drawn primarily from my own research, but wherever possible it will be substantiated by reference to other research studies.

The research design

The first major piece of consumer research in foster care was that of Weinstein[1] in the USA. This was an important study in that the findings were clear cut and lent weight to the prevailing theoretical view of the nature of foster home care. For example, Weinstein found that amongst the sixty-one foster children he interviewed, their 'well-being', as rated by social workers, was enhanced if:

1 the child had a clear understanding of his foster situation;
2 the child identified predominantly with his natural parents; and
3 the child was in contact with his natural parents.

Since these findings in America had clear implications for foster care practice there was a need to discover whether similar findings would emerge from a British study.

With the aid of a grant from the Social Science Research Council, I undertook a replication of Weinstein's work as part of a larger research project on 'The Social and Psychological Situation of the long-term foster child with regard to his natural parents'.[2] Basically this was a study of children in long-term foster care and their natural parents. In 1971 a sample was taken from one Midland local authority of all the children who had been in their current foster home with non-relatives for at least one year, and who were between the ages of five and seventeen years. Tape-recorded interviews were held with the 121 children in the sample, focused on how they thought and felt about their situation as foster children. At the same time the foster parents and social workers involved were also interviewed to ascertain their perception of the situation, particularly in relation to the involvement of the child's natural parents. The psychological adjustment of the foster children was measured by two scales; firstly, to be comparable with Weinstein's study, the somewhat subjective Total Well-Being Scale which he devised was completed by social workers; and secondly, the Rutter Behaviour Questionnaire was completed independently by the child's foster parents and schoolteacher. This is a more objective scale devised by Rutter and well tested for reliability and validity.[3]

In 1972 I attempted to trace and interview the natural parents of the sample foster children. Altogether tape-recorded interviews were completed with forty-seven natural parents, that is, at least one parent of 50 per cent of the children interviewed.

The foster children

Since the research project specifically looked at children in foster home care, what follows is mainly about foster children. However, some of the points made may be applicable to all children separated from a natural parent, whether by entry to care or by death or divorce, whether in foster home or adoptive home, residential care or boarding school, one-parent family or step-family.

Since the focus of interest is what constitutes the best interests of the child it is appropriate to look first at the emotional adjustment of the children studied to try to disentangle the factors which are related to good adjustment. This may then be compared with what seemed important to the children themselves, that is, their own view of their best interests.

Adjustment

Although foster home care is generally regarded as the best method of substitute care short of adoption,[4] as many as 39 per cent (almost two-fifths) of the sample foster children scored a seriously disturbed rating on the Rutter Behaviour Questionnaire. This compares with a proportion of 23 per cent of children in the general population, found when the scale was administered in the London Borough of Camberwell,[5] a community where the social class structure resembles the social class background of the sample foster children. Moreover, when the Rutter Behaviour Questionnaire had been used in two previous studies of children in residential care, the proportion of disturbed children was found to be 36 per cent[6] and 46 per cent[7] respectively, i.e. slightly below and slightly above the proportion found in this study. From these figures it would appear that children in care are more vulnerable to disturbance than children in the general population - which is what one might reasonably expect. However, additionally it appears that children in foster home care are as likely to be disturbed as children in residential care - which is not what one might reasonably expect, in view of the prevailing preference for fostering and the fact that the most disturbed children are more likely to be placed in residential rather than foster home care.[8]

This suggests that foster home care is not noticeably more effective than residential care. When viewed with the evidence from other research studies about the breakdown of long-term foster home placements[9] and the adult adjustment of former foster children,[10] then the unqualified association of good child care with foster home care is questionable. Clearly this has implications for assessing the place of long-term foster home care in the context of all substitute care provision. In child care there is a constant danger that placement decisions for a child are made according to the current vogue, rather than within a balanced perspective of a variety of resources. In particular, there is a danger that foster care is chosen when skilled residential care may be preferable. Recent research on residential care suggests that, contrary to prevailing professional opinion, residential care can be as successful as the natural family in providing an environment in which children can grow into successful and well-adjusted adults.[11]

Turning to the factors which differentiated the seriously disturbed foster children from the rest of the sample, other more specific practice implications may be drawn. For all except the very youngest of children, entering care is an experience of object loss in that, however inadequate or even neglectful natural parents have been, the child will have formed some attachment to them, and this attachment will be disrupted by the separation entailed in going into care. Studies in maternal deprivation suggest that such disruption of bonds may be related to subsequent emotional disturbance, but that the degree of damage caused by separation varies according to the child's age at separation, and the quality of care relationships experienced before and after separation.[12] It is therefore useful to look at the sample children in relation to these factors.

With regard to the child's age at separation, those sample children who entered care at five years or older were significantly less disturbed than those who experienced separation during the first five years of their life. And within this latter group, those children who were placed in their current foster home before the age of two years were significantly less disturbed than those who were placed between the ages of two and four years. Clearly, early admission to care is related to greater disturbance; and children who enter care between two and four years are especially vulnerable. This may be explained in terms of the theory of attachment,[13] which suggests that it is likely that children placed before the age of two years make primary attachments to their foster parents in contrast with children who enter care after the age of two years who have already made primary attachments to their natural parents. Of these latter children the attachments made by those over two but under school age may not yet be sufficiently strong for them to handle the experience of separation very well, whereas those over five are better able to retain firm attachments to natural parents in their absence, and hence handle the experience of separation more positively.

The implications of these findings for practice are extremely important and lend support to the arguments of Goldstein, Freud and Solnit about the significance of the passage of time for children at different ages.[14] A child placed before the age of two years will make a different sort of relationship with foster parents than one placed after the age of five. This must be an important consideration in making plans for the younger child's future since for him the distinction between his biological parent and his psychological parent is clear, and the right of the child to stay with his biological parent must be weighed against factors pointing to replacement or rehabilitation, including the rights of the biological parents.[15]

For children who were older at the time of separation or placement the distinction between psychological and biological parents will be less clear and accordingly will have a different influence on planning and decision-making. Moreover, because of the greater hazard entailed for children entering care between the ages of two and four there is a second equally important consideration; namely, the need to avoid separation if at all possible. This has social policy implications relating to day-care provision for the under-fives, which may be beyond the power of the individual social worker to effect. However, flexible and imaginative use of daily minders or part-time foster care could and should be seen as part of a whole range of available alternatives to substitute care, and there is scope here for development of the community child care worker role as envisaged by Holman.[16] Where it is not possible to support the child in his family in the community, then there is a need to take special care to minimise the damaging effects of separation by, for example, devising a process of reception into care in which the child's needs are not subjugated to administrative requirements.[17] For example, social workers should resist the practice of exposing children to dehumanising medical examinations *en route* from natural to foster home, as still happens in some authorities.

Apart from age at separation, the degree of damage resulting from separation is also influenced by the quality of care experienced prior to entry to care. In this study it was not possible to assess this retrospectively, but other research studies by Wolkind and Rutter[18] suggest that this is an extremely important variable. This may well be the case, since in my study so few of the variables concerning the quality of care experienced after entry to care seemed to have a major effect on the adjustment of the sample foster children. There was, however, some evidence of factors which might reduce the risk of disturbance. For example, although not significant in a statistical sense, disturbance amongst the children clearly increased with the number of changes of placement they had experienced since entering care and was proportionately less where there had been pre-placement visits in preparation for the placement. Older, experienced foster mothers were associated with an absence of disturbance and, similarly, the presence of siblings in the same foster home appeared to have a beneficial effect. In addition, those children whose future was assured in the foster home were better adjusted, as were children who had clear and full knowledge and understanding of their situation, and those who were in contact with their natural parents and/or siblings living elsewhere.

Although these latter two findings, which relate adjustment to self-knowledge and contact, were not statistically significant, the trends observed support the earlier findings of Weinstein,[7] and lend some weight to the concept of 'inclusive' fostering as advocated in the child care literature and conceptualised by Holman in another paper in this collection (Chapter 5). Conversely, they raise doubts about the value of 'exclusive' fostering, despite the encouragement of this model by the provisions of the 1975 Children Act. Furthermore, it is important to emphasise the last three factors mentioned in relation to the adjustment of foster children - that is, self-knowledge, contact, and the existence of definite plans for the child's future - as these are the factors which in the interviews the children considered to be important to themselves.

The foster child's perception and experience of placement: the need for security

All of the foster children interviewed in the research were long-term, and in fact most had been there very much longer, the mean length of stay being six years. Eighty-seven per cent of the children were expected by their social workers to remain in the foster home until and beyond their discharge from local authority care at the age of eighteen years; and 75 per cent of the children identified with their foster parents and wanted to remain living with them. Despite the extent of expected permanence, concern with their security of tenure in the foster home nevertheless coloured the interview responses of several of the children. For example, when asked to explain what they understood by the meaning of being fostered, the usual response simply implied that it involved living with people other than parents. However, some children chose instead to emphasise the fact that a foster child does not belong to the foster parents in the same way that their own or adopted children belong. And a trace of anxiety can be discerned in the responses of these children.

> *Brian* (14 years): The rest of the children belong to my mum and dad but I'm just brought up as another part of the family. I don't actually join it, I just fitted into it.

Some children reduced the anxiety inherent in the sense of 'not belonging' by defining the meaning of 'foster' accurately yet dissociating themselves from its implications; they did not perceive themselves as fostered.

> *Angela* (8 years): Some children come for a bit. Some mothers leave them and some mothers go to hospital. They all go back to their own mothers but I don't think that could happen to me. This is a foster home to some children who come, but not for me. For me it's a real, proper home now!

Other children harboured unrealistic fears about being removed from their foster home, despite the social workers' expectation that the placement was permanent. This was apparent, for example, when asked about their future.

> *Derek* (12 years): I think you're only out in a certain place for a certain length of time, say two to three years and then you're supposed to be moved. I don't know why – perhaps people get fed up with you.

Fear of replacement again cropped up when children were asked whether they felt being fostered was different in any way from children growing up with their own parents.

> *Lynn* (14 years): I don't think you should have to be extra specially obedient but you don't like saying things to foster parents that you might later regret. I argue because I like to stick up for what I believe in, but I think sometimes foster children are frightened to do this. They're afraid of being sent back.

Clearly this concern amongst foster children for their security of tenure has implications for working with and on behalf of foster children, although caution must be exercised in drawing very explicit conclusions from what was a specialised sample. Because of the length of stay in care of most of the sample children, many of them wanted to remain in their foster home and were anxious about the chance that this might not be possible. However, there were a few (mainly adolescents) who wanted to return home and who were afraid that this might not be possible. If the sample had been representative of all children in care then the proportion anxious to return home would probably have been greater.

Thus the first and major conclusion must be that children in care need to know what is going to happen to them, whatever it is. Whilst, clearly, those children who have already spent a high proportion of their life in a foster home may need to be assured that they can remain there, for other children it may be necessary to plan and work more positively than hitherto for rehabilitation or a more appropriate placement. And for yet other children there will be a need for them to be aware when their future is uncertain. For knowledge of uncertainty is shared and thus bearable, whereas uncertainty of knowledge can be frightening, even disturbing, since in the absence of facts, fantasies and fears will run wild.

Whatever their expected future the need of children to know what is going to happen to them implies, above all, a need for serious planning for children in care from the very time of their entry into care and, additionally, a need to involve children in the planning process. Sadly, the available evidence suggests that neither of these practices is widespread at present. As Rowe and Lambert put it, 'social workers still seem to be making plans *for* people and not *with* them';[19] and worse, in Parker's view, far too often social workers have no formulated plans and no plans to make any either[20]

The need of some children for a sense of security in their present foster home raises further implications, more specifically related to the provision of security to children in long-term foster homes. It is to the needs of these children that many of the new provisions in the 1975 Children Act relate. However, it is important not to lose sight of a broader perspective entailed in planning. There is a danger that attention may be too specifically focused on the provision of security, with too little consideration given to other, equally important, needs which may well influence the choice of the form of security offered to children in long-term foster care.

The need for a sense of identity

Weinstein suggested that in developing a sense of personal identity foster children need to be able to answer three questions for themselves.[21]

1 Who am I?
2 To whom do I belong?
3 What is going to happen to me?

In being concerned with the security of their future in the foster home, the foster children in this sample were attempting to answer questions two and three. However, it was clearly apparent that they were equally concerned with the first question, Who am I? (See also McWhinnie[22], Triseliotis[23] and Sants[24]).

Almost all of the children were concerned to know much more about their natural parents, and many were keen to retain or re-establish contact with them. For example, *Jane* (12 years), recently re-introduced to her natural mother, explained:

> I saw Mum last week – the first time for five years. I was ever so pleased. She's nice; she talks nice and looks nice and dresses nice – but I don't know really because I don't live with her. She's not really as I imagined her. I thought she'd be all fussy sort of thing, but she weren't – only a little. It's a bit confusing. I'm very pleased to have seen her and if I don't see her it bothers me a bit in bed at night sometimes. I think it's best to see her once or twice. I don't really know why. I just think so. I want to see her again; I'd like to see her. I like staying here but I'd like to see my mum occasionally.
>
> My dad, he's gone back to India. I've never seen him in my life. I would like to have seen him just once because I'd like to see my own dad instead of thinking someone else is my dad when they're not. It didn't bother me before when I was little, but I'd like to find out now that I'm bigger.

What Jane had to say highlights not only the need foster children have for a sense of genealogical roots in fixing the boundaries to a sense of self-identity, but also the way that, in the absence of facts, children will develop fantasies. Such fantasy pictures of natural parents may become extreme or bizarre, and this can lead to insecurity; this is further compounded by the fact that fantasies consume a great deal of emotional energy which cannot then be channelled into learning or making relationships. This in turn leads to the not unfamiliar picture of the child in care who is either under-achieving in school, or having difficulty in making relationships, or both. And this would account for the relationship between self-knowledge and emotional adjustment in foster children, mentioned earlier in this paper.

In view of the argument about the separated child's need for knowledge, together with the expressed interest of the foster children interviewed, it is perhaps surprising to find that in this research study the self-knowledge and understanding of foster children was very limited and that contact between foster children and natural parents was extremely rare.

A disturbing 22 per cent of children had no, or very little, understanding of their background and present situation, the majority had some but inadequate understanding, and only 26 per cent, i.e. a quarter, had what can be called a good understanding. In fact, three children were not even aware that they were fostered. As would be expected, the extent of understanding increased with age, but at all ages a majority of children had limited knowledge and understanding.

The need for contact between foster child and natural parent

Only thirty-three of the 121 children (27 per cent) had any contact with their natural parents and only less than half of these – fifteen children (12 per cent) – had contact as often as every three months, which, for a young child with an immature sense of time, can scarcely be considered frequent. Of the eighty-eight children (73 per cent) who had not seen a natural parent for at least two years, twenty-seven had some contact with siblings or relatives, and sixteen had a sibling in the same foster home. Conceivably this afforded some compensation for these children, but forty-five children (37 per cent) were without any contact whatsoever with a member of their natural family.

There is now considerable research evidence that lack of contact between children in care and their natural parents is related to poor emotional adjustment and delayed return home.[25] As outlined earlier in this paper, my research supports these findings; and in addition it suggests that lack of contact may lead to feelings of insecurity, confusion or anxiety about personal identity. For example *Andrew* (16 years) felt that:

> When you know as little as I do about your own parents, you do wonder. Your own father could have been a murderer – it's very doubtful but you wonder, 'Will this run in the family?'

In a similar vein there was some evidence from the comments of children interviewed that some of those who were not in contact experienced a sense of marginality or stigma in being fostered, which was not shared by those who had contact with their natural family. There is a popular belief that children in foster homes experience a conflict of loyalties between their natural and their foster parents and feel 'different' because of this. However, this was not substantiated by my research. When the adults – natural and foster parents – accepted each other, the foster children appeared to experience no conflict of loyalties and accepted the foster situation with equanimity, understanding the reasons why it had to be this way for them. By contrast, when children could not identify with their natural parents, through a lack of knowledge or contact, they seemed to experience a sense of stigma in being fostered. *Robert* (15 years) is perhaps a good example:

> It is probably slightly harder being fostered just because you've got to fight this conscious fact of being fostered and not having parents of your own. For example, if you have the micky taken out of you at school – or fear they might find out and take the micky. It's just your fact and you have to put up with it. It's really just mostly a joke – they don't mean to hurt, they only think it's a game – but others may not.

This experience of stigma in being 'different' links in with the theoretical view that children often experience the separation from natural parents entailed in coming into care as rejection, and that their feelings of rejection may undermine their sense of personal worth.[25] This was apparent in my research, in that those children who were in contact with their natural parents seemed reassured that they were loved, rather than rejected. They understood that the reasons for their being in care were not because they were bad, unlovable or 'no-good'; as a result they could tolerate the 'difference' implicit in being a foster child.

Implications for social work practice

These effects of lack of contact and/or self-knowledge have clear and important implications for social work practice in helping children in care to compile a real and positive picture of themselves. For a start, time must be devoted to talking with children, both on a factual and an emotional level. The evidence from my research suggests that not much of this is done by social workers, for only 30 per cent of the children spent time alone with their social worker. However, this is not necessarily bad provided someone with sensitivity is talking with the children, and in many cases it will be more appropriate for the person with daily care of the child to do so. In this case, however, it is imperative that social workers give foster parents sufficient support to be able to face with the child some of the painful and confusing feelings he is almost bound to have. Failure to help a child to sort out these feelings may well result in the child's growing up in a state of what Mandell calls 'emotional deep freeze'.[26] However, it is vital to recognise how much a child can face at any time, and to go at his own pace, whilst also being mindful of the tendency in us all to avoid facing the emotional suffering of children, and to rationalise this avoidance by arguing that the child will be too upset to face it.[27] The child already carries it within himself; it is the adults whose strength is invariably lacking.

In communicating with children about their feelings it is often a mistake to wade in directly. Far more effective is to make an approach via what Clare Winnicott[27] calls a 'third thing'; that is, an interest or activity that one can share with the child, thereby building a basis of trust which may lead to a sharing of feelings. Often the third thing may lend itself directly to talking about feelings, whilst at the same time meeting the need for factual information. For example, compiling a scrapbook or helping a child write his life story,[28] are essential for children in care who may have lost touch with the people, places and events of their earlier life. Because of the moves which children in care have experienced it is also crucial that photos, certificates, letters, paintings, etc. are kept and collected together so that the child can keep in touch with his personal past. This 'preserving the luggage of childhood'[29] is something which most parents spontaneously do for their own children and which, sadly, children in care so often lack.

Vital as information is to the foster child it can rarely replace the value to a child of retaining contact with the significant people from his past: parents, siblings, relatives, previous caretakers, other children from previous placements, and so on. All the evidence suggests that even where rehabilitation is not a possibility contact is invariably of positive value to the child's sense of identity and self-worth and to his emotional adjustment. In view of this, it is important to consider why there is so little contact between children in care and their natural families.

The problems of contact

As other research studies of separated and divorced parents have found, the dice appear to be heavily loaded against contact continuing between children and parents living apart.[30] So far as children in care are concerned in my research, I built up a picture of a constellation of factors which led to contact proving difficult and hence tailing off. On the one hand many foster parents were inclined to have an 'exclusive' view of their role; they found difficulty in accepting the natural parents, and the foster child's feelings for his natural parents. Social workers were then inclined to bend child care theory to fit the situation and collude with the foster parents' attitude for the sake of forestalling the risk of a foster home breakdown – with all the damage that might inflict on an already vulnerable foster child.

On the other hand, for reasons which will be explored later, natural parents often found difficulty either in having contact at all, or, in behaving well when they did have contact – thus reinforcing the 'exclusive' attitudes of foster parents and convincing social workers of the 'wisdom' of their stance in supporting and protecting the foster parents, all, of course, in the 'best interests of the child' concerned. As for the child, his 'distress' either before, during or after contact provided the ultimate justification for the curtailment of contact. This occurred regardless of his wishes, which invariably were in favour of retaining at least some contact, despite the emotional upheaval that this entailed for him – upheaval which was often, at least partly, due to living with the veiled hostility with which foster and natural parents viewed each other.

Whilst this pattern characterised many of the situations studied there were also several instances where contact clearly had been damaging to the child and had, perhaps rightly, been curtailed. However, this is not to say that, structured differently, contact could not have been a more positive experience for all concerned. What is needed is a more detailed study of the circumstances in which contact does or does not work positively, in order to disentangle the variables that make for more positive contact.

Meanwhile, it is possible to point to at least some implications for practice which might lead to more positive, and hence more frequent and enduring contact.

Fostering is a difficult and demanding job, whether 'exclusive' or 'inclusive', but the stresses involved in inclusive fostering are extraordinarily severe. People are asked to share their affection and inevitable attachment to a person (in this case a child) in a way that most people in our culture would find almost intolerable. It is too easy to criticise possessive foster parents. In order to gain some understanding of the strength and ambivalence of the feelings which may lie behind a foster parent's hostility to a natural parent it is a salutory exercise to get in touch with our own actual or potential feelings about sharing someone close: for example, husband, wife, lover or child. Clearly foster parents need considerable support in carrying out an inclusive role, with a commitment to maintaining contact between foster child and natural parent. The professional literature on foster parents is largely preoccupied with the selection of foster parents. If as much effort were focused on support – both emotional and educational – then this might do far more to guarantee the quality of child care provision than any amount of attention to selection, which, however rigorous, is full of uncertainty. By support it is implied that not only should social workers use more purposefully the encounters they already have with foster parents, but that serious consideration should be given to the provision of education and training for the fostering role. To this end some approaches to the provision of educational groups and courses have been outlined by the National Foster Care Association in a recent publication.[31]

With regard to the child's reaction to contact there is a danger of seeing any sign of distress as evidence that contact is harmful. Kline strongly refutes this view and argues, cogently, that distress is often a sign that the child is emotionally alive and amenable to help with his suffering and confusion.[32] He writes:

> A child's 'upset' reaction does not necessarily indicate that the visits are detrimental to his emotional health and development. . . . In this case visits do not cause the 'upset' but serve to bring closer to the surface the disturbed feelings that are buried inside the child. If the child can be helped to tolerate these feelings and eventually come to some peace with them, his capacity to relate to substitute parents and his emotional health will be better served than if he grows up under conditions that foster avoidance of them.

Although support for foster parent, child and social worker might go a long way towards increasing the extent of contact between children in care and their natural parents, it is unlikely to be wholly successful unless similar attention is focused on helping the natural parents cope with, what for them is invariably, an upsetting experience. (For a fuller discussion on parental involvement see Chapter 2 in this book.)

Conclusion

This paper has focused on the experiences of children and parents living apart, in order to shed some light on the consumer's view of what constitutes the best interests of the child. Implications and guidelines for practice have then been suggested in relation to social work with, and on behalf of, children newly entering care, and those already in long-term care.

References

1 E. Weinstein, *The Self Image of the Foster Child,* Russell Sage Foundation, 1960.

2 R. Thorpe, 'The Social and Psychological Situation of the long-term foster child with regard to his natural parents', unpublished PhD Thesis, University of Nottingham, 1974.

3 M. Rutter, J. Tizard and K. Whitmore, *Education, Health and Behaviour,* Longmans, 1970.

4 HMSO, *Report of the Care of Children Committee,* Cmd. 6922, HMSO, 1946; R. Holman, *Trading in Children,* Routledge & Kegan Paul, 1973, p.1; J. Rowe and L. Lambert *Children Who Wait,* ABAFA, 1973, p.15.

5 S. Wolkind, 'Children in Care – a psychiatric study', unpublished MD thesis, London University, 1971.

6 W. Yule and N. Raynes, 'Behavioural Characteristics of Children in Residential Care', *Journal of Child Psychology and Psychiatry,* vol. 13, December 1972.

7 Wolkind, op. cit., p. 166

8 Rowe and Lambert, op. cit., p.62.

9 G. Trasler, *In Place of Parents,* Routledge & Kegan Paul, 1960; R. Parker, *Decision in Child Care,* Allen & Unwin, 1966.

10 T. Ferguson, *Children in Care – and After,* Oxford University Press, 1966.

11 M. Wolins, 'Group Care – Friend or Foe?' *Social Work,* vol. 14, no. 1, 1969.

12 M. Rutter, *Maternal Deprivation Reassessed,* Penguin, 1972.

13 J. Bowlby, *Attachment and Loss, vol. 1; Attachment,* Penguin, 1971.

14 J. Goldstein, A. Freud and A.J. Solnit, *Beyond the Best Interests of the Child,* Free Press, New York, 1973, p. 40.

15 Ibid., p.99.

16 R. Holman, *Inequality and Child Care,* Child Poverty Action Group, 1976, p. 32.

17 O. Stevenson, 'Reception into Care: its Meaning for all Concerned', *Case Conference* vol.10, no.4, 1963; also in R.J.N. Tod (ed.), *Children in Care,* Longmans, 1968.

18 S. Wolkind and M. Rutter, 'Children who have been in care – an epidemiological study', *Journal of Child Psychology and Psychiatry,* vol.14, no. 2, 1973.

19 Rowe and Lambert, op. cit., p. 108.

20 R. A. Parker, 'Planning for Deprived Children', National Children's Home, 1971, p. 50.

21 Weinstein, op. cit., p. 21.

22 A. McWhinnie, *Adopted Children, how they grow up,* Routledge & Kegan Paul, 1967.

23 J. Triseliotis, *In Search of Origins,* Routledge & Kegan Paul, 1973.

24 H.J. Sants, 'Genealogical Bewilderment in Children with Substitute Parents', *British Journal of Child Psychology,* vol. 37, no. 2, 1964.

25 Weinstein, op. cit.; M. L Kellmer-Pringle, *Deprivation and Education,* Longmans, 1965; R. Holman, *Trading in Children,* Routledge & Kegan Paul, 1973; J. Aldgate, see Chapter 2 in this book.

26 B. R. Mandell, *Where are the children? A class analysis of foster care and adoption,* Lexington Books. D. C. Heath & Co., 1973.

27 C. Winnicott, 'Face to Face with Children' in *Child Care and Social Work,* Bookstall Publications, 1970.

28 Association of British Adoption and Fostering Agencies, 'The Story of Stephen Shore', in *Planning for Children in Longterm Care,* ABAFA, 1976.

29 W. Jones, 'Keeping the Memories of Childhood', *Social Work Today,* vol. 1, no. 5, 1970.

30 W. J. Goode, *Women in Divorce,* Collier-Macmillan, 1965; D. Marsden, *Mothers Alone,* Allen & Unwin, 1963; V. George and P. Wilding, *Motherless Families,* Routledge & Kegan Paul, 1972.

31 National Foster Care Association; *Education and Training in Fostering.* NFCA, 1977.

32 D. Kline, 'The Validity of Longterm Foster Family Care Service', *Child Welfare,* vol. 44, no. 4, 1965.

Nancy Hazel

7 Normalisation or segregation in the care of adolescents

Adolescents in need of help

Adolescents have always been a thorn in the flesh of their elders and betters, evoking feelings of both envy and righteous indignation. That adolescents behave in ways unacceptable to the older generation is unlikely to change, and some of them will always constitute a real threat to the health and happiness of other people, so that ways of limiting their unacceptable behaviour must be found. It is not, however, altogether clear that the provision of care and control under the present system in the United Kingdom does much to decrease anti-social behaviour, and there are hints that it may even serve to increase it.

West studied self-reported delinquency in boys aged fourteen, sixteen and eighteen to find out whether delinquent behaviour tended to increase or to decrease following an official conviction and sentence. His findings were:

> The results supported the hypothesis that, in comparison with equally badly behaved youngsters who escaped conviction, the convicted youngsters became still more delinquent. Further evidence showed that the deterioration was associated with being convicted between sixteen and eighteen, but not between fourteen and sixteen. In their case, no appreciable deterioration in behaviour, as indicated by self-report, occurred between fourteen and sixteen, but a marked deterioration occurred between sixteen and eighteen. This result obviously lends support to the deviance amplification theory, according to which the attachment of an official stigmatising label, at the stage of a criminal conviction, is likely to increase rather than to diminish delinquent behaviour. [1]

The social services themselves also appear to contribute to the creation of delinquency. A substantial number of boys and girls enter care at such an early age that no delinquent behaviour pattern could possibly have been established, and then progress through various forms of provision to end up in penal establishments. This population has not been studied, but the fact that delinquent careers may start or become consolidated during the period in care is not in doubt, as a high proportion of Borstal admissions have had previous residential experience, sometimes from an early age.

Evidence on the results of residential care for adolescent boys presents a discouraging picture. Cornish and Clarke, comparing community home regimes of the structural and therapeutic community types, found reconviction rates of about 75 per cent and suggest that 'only for about 20 per cent of those admitted to the school could it be argued that institutional intervention had provided more than a temporary interruption of their delinquent behaviour'.[2]

There seems to be a general feeling of even greater discouragement concerning residential provision for girls, although this is not so well documented.

It is probably true that too many deprived and delinquent adolescent boys and girls are removed from their homes because too little help is available to them in the locality where they live and in the schools which they attend. In most areas, intermediate treatment (i.e., a combination of support at home and limited periods away), as foreseen in the Children and Young Persons Act 1969, has been slow to develop. On the other hand, there is certainly a population of teenagers for whom life at home has become unbearable: broken marriages, rejecting parents, sick or inadequate parents; these produce stresses which become intolerable at adolescence when the boy or girl can no longer be dominated physically, and the unhappiness is acted out in delinquency or suicidal behaviour. Boys and girls in this situation need an opportunity away from home to come to terms with themselves and their life situation.

Another group of adolescents also need a kind of help which is at present seldom available. They are the 'casualties of the system'. Often they entered care as infants, and it is difficult to see why they could not have been adopted at that time. Instead they have moved from residential nurseries, through foster home breakdowns to a series of residential establishments, so that, as teenagers, they are totally rootless and unequipped to cope with the demands of normal life in the community.

There thus seems to be a clear case for help to be provided away from home, together with a reappraisal of the present system. For the majority of boys and girls with severe problems we now offer only supervision at home by overworked generic (and often untrained) social workers, or admission to one-sex residential establishments, generally with education on the premises. Supervision by a generic social worker may mean little commitment to the special needs of adolescents; and, where a residential placement is chosen, specialisation by age, sex and symptom means that local ties are broken, and that the principles of normalisation and localisation are abandoned.

The special family placement project in Kent

The Kent project grew out of the realisation that other countries had developed apparently successful alternatives to segregated residential placements. In particular Sweden had placed adolescent drug abusers from Stockholm in foster homes outside the city. The assertion generally made that so many English children and adolescents were 'unsuitable for fostering' did not seem well founded as, although 50 per cent of foster placements broke down, this was probably partly attributable to poor social work and inadequate financial support.[3] In the mid-1970s English social work departments contained virtually no child care specialists, training courses devoted very little time to the teaching of child placement policy or practice, and payments to foster parents were generally at a 'maintenance only' level.[4] In 1976, the Department of Health and Social Security stated that £110 million was spent on developing residential care but only £14 million on foster care.[5]

The Kent Project was established as an attempt to demonstrate that adolescents who had been defined as 'hard to place' could be successfully maintained in foster care. The project was set up as a five-year experiment, starting in January 1975. The organiser was a senior research fellow of the University of Kent, generous financial support was given by the Gatsby Charitable Foundation, and the running costs of the placements were paid by the Kent Social Services Department, which also acted as employer for the senior social workers and secretaries of the project team. The boys and girls to be placed were in the care of the Kent County Council.

Perhaps the first point which became clear to the project team was that innovation and experiment is much easier to implement in a semi-autonomous organisation than in any large social services organisation, which is inevitably constrained by tradition and agreed procedures. I will return to this point when considering the future of the scheme.

The project set out to place the most difficult group, which was defined as adolescents aged fourteen to seventeen years with 'severe problems'. Adolescents were referred to the project by the divisional social workers and the onus was on these social workers to persuade the project that the problems were severe. In fact the boys and girls referred fell into three rough categories: delinquent boys; 'beyond control' girls; and casualities of the system: i.e., boys and girls who had spent many years in care, moving through many placements and becoming increasingly rootless and alienated.

The 'methods package'

The project aimed to develop a methods package which could be replicated. The essential components of this package were:

1 *The concept of foster care as work for which a professional fee is paid*

One placement is estimated as equivalent to a part-time job, and two placements constitute a full-time job. This concept creates a new status for paid foster parents. They are now considered as colleagues working with professional social workers on a basis of equality of esteem and status, but at the same time their position as freelance operators rather than salaried employees places them in a rather ambiguous situation *vis à vis* the departmental hierarchy. Their sense of commitment and group solidarity has in practice produced a very sharp awareness of their own identity as specialist practitioners, and they are a noticeably articulate and independent group. They are inevitably critical of certain aspects of social work practice, and this can create tensions.

2 *The group as the focus of work*

All project families attend local groups which meet about every 2 or 3 weeks. Each group is composed of one project worker and at least five project families (when this number becomes too large the group will split). Groups tend to meet in residential establishments and to include a residential social worker. The link with field social workers is by means of regular 'open' meetings to which the local social workers are invited. The boys and girls in placement attend on a few occasions.

The groups have a number of functions. In the first place, they are concerned with self and group selection. By entering the group, applicant families learn to understand what is expected of them, and either become part of the group or are helped to leave it. Applicants are not formally 'approved', although the same written enquiries as to their health and reputation are made as in the case of normal foster placements, and visits are made to their home in order to see how the family lives and to ensure that all family members are fully consulted. The project worker is responsible for the decision to propose a placement to an applicant family. This step will depend on the family's feeling ready to proceed and on the availability of a suitable match. The divisional social worker must, of course, agree with the proposed placement of any boy or girl he has referred. As soon as a match appears likely and the adolescent appears interested in the plan, the family of origin will be drawn into the discussions and introduced to the project family. (There are, of course, occasionally circumstances where this is impossible.)

Preparation for placement is another function of groups. The group helps applicants to think through their future role and provides appropriate information. During the first phase of the project, when all project families were new to the work, it was not difficult to arrange a training sequence alternating between speakers and rather introspective discussion. With the present trickle of new entrants a new system is needed which it is hoped will have three components: the experienced families will act as helpers to newcomers; there will be study days on specific topics, which will also be open to social workers and other foster parents; and there will be a handbook and a library of cassettes, giving information on a range of relevant topics.

The group also offers a network for help, support and transfer. Help and support are given both formally and informally, and group members are able to help each other with quite severe crises. It is also possible for adolescents to transfer from one family to another in case of need, and they appear to accept these moves 'within the tribe'.

The development of policy is a matter for concern. Issues relating to present and future practice, financial matters, etc. are discussed and decided, or recommendations made, in the groups.

3 *Placements are for treatment*

The placements are intended to promote change rather than to provide a substitute home. The placements are essentially time-limited. A plan is made for the next piece of time – 'until you leave school' – or any other convenient period. The time-span can, of course, be reconsidered, shortened or extended. They aim at problem-solving. The objective of the placement is to deal with problems which the adolescent can identify. These are usually fairly simple to state, such as going to school or not running away, but sometimes more complicated, such as learning to form better relationships with adults or peers.

The objectives of the placement are written down in a brief contract for the adolescent and the foster family. The family of origin may also agree to specific tasks, but this contract has not so far been written. The project and divisional social workers also have brief agreements which divide the work between them. The general principle is that it is the responsibility of the project worker to make the match and set the placement going, but long-term maintenance should, as far as possible, be carried out by the divisional social worker.

4 *Use of Publicity*

The project staff believe that it is essential for the general public to understand what they are trying to do if people are to volunteer to help. The project started with a press conference, and has succeeded in retaining the interest of the media. Project staff, foster parents and adolescents have spoken to reporters, broadcast, and appeared on television. The parents of origin do not object to this publicity: indeed, why should these boys and girls in placement feel stigmatised in any way? As a result of this publicity there have been no difficulties in recruitment and, as far as we can tell, no one has suffered any harm.

Success and failure

Up to 1 December 1977, seventy-five placements had been made, forty-one boys and thirty-four girls. Until the results of the independent evaluation are available, an analysis of outcomes can only be impressionistic and subjective.

The word 'success' may be used in a very limited way to mean 'non-failure'; i.e., the adolescent is living in a foster family, is not in trouble with the law, in conflict with school or employer, is not physically or mentally ill, and appears to be reasonably happy. This is the sense in which we shall use the word, as success in a wider sense is much more difficult to define.

On 1 December 1977, forty boys and girls were living with project families where they had been for at least eight weeks. Of these, fourteen boys and eighteen girls seemed to be quite successful. In the case of four boys and four girls there was some cause for concern, but no suggestion that the placement was unworkable.

The other thirty-five placements are accounted for by new placements (under eight weeks), failure to settle, completions, transfers and failures. Four boys and one girl failed to settle within the first eight weeks, and no further attempt was made to place them in families as it was felt they were resistant to this type of placement.

Eight boys failed to complete their placement and were admitted to residential care. In seven cases the breakdown was the result of persistent delinquency. In one instance it followed violent behaviour within the foster home. The boy was readmitted to residential care and spends holiday periods with the foster parents. In almost all cases a friendly relationship between the boy and the family has remained after the breakdown. No girls have failed in this way, although two girls who were almost eighteen behaved explosively just before a planned move to independence. A third girl, aged sixteen, ran away to join a much older man with whom she had a long-standing and sincere relationship.

The difference in the failure rate as between boys and girls appears to be mainly a product of police activities. Girls can make a considerable nuisance of themselves, staying out overnight, getting drunk, etc., but are seldom prosecuted. The equivalent boys' activities are taking and driving away cars or mopeds, and stealing, which are more threatening to the public, and for which they are almost always prosecuted. Once the boy is drawn back into the criminal justice system, it may be difficult to prevent a feeling of 'in for a penny, in for a pound', and a reversion to a delinquent identity.

As the forty-one families actively working in the project form a network or artificial tribe, transfer from one family to another is not considered as a failure if it contributes positively to the adolescent's maturation. Since the beginning of the project there have been ten successful transfers, for two distinct reasons. In some cases, the assessment given to the project is misleading; new problems emerge in the intimacy of a family setting and old ones gain a different significance. This is inevitable, as most assessments take place either while the adolescent is unhappy at home or in a fairly large residential establishment. In other cases, the adolescent is sure that he would like certain things, such as life in the country or being the only child. When he finds himself in this situation, he discovers that what he really wants is something quite different – a legitimate discovery.

It is important to allow transfers, particularly of the second kind, as it gives the adolescent a sense of responsibility for his own life, but it is made clear that in the project's view one change is generally the limit.

The problem of aftercare

As the adolescents in placement grow older the problem of aftercare becomes more and more important. From the start it was predicted that leaving the placements would be the most difficult phase of the whole sequence, and this appears to be the case. Placements can have a number of different outcomes, which may be summarised as return home, and the move to independent living.

Return home: Four boys and five girls returned home or to the care of close relatives. This has not proved successful in the case of two boys and one girl. One boy and three girls seem to be all right. One return is very recent. Even where relationships within the family have improved, it is often not easy for adolescents to return to the same neighbourhood and former peer group.

Independent living: Two girls have married, and one of them has a baby. One marriage has broken down after a year. Three girls have moved into bedsitters, and two more are planning to do so. Girls long for 'a place of their own', and a bedsitter in a friendly house seems to be a good stepping stone towards independence. Boys seem to lack this 'nest-building' drive, but also want to show that they can manage as adults. They choose lodgings, but do not always succeed. Six boys moved into lodgings, but three got into trouble quite quickly.

In some instances the adolescent who got into trouble after the conclusion of the placement could return to the foster home, and one girl has done so several times. For the boys, however, the criminal justice system tends to take over, so that already one has been sent to a Detention Centre and another to Borstal. A third is in residential care, and has not been re-referred to the Project. Two of these boys remain in touch with their foster parents.

Some of the post-placement solutions look very promising. For example:

1 Girl aged sixteen at placement. After just over a year in the foster home she has completed a secretarial training and is engaged. She has moved into a 'flatlet' in the foster father's mother's house.

2 Boy aged sixteen at placement. Had lived in residential care since infancy. After eight months with a project family he joined his West Indian relatives in London and started work there.

It is quite impossible to evaluate how far a placement in adolescence can effect lasting change. The adolescents, almost without exception, enjoy normal family life and benefit from it to some degree. For many of them, however, this experience is both too little and too late, and after eighteen they are still ill-equipped for independent living. Legislation provides some forms of support, but we need to improve considerably our management of this transition.

To sum up, the 'methods package' seems to work well. The concept of a 'caring career at home' attracts families where the wife has had satisfying experiences of paid employment and now wishes to have the financial rewards, intellectual stimulation and social contacts of work without leaving her home, and where the husband and wife enjoy having a shared task. Families of all ages, with younger or older children or no children at home, can all be successful. Space is important, and practically all families are buying their own homes, in many cases older properties.

The difficulties presented by the adolescents can generally, but not always, be overcome by patient and persistent work. In the first two years of the project no family has rejected an adolescent because of unacceptable behaviour, although placements have been terminated by mutual agreement where it was felt that no further progress was possible, or an adolescent refused to remain in a particular family.

But the question of how much lasting improvement placements make to the adolescent's ability to survive in society remains. It is quite likely that the results of a follow-up would be no better than the results of similar studies in relation to residential care. Even if this were so, family placement is cheaper and more humane than institutional care for delinquents and does not appear to involve any greater risks to the community. Even where a placement has 'failed', the adolescent appears to have benefited from it rather than the reverse.

The pattern of interlocking roles

It has sometimes been difficult for the divisional social workers to accept a new concept of their role *vis à vis* project placements if they have been trained as caseworkers. Figure 7.1, prepared by the Parent

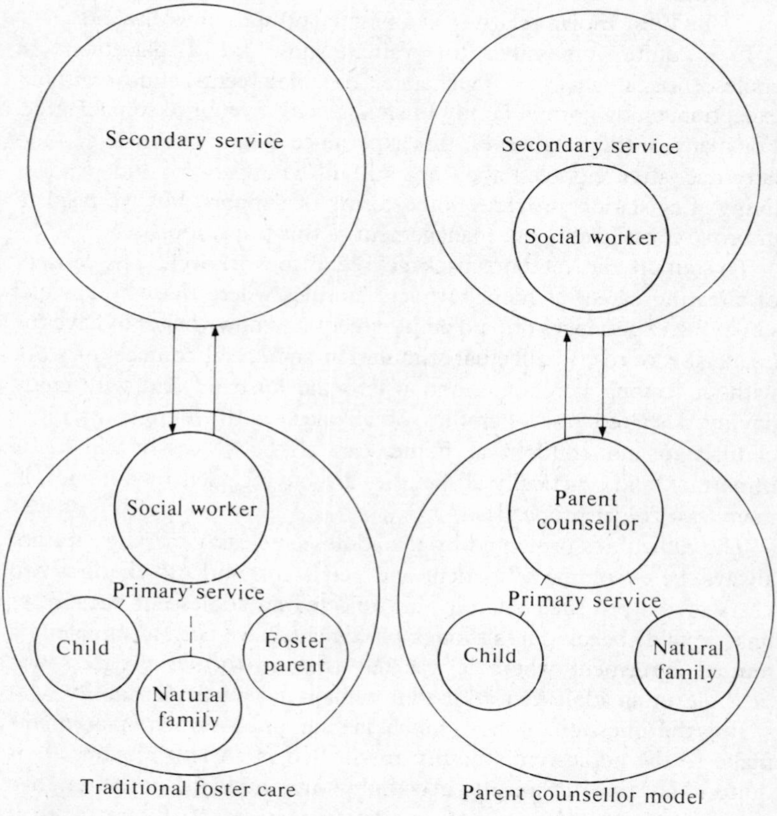

Figure 7.1: Administrative responsibilities

Counsellors Scheme of the Alberta Social Services, shows how the project families are expected to take responsibility for implementing the treatment plan which has been established at the inception of the placement, and to work with the family of origin. Kent echoes the role definition for the foster family made by the Alberta project:

> In summary, the role description, functions and expectations that were planned for parent counsellors (i.e., paid foster care workers) were significantly different than for foster parents. Their preparation included specially designed recruitment, selection, and training experiences; their primary function was the management of all services for the child and family in their care; and their accountability rested with clients, agency, and their parent counsellor colleagues. In short they were to be given responsibility commensurate with the capabilities that we believed they possessed, and they were to be provided with appropriate support, recognition, and financial remuneration.
>
> We began with a firm conviction that natural parents must be involved in the planning, goal setting, and service activities that would be characteristic of our programme. We assumed that natural parents would commit themselves to be involved in desired change activities, and that parent counsellors would aid in this process through frequent communication and resource acquisition where appropriate. We did not subscribe to the notion of a social worker managing or restricting communication between the two sets of parents as there seemed to be persuasive evidence from other programmes that such caution was both unnecessary and unworkable.
>
> Thus we began with a good deal of optimism that natural families could be involved productively in our service plans, and that while the specifics of this involvement would need later explication, we hoped our service model would lead to better results in this respect than are typically reported in foster care.[6]

The project worker appears to have three roles: recruiter, matchmaker, and trouble-shooter. As a recruiter he must find the families who will participate, ensure that the formal enquiries are completed, and that the families are enabled to discover for themselves if they wish to undertake this work and provided with the kind of training they need to equip themselves for the tasks ahead. The project worker runs the groups which provide training and support. As matchmaker the project worker will study the referrals which are made, he will suggest to the applicants which adolescents might best fit into their families. He will be responsible for enabling introductions to take place, for working out a treatment plan, obtaining the agreement of all parties and writing the contracts. He will be responsible for seeing that the placement gets off to a good start, and will then be expected to reduce his level of involvement. As trouble-shooter the project worker will intervene at any point during the placement to try to resolve difficulties or deal with complaints.

Although the role of the divisional social worker is not to provide direct treatment himself, he is responsible for providing reliable information at the point of referral, he retains accountability for the welfare of the adolescent, must assure himself that the match is appropriate, and must participate in establishing the treatment plan and drawing up the contracts. He must ensure that the appropriate financial and material support is available. He must maintain a relationship of trust and friendship with the adolescent throughout the placement in order to satisfy himself that a satisfactory service is provided. But the main service is provided by the project family, who will carry out the treatment plan, working with the adolescent, outside agencies such as schools, clinics and employers, and his family of origin. This is an area where it is particularly important for the roles to be carefully defined, as the divisional social worker may also be concerned with other problems in the family of origin which are not directly related to the welfare of the adolescent.

Sharing care is difficult for all concerned, but inevitable for each specific placement. In the long run, for the adolescent and his family, the placement may often be only an interlude in a long history of involvement with the Social Service Department, most of which has nothing to do with the project. For the project family, the current placement may be only one of a series, and each adolescent may have a different divisional social worker. Perhaps the most difficult part of the work for families who enter the project is to learn to collaborate with social workers within a large bureaucracy. It is difficult for them to avoid having unrealistic expectations of the social workers and not easy for them to share the responsibility for the adolescent.

Not unexpectedly, difficulties may arise where it is necessary to co-operate with other systems.

1 *Educational services*

It is extremely difficult for schools to offer appropriate individualised help to newcomers, in their last year at school, who have a long history of educational difficulties. On the whole they have shown great commitment and ingenuity in meeting these problems. A number of adolescents have wished to continue their education, but a further year at school often does not seem to offer enough impetus towards adulthood. Admission to technical colleges may be impossible for adolescents who want to continue learning but whose educational standard is not particularly high. When this occurs it is somewhat disastrous, as it means that past failures cannot be put right.

2 *The police*

We have learned that it is virtually impossible to place boys and girls where a prosecution is pending, as they feel so tense and insecure. In practice this causes considerable difficulties, as the time lag between the commission of the offence and the Court appearance is usually several months. During this period further offences may be committed, necessitating further appearances, not necessarily at the same court, so that a kind of chain reaction may be set up. In these circumstances the attitudes of magistrates are not necessarily consistent, so that no firm treatment plan can be made. Where Juvenile Bureaux have been set up, these difficulties have been markedly reduced.

3 *The health service*

On the whole general practitioners and psychiatric clinics are very helpful. However, the role of the psychiatric hospital at times of crisis or danger is not at all clear. For example, when girls take overdoses or attempt to injure themselves, or even make apparently serious threats against themselves or others, there is a need for instant admission to an environment where these threats can be acted out in safety. It is then to be expected that the placement can continue, provided appropriate multi-disciplinary support is available. However, hospitals do not necessarily accept the role of crisis treatment centres, and it is unlikely that most Social Service Departments can offer immediately available places with psychiatric supervision.

The future of the scheme

The scheme is likely to be incorporated into the Kent Social Services Department at the expiry of the five-year experimental period. This has raised considerable anxiety amongst the project families, who value their solidarity as a group of people engaged in sharing a difficult but worthwhile task. They feel that if they were to become part of a generic department, split among fifteen divisions, their special skills would be diluted and lost. It is nevertheless recognised that a greater degree of decentralisation will become inevitable as the project expands, and it is possible that specialist placement teams in three regions would provide an acceptable middle course.

At the same time as the project families have gained in skill and self-confidence, their interest has tended to extend from the day-to-day problems of managing a placement to the wider issues of managing the project within the Social Service Department. When the project was set up, an advisory committee was appointed, consisting of experts in child placement, senior members of the Social Service Department, and one representative of the project families. This committee has now been disbanded and replaced by an advisory, but not executive, committee consisting of six project family representatives (one from each group), and six 'professional' representatives, i.e., one member of the project staff and five senior members of the Social Service Department. Other people may be co-opted or permitted to attend without the right to vote. This plan was finally agreed at a general meeting of all project families and interested social workers in September 1977. It is hoped that a Committee of this kind will help the project families to feel that they are fully sharing in all plans for the integration of the project into the department.

Conclusion: normalisation or segregation in the care of adolescents

Policies for the care of any client group can be ranged along a kind of continuum. At the one extreme, reliance is placed on the care of experts in a specially constructed environment. Clients, selected by criteria such as age, sex and symptom, are placed together, and the care-givers are considered to be in the possession of special knowledge and skills which enable them to give effective help. For certain categories of inmate this model is clearly a valid one: the occupants of an intensive care unit in a hospital certainly need very specialised help from qualified personnel. For other groups, research casts doubt on the effectiveness of the model. One-sex community homes for adolescents, detention centres and Borstals seem to have a low success rate; and the personnel is largely unqualified and sometimes inexperienced, so that it is difficult to specify the 'special skills' or 'expertise' which are offered. Such a system, in which all services, even including education, may be provided on the premises, is extremely expensive to run. Yet in 1977 the United Kingdom relied on this model to deal with adolescents who needed care and control. The other extreme of the continuum would consist of a system in which the kind of service would be provided which would enable almost everyone in need of help or care to be maintained in his own home. For example, Sweden is currently conducting an experiment in providing care in the community without any residential back-up. Although it is not yet clear which clients cannot be maintained in the community, it has already been demonstrated in several countries that this type of care works well for groups who have traditionally been contained in specialised residential institutions of various kinds. However, placement policies are not static. A country may pursue the same strategy over a long period of time, improvement being limited to minor repairs or adjustments to the system ('tinkering'), or the system of care may be studied and evaluated, considered to be promising, and a deliberate policy of expansion and development may be set in motion (consistent development). Finally a country may decide that its present system is bad, scrap it altogether and make a fresh start ('all change'). Of course, these different courses of action are seldom so simplistic, but the trends can be detected, and stand out fairly clearly in policies for the care and treatment of adolescents.

In 1972 Massachusetts embarked on a programme of decarceration. This constituted a complete change of policy which is still being evaluated. The reformatories were closed, the staff were dismissed, and a wide range of other services was developed ('all change'). Sweden, following the publication in 1974 of the report of the National Commission of the Placement of Children and Young Persons, has endorsed the long-standing trend towards placement and maintenance in the community. The number of residential places, already extremely low, will shrink even faster, placement in the community will continue to develop, but, most of all, skill and resources will be devoted to helping families in their own environment in order to avoid removal of any kind (consistent development).

The policy in the United Kingdom has generally consisted of 'tinkering'. Reliance traditionally has been on one-sex residential institutions, with very little use of family placements and very few resources devoted to care and treatment at home. From the mid-1960s there was anxiety about the increasing number of adolescents entering care through the juvenile courts, and there was a demand for more residential places and particularly more secure places. Although 'intermediate treatment' was envisaged in the Children and Young Persons Act 1969, it developed very slowly, and fostering was virtually never considered for disturbed and delinquent adolescents.

As the country moved from the expansionist social policies of the 1960s, into the economic crisis of the mid-1970s, local authorities became more and more aware of the spiralling costs of residential care. At the same time, research studies showed consistently the failure of residential establishments to provide effective help to delinquent adolescents. Several working parties expressed the view that a change in policy was needed to give greater emphasis to care in the community, and in particular to develop and modernise the concept of Intermediate Treatment.

One of the promising features of intermediate treatment was that it led social workers to work with groups of young people and to place less reliance on the one-to-one casework methods in which many of them had been trained. Intermediate Treatment groups provide various kinds of help and activities, and are serviced by unpaid volunteers, paid volunteers and social workers. The groups perform a number of functions, which can roughly be divided into two main areas: assessment and screening; and treatment and help.

The adolescents for whom the group programme is both acceptable and appropriate will continue to attend, but for a minority it will become apparent that their needs cannot be met in a group situation, either because they are unable to tolerate group pressures or because they have intractable and often complex individual problems which cannot be tackled in a group setting. For these adolescents an additional service must be made available. Traditionally, this service has been the prerogative of social workers, who have sometimes involved unpaid volunteers. But a case can also be made for paid volunteers who would commit themselves to working intensively with one adolescent, who would continue to live in his own home. These freelancers would require group support and could use contractual, problem-solving, and time-limited methods, as developed in the Kent Project.

Finally, for a relatively small number of adolescents, removal from home would appear to be unavoidable, either because their family conditions are intolerable or because they cannot resolve their difficulties without a change of environment. For these, specialised family placements would be appropriate. It is also possible that where a family placement has been successfully completed the adolescent might be encouraged to join an intermediate treatment group as a helper, thus acquiring a legitimate reference group and a new adult status.

Thus a system of care and treatment for adolescents in the community should consist of three main components:

1 Groups for boys and girls accepted for intermediate treatment.
2 Non-resident individualised intensive help.
3 Specialised foster care.

In developing a continuum of care of this kind, considerable work on the screening and assessment functions of the groups is needed. This would appear to be the task of the social worker, who would also carry the role of organiser. Normally the social worker would not carry the role of caseworker or therapist, as the main treatment tasks would be undertaken by volunteers.

The whole trend towards maintenance in the community focuses on the need for a re-definition of the social worker's role. If we accept that lay people, acting as volunteers, paid freelancers, foster care workers, etc. can be trusted to carry out complex tasks which were formerly considered to be the prerogative of 'trained experts' such as field or residential social workers, and that these volunteers and freelancers can support and help each other, then the social worker's role becomes primarily that of facilitator, rather than attempting to provide a direct face-to-face casework or therapeutic service.

References

1 D. J. West and D. P. Farrington, *The Delinquent Way of Life*, Heinemann, 1977, pp.138-9.

2 D. B. Cornish and R. V. G. Clarke, *Residential Treatment and its Effect on Delinquents*, HMSO., 1975.

3 National Children's Bureau, *Highlight*, no. 6, 1973.

4 National Foster Care Association, *Education and Training in Foster Care*, NFCA, 1977.

5 Department of Health and Social Security, *Priorities for Health and Personal Social Services in England*, HMSO, 1976.

6 Alberta Social Services, Parent Counsellors, 'Casework Service Model', 1977.

Christine S. Reeves

8 Foster care: a partnership of skill

We care what happens to people only in proportion as we know what people are. *Henry James*

Foster care in all its facets is about that most complex feature of life and human interaction: it is about relationships. For the foster parent, there are many possible relationships. Besides the relationship with the child, its natural parents, the various relatives and other professional people, the most important of all is the relationship which exists between the whole foster family and the Social Service Department. Winnicott [1] highlights one important element in the relationship between the social worker and the foster family by commenting that: 'If the relationship becomes the worker-client relationship we know in casework, something has gone wrong in our selection of foster parents. We have taken on a client not a working partner and our work with the child will suffer in consequence.' Just as this factor is so critical in individual cases, so it was a dominating feature in the establishment of the National Foster Care Association (NFCA).

The association: its origins and aims

It is not surprising that the Association emerged at a time when there was a great deal of discussion and interest in child care. However, many people at varying levels in Social Service Departments were both surprised and sometimes disturbed by the establishment of such an organisation. The anxiety expressed might have been well founded had the Association become a destructively critical organisation. On the contrary, it has tried to comment and add its thinking for the improvement of a system which to many had already been showing signs of decay. The system needed a penetrating injection of renewed vitality, new foresight and new perceptions of foster care. Foster parenting at one time was very much for those full of kindly mothering instincts, their needs being fulfilled whilst a child, or children, was placed with them. At the same time foster parents themselves were treated as subservient in the caring partnership. In the last few years there has been a growing appreciation of the potential in foster care, along with more symmetrical relationships developing between foster parents and social workers. There has also been a developing awareness of the different ways in which foster care can be used. The new developments imply increased demands on both foster parents and social workers for specific knowledge, better understanding, and more skills to tackle the increasing problems displayed by children coming into care.

Foster parents play an intensive as well as an extensive part in the caring partnership. It is not surprising therefore that they express the desire to be more involved with the child care service as a whole as well as with the individual children.

The association: a partnership in caring

Implicit throughout the germination, growth and naming of the National Foster Care Association is the concept of foster care as a partnership. The name itself sees foster *care* as all important, not foster parent. The founders of the Association represented the three main service-giving partners in the system: foster parents, social workers and residential care staff. As the Association has developed, emphasis has continuously been placed upon its role as co-participator in developing an improved service for children in care, particularly foster care. By the same token local groups are encouraged to see themselves in a similar light and to work in partnership with the local authority towards an improved service. Even the individual foster parent should be encouraged to be co-participator with the individual social worker in pursuing the best care for the individual child.

At all levels, foster care should be seen only as a coalition. Whilst pursuing every opportunity for foster parent representation, the Association is acutely aware of the many other people that need to bring their skills to bear if sound planning and development is to be available to children in care. The foster parent, perhaps more than any other partner, sees the coalition at first hand and is aware of the interaction, or lack of it, that helps to form and mould the child's life patterns. Other professionals should be included, such as representatives of the medical, educational and psychological services. Too often, however, it is the foster parents who find themselves at the centre of differing opinions about some future plan for the child. In one case the foster parents had cared for a child for several years, coping with educational subnormality as best they could. A stage was reached when they felt something more needed to be done, and at their instigation the child was examined and assessed over a period of time. The medical and psychological services strongly recommended a form of care which would allow the child to remain in the secure environment of the foster home. This form of security was considered to be an extremely important feature of any treatment. The Social Service Department completely disregarded these recommendations, and the foster parents were left feeling anxious for the child, frustrated about the situation, and angry with the department. No really satisfactory explanations could be obtained from the social services.

If sufficient credence is given to the partnership concept, a lot could fall into place. We should then learn much more from each other, thereby giving a basis for improving service and even establishing joint training programmes. Foster care needs to be removed from its present rather detached and isolated position and be included with the rest of the child care services.

Historical perspectives

Many of the confusions existing in foster care are the inheritance of a past system. Its origins lay mostly in people who were willing to take children for very little or no financial remuneration. Such children were usually orphaned or destitute, with the foster parents frequently placing themselves in a pseudo-adoption situation. There was little likelihood of parental involvement or 'interference'. Whether foster parents were 'good' or 'bad' was often judged on whether they accepted any financial assistance or not! In the seventeenth century parents unable to care for their offspring were discouraged from abandoning them in the workhouse with the threat that the children would be fostered out. Fostering was mostly outside the 'Unions' boundaries, which caused parents to lose contact with the children. In 1870 a Poor Law Inspector made the recommendation that children should not be 'boarded out' with relatives, and should be discouraged from contact with parents. The idea behind this move was for a fresh start away from 'pauper parents'.

This pattern of care left foster parents in the role of substitute parents, often having little or no contact with the child's own family, or even the agency placing the child. The task was in one respect isolated and yet clearly defined. By the end of the Second World War, society's awareness of the needs of children began to develop and consequently change. The 1948 Children Act established child care departments and staff specialised in problems of child care, including foster care. Short-term foster care began to emerge, helping to present an entirely different picture of the potential and overall nature of the service. The element of permanency dwindled and there developed a growing realisation that foster care was no longer (if indeed it ever had been) a simple task of extending one's family by one, two or more.

Foster care was now beginning to be recognised as a skilled undertaking, but mostly in respect of new knowledge and skills needed for social workers. The foster parents' need for similar training was not recognised until very recently. Though new demands are being made upon social workers and foster parents, the tools required to meet them are not being sufficiently or effectively provided. Dinnage and Kellmer-Pringle [2] comment that 'foster parents are faced with a task which would tax the skill and understanding of a highly trained and experienced caseworker, let alone someone who is (and should be) emotionally involved, rather than skilled in detached professionalism.'

Given this kind of historical background and no positive dynamic development, it is not surprising that so many placements break down. These are ill-defined roles and relationships, widely differing expectations and assumptions; in short, 'conflicting perceptions of the foster care situation have continued to exist for close to a hundred years and to this day there is no consensus'. [3]

Preparations

Preparation for foster caring is as much in need of radical reappraisal as other areas of the service. For foster parents we need to look at recruitment methods and policies, assessment procedures, basic training, and methods for early introduction to the types of child as well as to the individual children whom they will foster. For social workers there is a growing awareness of the inadequacy of basic training programmes. Generally courses do not seem to equip social workers for their various tasks in assessing, placing and supporting children in foster care.[4] There is at present a great danger that an imbalance of skills is being created in a different direction compared with the post-1948 period. Whilst foster parents increase their demands for training and for more knowledge, social workers, bound by their generic responsibilities, become less specialised and fall behind. The hitherto subservients of the relationship are becoming the knowledgeable advocates for an improved and more imaginative foster care service.

If we accept the premise that foster care has changed and is continuing to change in its demands and its very nature, then we must look at the people involved in the task with a more enquiring and skilled eye. It can no longer be considered that all foster parents need is a large heart and matching-sized house. Much more is needed, including more understanding of the circumstances surrounding admission to care and of the consequent traumas and behaviour problems which might ensue. A greater knowledge is required about how other agencies can be used and how foster parents can obtain advice and support from them in the interests of children. Above all, the foster parents are the full-time partners of this caring team: as such they must know what goals other partners are working towards, so that the best can be given to any child in care.

First impressions

Recruitment is often the poor relation of the foster care programme. Yet it is during this initial stage that the scene is set and the foundations are laid for future relationships. It is at this early stage that basic understanding or misunderstanding about what foster care really entails is communicated. In general, Social Service Departments need to review the methods they employ in approaching the highly skilled and complex task of recruiting foster parents. The need to identify the children who could benefit from different forms of fostering is still not fully grasped. There are still many children stagnating in residential institutions because their needs have not been satisfactorily assessed and therefore alternative care has not been sought. Rowe and Lambert[5] outlined this problem explicitly in *Children Who Wait,* and yet this knowledge of how many and which children need foster care, etc. is still not readily available in many local authorities even at the time of mounting recruitment campaigns.

Without this basic information, resources in the community must remain untapped, or unused even when found.

Few families stand still in character, interests or skill. The foster family too may well be prone to change, affecting attitudes and skills. This makes the need for some form of regular reassessment of vital importance. Sometimes the family who were initially approved to foster pre-adoption babies later develop an interest in teenagers. This kind of change in preference needs to be reviewed and reassessed. A large child care agency in Toronto has a mutual assessment system whereby once a year the agency worker and the foster parents make an assessment of each other's performance over the year. This allows for honest, frank and open discussion. If things are not working out too well it is as important that these should be talked about as much as the successes of placements. Such action may avoid further incidents or the most disturbing features of foster care. When placements break down or a family suddenly ceases to be used after some years of service, one of the stock replies tends to be, 'Well, we've not been too happy about this placement for some time.' However, rarely does this factor seem to be adequately communicated to the foster parents. If the department is unhappy with the standards of care foster parents provide, they should be told this and not shielded. Evasiveness can only cause problems later.

Central to the issue of recruitment is assessment. Too often these two facets are handled as separate entities, giving rise to such statements as: 'We applied weeks ago and have heard nothing;' 'They can't want places very badly if we need to wait this long;' 'I gave up trying to contact them (meaning the social workers) and went and got a job.' From the social services side the usual comments are: 'We apologise for the delay in contacting you, the worker was on leave;' 'We did not expect such a response, we could not cope as we are short-staffed;' 'Sorry, we only want homes for *x* type of children;' 'We have a policy of not accepting *y* types of people.' This kind of response is extremely damaging to the image of foster care as a whole. It tends to lessen the impact of understanding the needs of children in care and to reduce the respect not only for the agency concerned but for others who may be involved. Here in particular I refer to foster parents who often unwittingly take on the responsibility of recruiting other foster parents. If they come to feel they are bolstering a disorganised service, they too will become disillusioned and lose respect for the service.

The assessment of foster parents is a highly skilled job. It is on the judgments made at this stage that the lives of many children will depend. When we read accounts of the skills involved in such assessments we should question where such skills are learned. The study of the NFCA, referred to earlier, showed that in today's training programmes for generic social workers, many leave courses having had little or no special training on foster care.[4] This must mean that the whole area of foster care assessment and its specific knowledge base are left untouched. How do such workers then interview prospective foster parents, as clients or as colleagues?

Training needs

Although there is an increase in the availability of training courses for foster parents, sadly many of these are ill-prepared and do little to enhance an understanding of the skilled tasks being undertaken. In the USA the Federal Government, acknowledging the need for training programmes for foster parents, promoted the production of learning packs which were extensively tried and tested before being marketed. Ambivalence towards training is not difficult to understand when reminding ourselves of the historical basis of foster care as 'simple' parenting. A study carried out by Ambinder and Sargent[6] into foster parents' technique of management suggested, even as far back as 1965, that effective foster care requires that prospective foster parents be given some training. Parker[7] added: 'is it fair to ask unskilled and untrained foster parents to do a difficult job in what for them may be an unnatural and naturally difficult way, by eschewing the role of parent?' We seem to be asking more of foster parents whilst giving less, and thus showing a basic ignorance of the complexity of the task. I have already touched upon the concern expressed by the NFCA about social worker training in foster care. Too often they are left to learn by trial and error, increasingly finding themselves supervised by non-specialist child care trained personnel.

The present task

Before any foster care placement can be successful there is a need to define the objective. Many projects which fail to reach their goals appear to pay insufficient consideration to such questions as: on what basis and towards what end will who do what to whom, for how long, with what effect, at what cost, and with what benefits? It is, of course, often difficult to predict the outcome of situations so entangled by the complexity of human relationships and the unpredictability of human behaviour. However, if mutual trust is the basis for successful fostering, then success can be worked for and expected only when there is a measure of certainty and predictability in the situation.[8]

The social worker-foster parent relationship has been described in varying ways, and however it might be defined there is still one very basic essential element: i.e., that of the identification which takes place between foster parent and social worker. Also there is the need for each to understand that the foster parent's ability to accept a child and to give to it is greatly dependent upon the experience of the worker as accepting and giving, towards those foster parents. Wires[9] described the social workers' interest in the foster parents as a 'selfish' one, placing the concern for the child as paramount in their interests in the whole relationship. Of course this is true of foster parents also, it is the child who is the common denominator in the partnership. It is therefore essential that each partner is working to a common goal. Foster parents are no longer prepared to be viewed as puppets whose strings are pulled by the social workers at any given time. They are developing and extending their sense of responsibility in this caring process, demanding an input into the decision-making process surrounding the children they care for. They will not be treated simply as a depository for children. Foster parents must be intimately involved in the total caring process for those children to whom they open their hearts, their homes, and often their purses. From the social worker's point of view the foster parents should be seen as a help in the making of plans for the children, not as an obstacle to be overcome.

In order to be a help there is a need for support. Support should be mutual, but it is often spoken of as a very one-sided 'prop'. Foster parents feel a burden on the social worker if they need to ask constantly for information, or wish to discuss areas of concern. Surely much of this could be better tackled if a more professional relationship were pursued. 'The foster parent becomes a sort of professional colleague when the worker shares with her case material pertaining to the child's family.'[10] If the social worker involved in a placement is inept in his/her approach to a case it should not be expected that this will either not be observed by the experienced foster parent or upheld. The demands for better practice should come as much from the foster parents as from the social workers.

It is also time for much more attention to be paid to findings from research. In 1966 Parker[7] claimed that a successful foster care placement of a long-term nature correlated with cases where there had been five or more meetings before actual placement. In a later study George[11] spoke of the trauma and depression suffered by children on being dumped in unknown foster homes. However, even today the following case is not untypical of placement arrangements:

> A foster family was asked to take a child on a long-term placement. The couple had asked for such a child some considerable time earlier and had waited for a long time for it to happen. It was very tempting for them to agree to the suggestion, but on second thoughts they refused to have the child at such a short notice. They insisted on a proper period of introductory meetings. What was finally arranged was planned totally by the foster parents concerned: they came to call the situation a 'do-it-yourself placement'. The transfer was eventually completed. The foster parents never saw the social worker throughout and the very inadequate information about the child was conveyed briefly in writing.

This family was able to cope and mould the transfer to meet the needs of all concerned. Many questions can also be raised about the kind of relationship that follows. Officially foster parents cannot sign for injections, dental treatment, medical or educational care, etc. There is no way that the best interests of the child can be served whilst such Dickensian attitudes are allowed to continue. The minute-to-minute care of children cannot, on one hand, be entrusted to foster parents, and on the other leave them in such a subservient position. It is also important to understand each other's language. Support means sharing the care and planning for the child. It does not mean propping and forever feeling that a call from the foster parent spells doom. One foster mother rang her social worker expressing concern that the bed-wetting, about which she was told nothing prior to the placement, was still continuing. She was trying to say that time had not brought about a settling of this problem, and perhaps they ought to look at other help which might be available. She asked the social worker to talk about it and agree on a plan of action. The social worker's reaction was: 'Oh my God, this is going to break down. I'd better look to moving the child – the foster mother can't cope.'

Foster parenting is often an extremely isolated task; so channels of communication for sharing concern are very important and should be clearly established. These may not always lead to the social worker, but at times to the Health Visitor, GP, or teacher. Foster parents need to know who the agencies are which might assist towards wholesome development of the children they care for.

Local foster care groups

It is very much hoped that the growing trend for foster parent associations to be established across the country will eventually be for the betterment of services to children in care. These groups serve a variety of functions, each having valuable traits. Where such groups exist there is a corporate voice which can be heard and referred to on all matters of foster care. Some will want different and greater involvement in the overall foster care service for their area, others will be content to organise social activities for themselves and the children. Many groups begin with one objective in mind and extend their interest to other areas. Whatever their style, they are viewed with mixed feelings by social workers and Social Service Departments. These feelings range from suspicion and scepticism to encouragement and complete support. Because of the long period of time without opportunity to meet each other, the first meetings are bound to be something of a watershed of views, anxieties, opinions and antagonisms. This is something which social workers will have to work through.

Foster parents have been on the outside for so long that understandably they have in many cases built up a great deal of anger against social workers in general and the Social Service Departments in particular. Eventually each foster parent has got to learn to cope with his own and other people's feelings and use their anger constructively. Social workers on their part need to see through this anger and frustration and try to understand the underlying concern and anxiety. In the long run paths are bound to merge and a working partnership to emerge. Wires[9] elucidates this point, citing a graphic example of foster parents and social worker relationship which begins in such a frame of antagonism and mistrust. She comments that as the foster mother expresses in a variety of ways, and often with resentment, her own needs as a human being and the worker responds to her, sensitively and fulfillingly, then the relationship between them grows with mutual change in feeling towards each other.

The formation of local foster parent groups has been encouraged by the NFCA, whose main contacts with the coal-face workers comes through these member groups. Approximately 200 groups exist; this figure represents an enormously rapid growth over the past four years. One of the most important roles which these groups play is that of support on all aspects of foster care. Such support is either readily available from within the group's usually quite extensive experience, or it is sought from outside sources, including Social Service Departments. This is a point at local level where real partnership can exist, and where social workers and foster parents alike can learn from each other. Used constructively, such groups should be a valuable asset to any area. Corporately they can assist in the organising of recruitment, introduction of potential foster parents, and formulation of policy on the foster care service.

At the personal level foster parents expect to be involved in the reviews, case conferences and general planning for the children they care for. Without this active participation the foster parenting task becomes isolated and often incompatible with the social work task in the partnership.

New trends

There are now many schemes being run by agencies involving new programmes in foster care. Unfortunately, such schemes are often conceived, planned and executed without any effort to seek the views of established and experienced foster parents. Where there is a local association there is no excuse for not involving them. Many foster parents today see their role as something beyond that of actually caring for a child or children with whom they may be sharing their home. Foster care is not merely the taking of children, placing them or putting a roof over their heads; it is something much bigger than that, and for those who commit their interest to it has far-reaching effects. Foster parents are becoming actively concerned for all children who for some reason are unable to live with their own families. A responsibility also falls upon all those who care for children in one way such as fostering, to broaden their concern to ensure that child and family services do not suffer in the general apportioning of resources.

It is not unusual for foster parents to be seen as selfish because of their fervent efforts to improve the circumstances in which they are trying to care for children. They need, however, to add their voices to those of others who are speaking out on behalf of children whose destiny is often decided without prior consultation. The children are often too young to be heard when it counts. Their rights need to be protected, but they can be pushed only as far as the adults are prepared to champion them. The National Foster Care Association exists to help and encourage this trend. The aim is to work for an all-round improved service to children and their families, and particularly to those children who happen to come into care. Children in care are one of the most powerless groups of consumers of service. There is no identifying body yet acting on their behalf and promoting their right for the best possible service.

Slowly foster care will become more respected as a community activity and as a social work function, without some of the undercurrents of stigma that one comes across. Training, support and a partnership relationship should be the basis for a sound foster care programme, allowing individuals within it to develop their interests and skills into the variety of areas which are emerging. These include not only the fostering of handicapped children or delinquent teenagers, but also of unmarried young mothers or mothers-to-be, support systems to families at risk, and the caring for family groups. Many experienced foster parents feel that in many circumstances it is the parents who need 'fostering' more than the children, and they are prepared to take on such a role.

Conclusion

Whilst this chapter may have seemed somewhat critical of the system as a whole, it is simply a statement of facts as they are known. These observations may not reflect the situation nationwide, but neither are they isolated. It is the intention of the National Foster Care Association to help to improve services to deprived children. The next step is to be more specific about the areas in need of improvement. More systematic study will be necessary. It is recognised that there are inadequacies in the quality of care provided by some foster familes. In the end, however, the whole service will be as good or as bad as the social workers and the Social Service Departments will develop it, through their whole approach to recruitment, assessment, placement, and maintenance of the arrangement. The NFCA is prepared to join in these efforts to raise the general quality of the care of children and particularly of foster care.

References

1 C. Winnicott, *Child Care and Social Work,* Bookstall Publications, 1970, p. 23.

2 R. Dinnage and M. L. Kellmer-Pringle, *Foster Home Care: Facts and Fallacies,* Longmans, 1967, p. 28.

3 M. L. Kellmer-Pringle, *The Needs of Children,* Hutchinson, 1975.

4 National Foster Care Association, *Education and Training in Foster Care,* NFCA, 1975.

5 J. Rowe and L. Lambert, *Children Who Wait,* ABAFA, 1973.

6 W. Ambinder and D. Sargent, 'Foster Parents' Technique of Management of Pre-adolescent Boys' Defiant Behaviour', *Child Welfare,* vol. 44 no. 1, 1965, pp. 90-4.

7 R. Parker, *Decision in Child Care,* Allen & Unwin, 1966.

8 Dinnage and Kellmer-Pringle, op. cit. p.29.

9 E. M. Wires, 'Some Factors in the Worker-Foster Parent Relationship', *Child Welfare,* vol. 33, no.8, 1954.

10 Dinnage and Kellmer-Pringle, op. cit. p.28.

11 V. George, *Foster Care: Theory and Practice,* Routledge & Kegan Paul, 1970.

John Triseliotis

9 Growing up in foster care and after

This chapter describes a follow-up study of forty young people born in 1956-7 who spent between seven and fifteen years each in a single foster home before the age of sixteen. At interview the former foster children were between twenty and twenty-one years old. The main aim of the study was to throw some light on the foster care experience as seen through the eyes of foster parents and former foster children; also to evaluate the latter's current social and personal circumstances and relate them to background characteristics and experiences. The number of forty was reached from a possible sample of fifty-nine. (Details of the sampling process, methodology and rating questionnaires and other information will be found in the main report submitted to the Social Science Research Council.)

In spite of the fact that in this country children have been fostered for almost 200 years, there is no significant study to show how people who grew up as foster children cope in adult life. Most studies in foster care so far have focused on children under the age of sixteen and on factors contributing to the breakdown of placements. One somewhat relevant British study was by Ferguson,[1] who looked into the circumstances of 205 young people, two to three years after they had left the care of Glasgow Corporation. Ferguson's overall conclusion was that on a range of items such as employment record, scholastic achievements and intellectual ability, the young people who grew up in public care were poorer compared with a group of working-class Glasgow boys not in care.

The first study of this kind in the USA was by Theis[2] of the State Charities Aid Association of New York. Theis published a study of children who had been placed in long-term foster homes and were then over eighteen years old. She found no significant difference in the social adjustment of children from 'good' and 'bad' backgrounds.

Again in the States, Meier[3] followed up former foster children to assess their social effectiveness and its relation to childhood experiences. His overall findings were that the vast majority of his subjects had found places for themselves in their communities. Theis'[2] and

Meier's[3] findings are also supported by Salo (Finland)[4]. Salo compared the adult adjustment of individuals who as children had been removed from neglectful surroundings with that of persons who as children remained in neglectful surroundings. Some of the former children went into foster homes and others into institutions. Salo found that those who were removed showed consistently less maladjustment in adulthood than those who remained.

People who have spent most of their childhood in substitute forms of care are the obvious target of researchers keen to find answers to such questions as: the relative influence of heredity and environment, the possible transmission of forms of behaviour (e.g., crime, alcoholism and mental illness), and the reversibility of psychological trauma. Social workers engaged in work with children act in the belief that, given an enabling environment, earlier adverse experiences can be reversed. Clarke[5] adds that early learning has immediate effects, which, if not reinforced, will fade in time and that it will not *per se* have any long-term influence upon adult behaviour, other than as a link in the development chain.

Some characteristics of the children

Table 1 Children's age at reception into care and age at final placement (N. 40)

age	under 12 months	1–3 years	4–7 years	8–9 years	total
into care	16 (40%)	13 (32 %)	8 (20%)	3 (8%)	40 (100%)
final placement	4 (10%)	16 (40%)	6 (15%)	14 (35%)	40 (100%)

Though four out of every ten children were received into care when under a year old, only one out of every ten was placed before this age in what was to be his or her final childhood home. Whilst on average the children had a mean number of four moves before final placement, four out of every ten had from five to nine moves. Most of the moves were between different residential nurseries and foster homes, and in twelve cases the children had returned to their families of origin before final reception into care. Nineteen of the children were placed with siblings in the same foster home.

Characteristics of the families of origin

Almost all the forty families of origin shared three major characteristics: chronic marital and other forms of disrupted personal relationships, lengthy periods of unemployment, and economic dependence. In addition, over half the families experienced more than one period of homelessness, and about a quarter had a history of crime and alcohol abuse. Characteristics such as disruptive relationships, unemployment, economic dependence and homelessness were of a chronic nature rather than due to a recent crisis or upheaval. Chronic disharmony in personal relationships and long-term economic dependence appear to be characteristics of parents whose children stay in long-term foster care. Given the characteristics of the families of origin, it is unlikely that the children in the study had the best start in life.

Characteristics of the foster families

The overall picture that emerges of the long-term foster parents is of couples mostly in their forties and early fifties at the time of placement; having no children of their own, or their own children beginning to grow away from the family home; holding steady semi-skilled and skilled jobs, and living in council accommodation. Their financial situation was marginally better than that of the families of origin, its main difference being the regularity of job and income.

The growing-up experience

The foster parents and the young adults were asked, separately, to talk about the foster care experience. Whilst the foster parents were encouraged to describe the experience of being caretaker to the foster child, former foster children were asked to give their perception of the growing-up experience in the foster home. Areas that were explored included the quality of relationships, the presence of tension, behaviour and emotional problems, parental visiting, acknowledgment of the child's status, and the general impact on both parties of the fostering experience.

In this kind of retrospective evaluation and of reminiscence, there is a tendency on the part of the subjects to telescope past events and to put across mostly the overall impression left by the experience. It was found that, occasionally, important recent or current events may colour some of the earlier experiences but they do not radically alter them. For instance, where experiences in the past were predominantly satisfying and enjoyable, current upsets were not enough to change them significantly. There was considerable congruence between the views and perceptions of the young adults and those of their former foster parents. Where, however, the growing-up experience was not always mutually satisfying, the two parties offered different explanations for this. With the aid of an independent assessor, a former senior social worker, the responses of the two parties were classified into four categories based on the quality of the relationships and experiences described.

Group A: Mutually satisfying relationships (14 children out of 40)

The experience of caring and of being cared for was perceived by both parties in this group as having been most satisfying. Both foster parents and the young adults viewed the growing-up period as one of enjoyment, of warm and caring relationships, of children being integrated into the family and with both foster parents playing an active parenting role. Within these relationships there were periods of strain and tension but they were not allowed to disrupt the otherwise strong and affectionate ties that had developed. The main characteristics of the caretakers as perceived by the young adults were: relaxed people, patient, warm and caring, but also controlling when necessary; a stable relationship between the foster parents, and active involvement with the children by both of them. An added characteristic of these foster parents was their predominantly positive feelings towards the families of origin and a general enjoyment of the children. They talked about the children in warm affectionate terms, and the former foster children spoke about their caretakers in the same way.

> *Foster mother:* . . . I took the girls in after my own daughter left school. The house felt empty then . . . they were a bundle of nerves when they came at the age of five and four. It took a lot of patience but it was rewarding. Once the girls got to know us they felt more settled and we were more relaxed with them . . . you get great comfort out of having children. After a while they are like your own. You do not feel they are different because they are fostered. My daughter is their sister and this is the home for all of us. . . . My husband was thrilled with them and the girls have grown very fond of him. . . . We are the only parents

> they have now. . . . We tried to give them all the love and comfort we could. . . .
>
> *The foster child:* I have been living with my 'parents' since I was four. My sister was also with me all the time. . . . They are my 'mum' and 'dad'. I know nothing else. I never think about my other parents because I never saw them since we were left in the Home. I must have been three at the time. My natural parents do not mean anything to me now. . . . Before we came here we were messed about. But with my 'mum' and 'dad' here we had a good life and always felt as part of the family. We had a lot of fun together.

Similar sentiments were expressed by other foster parents and former foster children in this group. The way foster parents and children blended together and developed strong emotional ties was impressive.

> *Foster parents:* I was 38 and I knew when I had my boy that he would be the only one and we wanted to adopt. But we were told we were old and would we not prefer to foster. . . . Then Helen came. She had many changes before she came to us. We were asked to take her in temporarily! She stayed ever since. She needed a lot of attention. I think if you are content in your home life everybody else who comes in just accepts these conditions. I am one of a big family and there are all these aunts and uncles and they have all accepted Helen. Nobody has ever said that Helen is not 'our' child. I mean that they have looked upon her as one of us. My husband has been thrilled helping her with her homework. He used to plan holidays and weekends for all of us. Jimmy, my son, always talks of his 'wee sister' . . .
>
> *The foster child:* I call my foster mother my mum. . . . It is as simple as that. When my natural mother left me in a Home it broke my heart. I was mucked about for some time before I went to live with my 'mum' and 'dad'. It has been such a happy life. I forgot all about the previous upsets. I made roots. . . . It is difficult to explain perhaps but I grew up feeling this is home and this is where I belong . . . I don't know how else to put it.

Some foster parents who had backward, epileptic children or children of poor health placed with them put a lot of effort and patience into their parenting. This included regular visits to doctors and hospitals, making sure that the child was taking its tablets, putting up with disruptive behaviour or teaching an eight-year-old the kind of things that a normal child learns much earlier, whilst also offering a caring experience to children who had known none. The former foster children valued this kind of attention and were very appreciative of the quality of care they had received. Individual attention and devotion were of immense value to another child who had never known a family before, having spent most of his formative years in a big institution.

> *The foster mother:* David came to us after spending almost six years in a special Home. I was only to have him for three months! He spent nine years. He was very backward; he could hardly speak and had no schooling. He needed all the attention he could get. He was like a baby. I and my husband tried to give him all the love we could. He used to follow me everywhere. It was very distressing at first but he improved and grew up . . .

> *The foster child:* My first six years were just matrons and nurses. I knew nobody coming to see me. People forgot I was there. I have never known what other children have experienced. I had lost a big part of my life. . . . My lot then was a poor one. If it hadn't been for my social worker I would still be in the Home. Coming out into the world, I didn't know where I belonged. I still remember the first cuddle of my foster mother. They taught me almost everything I know. They cared for me. . . . I owe a lot to them.

Child's knowledge of his foster status and background

Foster parents in this group were fairly open with the child about his foster status. They were also not unwilling to share the little information available to them about his origins and to encourage the child to retain contacts with his natural parents. Their readiness to do this was greatly appreciated by the former foster children and was experienced as positive and helpful. Knowing some unpalatable facts about their natural family, though experienced as painful, was preferable to not knowing. In some cases the children had memories of their first families, including times when they felt let down by them. In some instances the natural parent(s) had disappeared by the time the placement took place. In others, parents visited in the first or second year, and were not heard of again. There was no evidence to suggest that the foster parents kept the natural parents away. The foster parents in this group saw themselves mainly as the psychological parents, whilst allowing the child to develop awareness about his first family. The fact that they were ready to talk to the children about their natural parents and to encourage contact did not prevent their being very upset and distressed if the children were removed, especially a couple of years or so after placement.

Foster parents claimed to have been given little or no information about the child or the family of origin at the time of placement. Such information would have been necessary to pass on to the child to help him not only to satisfy his curiosity but also to build his self-image on the concept of his family of origin, and to connect past and present. The foster parents' readiness to 'include' the family of origin, and also the fact that some of the children had visual images and experiences of the natural parents, may account for the absence of any significant curiosity, among this group, about their origins or of any desire for reunions.

> *Foster mother:* When the girls arrived we started writing to their mother. She kept in touch and visited. She would often say in front of them, 'I don't want them. I have no room and my new man will not have them.' When the girls started calling us 'mum' and 'dad' I would say, 'Yes', but never forget you have got your own mum and dad up in Glasgow. You are just a wee loan to us.' Their mother continued to visit in the first year but stopped. . . . As time went on the girls didn't want to hear any more . . .
>
> *The foster child:* My mum and dad – that is my foster mum and dad – always talked to us about our first mother. They used to urge us to write but we lost interest. They told us that some parents couldn't help not caring for their children. My natural mother visited us only once or twice. She brought a man with her. She promised to visit again. She didn't. . . . My mum and dad are the people who brought me and my wee sister up. . .

Psychological bonding

It is difficult from this small study to draw definite conclusions about the stage at which foster parents and foster children become closely identified, with strong psychological bonds developing between them. Children who were placed as infants seemed to blend into the family very quickly. Their memories and experiences were about a single family, the foster family. Children placed at an older age developed deep psychological bonds at varying stages, depending on age at placement, past experiences and parental visiting. The available evidence suggests that the strongest factor which affects attachment to a new family is the involvement and pattern of visiting by the natural family. Whilst the parents kept visiting regularly, the older children at least seemed to retain a lot of attachment and feelings towards them.

As the parents' involvement and visits diminished or disappeared altogether, the children transferred their attachments to their caretakers, especially where these found response.

Removal of the child after the transfer of such feelings and the development of psychological bonds would have been experienced as traumatic. When bonding takes place both child and foster parents need greater security of tenure and guarantee of permanence to prevent disruptions. In this respect, the former foster children's loyalties were with the people who cared for them, and not with those who gave birth to them. Removal from their carers would have been experienced as very traumatic.

> *Former foster child:* It was only recently I was told that my natural parents could have removed me at any time if they wanted to. Even now when I think of it I shudder. . . . For me they would have been total strangers. Why remove me when I was so happy? I have met my natural mother recently and I see her from time to time. There is no bond between us. My 'mum' is my foster mum and my 'dad' is my foster dad. If I call my natural mother 'mum' when I meet her it is just for saving face. . . .

Some young adults were feeling bitter that their adoption by their foster parents was blocked either by their natural families or by the 'authorities'.

> My foster parents have wanted to adopt me and my brother but they were told that our father wouldn't let us go. I remember thinking at the time, 'Why won't he let us go, he never comes to visit us. If I were adopted or not what did it matter to him?'

Another commented on the local authority's refusal to allow the foster parents to adopt him:

> If my 'parents' were good enough to foster me they were also good enough to adopt me. If you are adopted you cannot be taken away.

The children's characteristics

At the time of placement in the foster home, eight of the children who experienced the growing-up period as fully satisfying were between one and three years old, and the remining six between four and nine. The children's mean number of moves before final placement was four. Most of the children who were placed with siblings appeared in this mutually satisfying group. The older-placed children displayed some problems at placement, but these quickly disappeared. Subsequent problems were relatively minor and included occasional temper tantrums, two episodes of truancy, some pilfering and passivity.

Characteristics of the families of origin and of the foster parents

A major characteristic of the families of origin was chronic and disruptive relationships, social isolation, lengthy periods of unemployment and homelessness. In four of the families there was a history of crime and alcohol. In spite of the amount of strain the natural families must have laboured under, as well as the incapacitating indices of social deprivation they shared, their children appeared to make a remarkable adaptation in the foster family.

The general characteristic of the foster homes was of integrated, stable and flexible families with a lot of warmth, where the fostered children seemed to have found a definite place. Whilst four of the families were childless, the remaining ten had one or more own children who were either living at home or had already moved away. At the time of placement they were mostly in their forties and early fifties.

Group B: Possessive type relationships (8 children out of 40)

The description 'possessive' relationships is used here to describe over-protective and largely 'exclusive' type relationships. These relationships contained considerable satisfactions but some of the former foster children made qualifications about the degree of possessiveness shown by the foster parents and their tendency to deny the child's status and family of origin. The young adults in this group, whilst careful not to sound critical, implied that their independence and autonomy were somewhat curtailed as a result of these attitudes. At least six of the eight young people expressed very positive feelings towards their foster parents, whom they came to regard as their parents and the foster home as their home. The foster parents expressed greater anxieties, compared with foster parents in the previous group, about the possibility of losing the children and therefore their reluctance to talk more openly about their fostered status. The evasiveness about including the child's family of origin and helping him to integrate this reality into his self-concept did not appear to be accompanied by serious ambivalent or rejecting feelings towards the child, except perhaps in one case.

The over-possessiveness referred to above spread to a number of other areas of the child's life besides the reluctance to be explicit about the natural family. The same foster parents were also more hostile to the idea of parental visits or contacts. It could be claimed that the petering out of the few parental visits in the very early years was perhaps due to this unconcealed hostility. As a result of the secrecy surrounding their foster status, the young adults in this group were more curious than any other group in the study to know about their first families. In contrast, however, to the writer's experience from interviewing adopted adults from whom information about their adoption was withheld, these fostered young adults were less critical of their foster parents. This could be explained by the fostered adults' less secure position in relation to their foster parents.

Holman[6] puts forward two contrasting models of foster parenthood, claiming that there is an 'exclusive' model where the ultimate goal is for the foster parent to become the child's psychological parent to the exclusion of the natural family. The child is then encouraged to drop all ties with his previous life. On the other hand, he postulates the 'professional' or 'inclusive' model where foster parents aim 'to offer love without having to regard themselves as the real parent'. This conclusion needs modification when referring to long-term fostering of the types described here. Though such possessive and exclusive relationships were undesirable, they also had strengths in them which seemed to compensate for the drawbacks. In effect, if possessiveness and exclusiveness are only one characteristic in a family that offers other satisfactions, e.g., where the basic relationship is secure, the child still retains strong feelings of satisfaction. It should also be remembered that the terms 'exclusive' and 'inclusive' as postulated by Holman rely heavily on Weinstein's work, which is based mostly on children going in and out of care.[7] Most of the children in this group managed subsequently to lead a more independent life without destroying a basically satisfactory relationship with their foster parents. Obviously these relationships were not as fully satisfying as in those where the foster parents were open and 'inclusive' from the start.

This form of possessiveness or exclusiveness featured largely among childless couples with whom social workers tended to place illegitimate children. It was perhaps thought that parental interference would be minimal, and that a *de facto* adoption situation would develop. At least five of the eight couples in this group would have liked to adopt the children. Social workers often colluded with foster parents instead of using their authority, knowledge and skills to help them over these issues.

The following is an example of what started as a fairly possessive, exclusive, relationship which was not sorted out until the child's late teens. It is a relationship that contains many satisfactions in it, in spite of some conflict and inexplicitness about the fostering status. It does raise, of course, the serious question of whether the placement should have been arranged at all in view of the foster parents' attitude at the time. More important, nothing was done either to explore these attitudes further or to attempt at least to help the foster parents over them.

> *Foster mother:* Douglas came to us when he was just under a year old. The social worker said that his mother was unlikely to show up again. I did say to her that I didn't want to have much to do with her. . . . She showed up once. I did not invite her in and that was the last I saw of her. To be honest with you we wouldn't have taken him otherwise. I mean we were told he would never go back to his mother. I couldn't keep a child and then have it taken away from me. . . . We did tell him when he was about seven or eight, I don't remember exactly, that he was fostered with us but we didn't hark back on it and he never asked. . . .

> *The foster child:* I remember having a hazy idea that I was 'adopted' because my 'parents' couldn't have any of their own children. But it was not something we talked about and I never raised it until I was fifteen. It was only recently I found that I was only fostered. Not that it bothered me, but I wish my parents were more straight about it. I didn't want to ask because I didn't like to upset my mother. I would have liked to know why my parents could not keep me and all that. . . . I was very much a mother's boy and I suppose she was over-protective and fussing over me. Sometimes too much. . . .

Psychological bonding

As seven of the eight children in this group were placed when under four years old, psychological bonding seemed to develop at an early stage. In spite of the drawbacks referred to earlier about over-possessiveness and the exclusion of the family of origin, six of the eight children developed strong feelings of belonging and came to view the foster family as their family. They applied the term 'parents' to their foster parents and maintained that this was how they were made to feel. There was no dispute about their attachment and loyalties to these foster families. There was no obvious wish to search for or seek reunions with the family of origin, though they would have appreciated more information about their backgrounds and the circumstances of their fostering.

> I'm here, I've got my 'mother' and 'father' and they have done all they can for me. I have a happy home. I would go through it again even if my 'parents' have been rather evasive about my fostering. . . . I would like to find out a bit more about my roots. . . .

The remaining two of the eight children were somewhat confused about their status in the foster home and somewhat less certain about their place. Their difficulties seemed to reflect relationship problems within the total family and were compounded by the confusion concerning their origins. However, they still viewed the foster family as their family, having no other base.

The children's characteristics

Compared with the rest of the sample, these children were the youngest to come into care and the youngest to be placed with their foster parents. All were placed when four or under, and none was brought up as an only child. Children in this group exhibited somewhat more persistent emotional problems compared with the previous group. Difficulties included 'nerves', sleep walking, persistent 'rash', and some were described as 'highly strung'. One had psychiatric help as a child, whilst another had a history of pilfering money from home which coincided with his sudden awareness about his foster status. Apart from the last person, the problems with the rest seemed to clear by the mid-teens.

Characteristics of the families of origin and of the foster home

The home background of these children was not dissimilar to that of the rest of the sample. Similarly the age, occupational and economic background of the foster parents was not dissimilar from that of foster parents in the rest of the sample. One main difference from all the other groups was the greater secrecy and evasiveness they displayed concerning the child's status and the family of origin. Also this group had a significantly higher percentage of childless couples (five out of eight).

Group C: Professional type relationships (9 children out of 40)

At least nine of the children were brought up in foster homes which could be described as 'professional'. Though none of the foster parents in the previous two groups saw themselves or wanted to be seen as professionals doing a job, foster parents in this group accepted that their role developed into a kind of job, but they hoped they had not lost their caring qualities. The majority started as long-term foster parents with one or two children, but were persuaded to take on more than they originally intended, some of these for short and some for long periods. By the time of this interview, some had cared for up to 100 or 200 children. The arrangement developed into a form of group foster care. They had children to stay for a few weeks, or a few months, sometimes up to a year or two, and some staying until they became independent.

The foster mothers had mixed feelings about the change of their role, which was a departure from their original intentions. They attributed this to pressures exercised on them by hard-pressed social workers who had children on their hands and nowhere to place them. Though George,[8] Holman[6] and Aldgate[9] argue for the extension of professional type fostering, its value is more doubtful for long-term fostering, unless the drawbacks identified in this study can be coped with in other ways. Similarly, these findings suggest that it is inadvisable to mix short- and long-term stay children, as it seems to work to the disadvantage at least of the long-term ones.

A further general finding is that though many foster parents can care for one, two or three children on a short- or long-term basis, it is dangerous to pressurise or encourage them to go beyond what they see as their coping abilities. Some breakdowns, we found, occur when foster parents are pressed to go beyond their limits. Foster parents seem to find it difficult to refuse hard-pressed social workers when the latter are also in a position of authority over them. It is a short-sighted policy that stretches the limits of existing efficient resources for short-term expediency.

The foster parents whose role was a professional one and developed into group-caring were seen by the young adults as mostly caring people, but (to use one phrase) 'there was not always enough to go round'. Compared with the young adults in the previous two groups, those in this group experienced the foster parents with less intensity, had less individual attention, were aware that they had to share them with a great number of others, and were critical of the ever-changing number of children in the family. More serious were the young adults' views about what happened to them after the statutory period of care was over. However, in spite of some serious reservations, and with the exception of one foster mother who was experienced as rather hard and distant, the remaining children retained a lot of affection for their foster families. Whilst being glad and even 'grateful' for being offered a home for so many years, they still felt that it was 'not like a real family. It was like one and also different'; 'more changeable, more children, more arguments, more upsets, more of a job'.

> *Foster child:* I hated to see new children coming. I always felt they took my place away. . . . You thought it was your place and nobody else's and then taking it from you. . . . When I was getting on to eighteen, my foster mother didn't say it in so many words, but it was clear that the bed was needed for the new ones. . . . I decided then to join the Army. Perhaps I could have stood on my own feet if I went into digs, but I thought the Army was a way of seeing the world. It gives me time to mature and work out things for myself. . . . If I were adopted when young I would have had a proper mum and dad.

> *The foster mother:* I never thought of fostering so many children. It all started very differently, but the social workers would come and press me to help them out. . . you cannot refuse them. I've had nearly 100 children. I've had them for six months, for a year, two years, three years and for sixteen years. The long-term ones resent it when they see the new ones. They imagine they will be pushed out but I say to them, 'These children are needing help like you did'.

Foster mothers in this group were understanding of children's needs, but perhaps their commitment to each child was not as strong as that of foster parents who had one or two children on a long-term basis. The young adults in this group referred to their foster parents less as 'mums' and 'dads', had fewer contacts after leaving school; and only two continued to live in the foster parents' home, regarding it as their home.

The concept of professional fostering, as portrayed in social work literature, may fit other forms of fostering, particularly in situations where there are serious chances of the child's being restored to his original family or rehabilitated in some other way. In the light of these comments and findings, professional fostering carries risks for children who need families for a large part of their childhood and a base for use in adult life. To a large extent professional group foster homes are not very different from residential Homes. Their biggest advantage over institutions is perhaps the permanency of the caretakers, but they lack the facilities and assistance available in a small Home. It is apparent from these findings that no single type of foster home can meet the diversity of need in children. Much more detailed work is necessary to enable us to identify which kinds of need can be met by particular forms of care. Professional foster parents can be a valuable resource for meeting a particular need at a point and time but they cannot be used as an answer for all the problems in fostering.

Child's knowledge of his foster status and background

As all nine children in this group were placed when aged between eight and nine years old, they all had some idea about their status. Information and knowledge about their antecedents was more patchy, but foster parents themselves were given little information to pass on. Professional-type foster parents in this group appeared more open with the child about his status and were generally more sympathetic towards the natural parents. They also seemed less threatened by the very rare parental visits.

Psychological bonding

In spite of the earlier disruptions in these children's lives, the great number of moves they experienced between reception into care and placement, and the older age at which they were placed, and the insecurities identified in these professional-type group foster homes, the children seemed to make a satisfactory adaptation. Their adaptation and overcoming of many handicaps was a demonstration of how older children can transfer and settle satisfactorily under a more permanent type of arrangement. If no stronger bonds developed between them and their carers, this was related to the type of foster homes chosen on their behalf.

The children's characteristics

A major difference between this group of children and those in the rest of the sample was the older age at which they came into care and were eventually placed. No child, for instance, was received into care when younger than eighteen months, and all nine in the group were placed when aged between eight and nine years old. Between them they had an average of five moves from first reception into care and final placement. This was a somewhat higher number of moves compared with the rest of the sample. The older age at which these children came into care and were eventually placed possibly influenced the social workers' selection of professional group-type foster parents. Perhaps these caretakers were readier than others to accept older children who had already had a chequered life. Considering the background and the needs of these children it might have been thought unwise to place additional children in the same homes, thus increasing the insecurity of the children already there.

All the children in this group were described as having displayed more emotional problems whilst in foster care, compared with the previous two groups. The problems included persistent bed-wetting, temper tantrums, dependency, sleep walking and general 'immaturity', i.e. 'not acting his age', 'behaving like a toddler'. However, no child from this group was in trouble with the law whilst in foster care or after, in spite of the fact that two of the natural fathers had lengthy criminal records.

Apart from one foster home, the rest coped well with these problems and there was no occasion when they felt like asking for the child's removal. Within the role assigned to them the foster parents tried their best to care for the children. With one exception, by the time the children reached the age of sixteen, all the problems noted above had to a large extent disappeared. There was more sadness, therefore, that the impermanency of the foster homes left many of the former foster children in this group rather rootless in their late teens.

Characteristics of the families of origin and of the foster home

Again the characteristics of the families of origin were not in any way different from those of the rest of the sample. Because of the older age at which these children came into care, they had spent on average four and a half years with their natural families and been exposed to the tensions and conflicts going on there.

The main difference between foster parents in this group and the rest of the sample was that these foster homes had the characteristics of a small group home, having sometimes up to ten children.

Group D: Ambivalent type relationships (9 children out of 40)

Both parties in this group felt that the arrangement had not worked out well and that things went wrong somewhere. There was no agreement as to what went wrong. Both foster parents and those fostered were left with mixed feelings of sadness, disappointment and sometimes distress. Overall the nine young adults in this group experienced their growing-up relationships as having 'some good' in them but with a fair amount of tension and squabbles. Whilst recognising the foster parents' efforts to make a go of the arrangement, the former foster children also referred to subtle forms of rejection and occasional threats of sending them 'back to the welfare'. No close bonds seemed to have developed between them and the foster parents. Friction, especially in early and mid-teens, was frequent, before eventually most of them broke away to set themselves up on their own, with siblings, relatives or in hostels. Though it did not always lead to complete separation, contact with the foster parents was reduced to a minimum. There was a mutual absence of loyalty and commitment between foster parents and foster children.

The young adults claimed to have found their foster parents rather impatient, emotionally inaccessible, not understanding and often unpredictable. The foster parents in their turn complained mostly of difficult behaviour which they tended to explain in terms of the child's background and 'bad blood'. It would be wrong to give the impression that poor relationships and friction were a constant characteristic in these children's lives. On the contrary, there were many good moments too, otherwise the arrangement would have totally collapsed at an earlier stage. Foster parents still cherished a lot of feelings towards children who were placed with them when very young, and some of the former foster children also wished things had worked out differently. At the time of interview, it seemed too late to try and salvage these damaged relationships. The fact also that a number of young people in this group were currently involved in some kind of trouble, may have clouded the attitudes of both sides about the nature and quality of earlier relationships.

> *Foster child:* I must have been seven when I went to live with my foster parents. They were the second family I went to. The first family went abroad after promising to take me with them. They didn't, and it broke my heart at the time. . . . The N's (foster parents) had two of their own and another foster child. Somehow I never felt I belonged there. We foster children did not fit in very well. I cannot say that I developed much attachment to them. My foster mother often threatened to send me back to the Corporation. Sometimes she would ring them but they would make her change her mind. I suppose I was difficult too, and I would hark back or argue. She would then smack me and send me to bed. . . . I could be nasty and so could my foster mother. . . . I left at seventeen when our quarrels became worse, and I went to live in a hostel.

> *The foster mother:* Nancy was difficult from the start. How I put up with her all these years God knows. She would argue and answer back. Once or twice I 'phoned the corporation to have her back but they made me change my mind. . . . I shouldn't have done. When she was fourteen or fifteen she started staying out late and we had to call the police. . . . It was difficult to get through to her. . . . In the end she left to live in a hostel. That was as well, as we couldn't go on like that.

Nancy obviously felt very rejected and let down by the first foster family who were promising to adopt her. Perhaps some of her resentment and bitterness were transferred onto the new family. Maybe she needed time to settle before she was eventually placed again. The fact that the placement lasted for almost ten years was an indication of some strengths in the relationship. As in other cases, the social workers were recording 'good progress' until about the age of twelve, when for the first time conflicts and arguments were noted in the records. Intervention did not seem to help to iron out the difficulties.

Unlike foster children in the first two groups, those in this group rarely referred to their foster parents as 'mum' and 'dad', and made few references about the foster home being 'home' or 'my family'. The difference in quality between their comments and those of young people in the other groups was indicative of the different quality of the relationships and experience. Equally foster parents did not refer to these children as being one of them or as 'one of the family'.

Child's knowledge of his foster status and family background

Four of the five children who were placed when three or under were kept ignorant of their foster status until around the age of seven and over, when some of them were exhibiting difficult behaviour. Information about the child's foster status was then used in a rather attacking way. Both with the young and older placed children, there was then a tendency on the part of the foster parents to stress the child's foster status as an indication of difference. It eventually became a form of explanation to themselves and to the child about his behaviour.

Aggressive references and comments about the family of origin were not only confusing to the child but also reinforced a negative self-image.

> *Bill:* I went to live with my foster family when I was about eight. . . . Sometimes I was difficult, I suppose, and my foster mother would often make comments about my 'bad blood'. I didn't know what to say as I knew nothing about my own family. Nobody ever told me. All sorts of things pass through my mind. . . . I still don't know anything about my background. . .

Psychological bonding

There was little evidence of lasting psychological bonding between the children in this group and their foster parents. Neither side claimed to have experienced periods of intense reciprocated attachments or of lasting loyalties. The children failed to develop a strong sense of security, and the foster parents were aware of long periods of tension and strain. There was an absence of physical and emotional contact between the two parties, in contrast to the other three groups. If there are certain possible explanations of why the older placed children failed to settle down in these foster homes and develop more lasting attachments, no similar explanations can be offered for the younger placed children.

The children's characteristics

An important question is how far the characteristics of these children were similar to or different from those of the rest of the sample. Broadly, their age on coming into care was similar to that of Groups A and B, but younger than Group C. At final placement, five of the nine children were three or under, similar to Group A, but three were aged between eight and nine. In effect, poor experiences were described by children who were placed both very young and very old. The experiences of the older placed ones were, however, more sad compared with the rest. The three older placed children who never settled properly in their foster homes had one common feature in that all three had experienced a broken-down fostering arrangement that had lasted for at least three years. All three young adults had memories about the earlier placements, and underlying these were feelings of disappointment and rejection about what followed. It is possible that some of these feelings were transferred on to the foster parents.

A further characteristic of this group of children, compared with the rest, was the surfacing of more intense emotional and behavioural problems. Their onset was around the ages of seven to nine but was accentuated particularly from early adolescence onwards. Difficulties included stealing from home and outside, setting fire to things, school truancy, attention-seeking behaviour, and running away from home. Child Guidance help was sought for two of the children when they were in their early teens. Some of these problems continued in adult life in the form of brushes with the law, and in the case of two young people the seeking of psychiatric help for anorexia and depression respectively.

Characteristics of the families of origin and of the foster home

The characteristics of the families of origin of children in this group did not differ significantly from those in the other groups. The main exception was that two of the three children who were the offspring of women with psychiatric disorders themselves developed a psychiatric condition for which they received treatment.

The overall impression formed about the foster families in this group compared with the rest was that they were functioning under greater tensions and pressures. Housing problems, financial difficulties and marital discord were not missing; there was a low level of tolerance of difficult behaviour.

Self-rating of the fostering experience

After talking about their growing-up experience, the former foster children were asked to rate its quality from a five-point scale. All fourteen whose descriptive responses were earlier classified as *mutually satisfying* rated the quality of their fostering experiences as 'very satisfying'. Similarly, six of the eight whose relationships were classified as *possessive* perceived their experience as 'very satisfying', one as 'satisfying', and the other as 'rather poor'. A more varied picture emerged amongst those who grew up in *professional* group-type foster homes. Three of the nine in this group rated their experience as 'very satisfying', four as 'satisfying', one as 'about half and half', and the remaining one as 'poor'. Finally, six of the nine in the *ambivalent* group rated their experience as 'poor' or 'very poor', and the remaining three as 'about half and half'. Overall, seven out of every ten of the former foster children rated their total experience in the foster home from 'satisfactory to very satisfactory' and only one in five described it as 'poor' or 'very poor'. The former foster children's evaluation of the growing-up experience was not too dissimilar from that of the foster parents themselves.

Current circumstances and social functioning

Whilst some aspects of current circumstances can be examined in terms of facts, others, and particularly those involving relationships or a sense of well-being, are more intangible. Whether reference is made to concrete or tangible factors the two cannot be rigidly divided, as difficulties in one area can affect the other. In the end the following areas were selected as reflecting the current situation: education, employment and economic independence, living arrangements, marriage, and overall capacity to cope with current life situations, including a sense of well-being. Apart from descriptive and factual information, a number of rating and self-rating questionnaires were also administered.

1 *Education*

Almost all the former foster children terminated their education at fifteen. The wish for quick economic independence, maximum earnings and the lack of guidance or incentive were the main explanations offered for the non-pursuit of further education or trade. The former foster children's educational aspirations were broadly within the aspirations and expectations of their foster parents. Compared with their social background and experiences the children performed as well as could be expected, though education furnished them with very little that might stand them well in adult life.

2 *Employment and economic independence*

In view of the lack of educational and vocational preparation it was not surprising to find that most of the former foster children were now holding unskilled and semi-skilled occupations. The occupations held by them were broadly similar to those held by the natural parents. There was no evidence of upward occupational mobility and it was difficult to see how this could come about. Four out of every five of the young adults had a steady work record but many of the jobs, because of their nature, had a precariousness about them. The former foster children's economic position was reflective of their work pattern and record.

3 *Living arrangements*

Fourteen of the forty young adults were still living with their foster parents looking on them as their family. Ten, though living and working away from home, still regarded the foster parents' home as their own and visited regularly. Those married would frequently visit with their spouses and children. Whether they lived at home or independently, for those young people the foster home was a source of support and emotional nourishment.

> *Foster mother:* The girls are part of our family and this is their home, like it is for my own two sons. They are our children. They will go if their jobs take them away or if they marry, but until then this is their base.
>
> *Foster child:* It never occurred to me that after so many years I should now try and find a new home. This is my home. . . .

The living arrangements of ten young people who lost contact or became estranged from their foster parents were more precarious. Some lived in a succession of digs or tried to set up with relatives from the original family, but it had not worked out. They had an unstable work record and were generally feeling rootless and drifting. Finally, six of the nine who grew up in professional-type foster homes still kept some form of contact with their foster parents, but felt somewhat disappointed and sometimes bitter because of the absence of permanency.

4 *Marriage*

Two young men and three women married and had one child each. The marriage of one young woman who married at sixteen, against her foster parents' wishes, broke down. The young couples received a lot of help and support from their foster parents when trying to set up home, and the existence of the latter in the background served as a boost to the morale of the young couples. The only exception was a young woman who became estranged from her foster parents at sixteen, and she was now finding herself isolated and rather forlorn. All five couples felt under some pressure because of what happened to their families of origin. They were determined that this would not happen to their own children.

5 *Overall capacity to cope with current life situations and sense of well-being*

In this part of the study an attempt was made to look at the young adults in terms of their current personal and social functioning and general sense of well-being. The study focused on the young adults' capacity to cope with issues of daily living, including social behaviour outside the family. They were also asked to rate and describe how satisfied they felt with themselves and with their general life situation.

Twenty-four of the forty former foster children were rated, or rated themselves, as coping well. The same young people expressed considerable satisfaction with themselves and with their life situation. They generally had good relationships with their 'mums' and 'dads' and with peer groups and retained a positive image of themselves. Questions about their origins and identity such as 'Who am I?' did not unduly bother them. They had no desire to set out on a search for their natural families. Those featured in this group were mostly people who expressed satisfaction with their growing-up period. Six of the young people were seen coping about half and half. They made a number of qualifications concerning their situation or their feelings about themselves. Five of the six grew up in what were earlier defined as professional-type relationships.

Ten of the forty former foster children were seen, or saw themselves, as doing 'less well'. Their general characteristic as a group was the absence of a settled way of life, unsteady employment record, economic dependence, no fixed residence, and being in a continued state of transition. They expressed dissatisfaction and disappointment with their present and past circumstances. Some were critical of their foster families, and a minority blamed themselves for 'messing' their lives. There was anger, disappointment and in some an element of desolation. They were pessimistic about the future and did not think that their circumstances would change all that much. They generally had a poor self-image, which they attributed to being fostered and to other people's negative perceptions of fostering. Those expressing general dissatisfaction were mostly among those whose foster home relationships were described as 'ambivalent', ending up in disruption. The evidence seems to indicate that where the foster home relationships break down in mid- or late teens the chances of the young person subsequently leading a settled way of life are considerably reduced.

6 *Criminal behaviour*

Of the forty former foster children in the sample, four had a Hearing appearance between the ages of fourteen and sixteen, and eight (or 20 per cent) had a Court appearance between the ages of seventeen and twenty-one. Three of them were currently on probation. Most of those in trouble were in the group where relationships in the foster homes were mutually experienced as unsatisfactory. At least five had a history of emotional and behavioural problems going back to their early teens. Criminal behaviour amongst these young people seemed unrelated to similar behaviour amongst the natural parents. Though seven natural parents had a conviction, only one offspring was involved in similar behaviour so far.

Perception of social workers

Social workers in general seemed to have left little or no impression on the lives of most of the former foster children. Most of the young adults had only very faint memories about their social workers and very vague ideas about their role and function. They had some notion of 'the welfare' or of 'the corporation' being responsible for them, but not always of a specific person. The records also confirmed that most contacts were between the social worker and the foster parents. The association of social workers as people who had been instrumental in shaping their lives was rather hazy. The records pointed to the absence of frequent, continued and planned contact, qualities which some, but not all, foster parents and children would have liked. It is recognised that social workers may often find it difficult to know how to respond in situations of long-term fostering, but there was no evidence of planned visits to suit the needs of different children and foster families. For instance, if a crisis occurred in one of the more troubled placements, the tendency was to respond to it on an emergency or crisis model. Yet the needs of the situation appeared to demand a more sustained form of intervention. In general, however, those foster parents who became the children's *de facto* parents did not miss the absence of more visits from social workers. Similarly they were uninterested in the educational and other programmes put on by the agency for the benefit of foster parents, and they put little emphasis on the low level of the boarding-out allowances. In fact they would not have been prepared to act as 'professional' foster parents with considerably increased fees in return. The motivation for the two roles seemed different.

Summary and discussion

This was a follow-up study of forty former foster children born in 1956-7, who spent an average of twelve years in a single foster home. The study set out to answer two basic questions. First, what is it like to grow up fostered; and second, how are former foster children coping in adult life? Watson[10] commented that '. . . to an agency children who remain in foster care often represent its failure.' Success is viewed as rehabilitation with the natural family or adoption. Has long-term foster care then no place in agency programmes?

Half of the subjects in the study were aged three or under at the time of the final placement, and the remaining half between four and nine. All the children came from socially disorganised and deprived families and had experienced an average of four moves between reception into care and final placement. Narrative descriptions by the foster parents and the former foster children about the fostering experience were classified by the researcher and an independent assessor into four types of relationships and subsequently correlated with ratings concerning current coping. Twenty-four (or 60 per cent) of the former foster children enjoyed their fostering experience and were generally coping well at the age of twenty or twenty-one. For another six (or 15 per cent) the experience had many satisfactions but also some identifiable difficulties. These were young people who mostly grew up in what were perceived as professional-type foster homes. Finally ten (or 25 per cent) of the subjects had mostly negative feelings about their fostering experience and their current level of functioning gave cause for some concern.

The overall findings suggest that people who grow up in long-term foster homes, within which they are wanted and integrated as part of the family, generally do well. Those who were perceived and judged as doing well, were placed in the foster homes at different ages. Most children were able to overcome the serious social handicaps of their natural families and the traumatic situations to which they were exposed before and after coming into care. Even the nine children who were placed with professional-type foster parents when aged between eight and nine and after an average of five moves did well. It could be argued that social workers mostly placed children with no pronounced emotional and behaviour problems, leaving others in residential institutions. This may have been true of some children, but not of all.

Foster parents had to cope with a fair amount of difficult behaviour at the time of placement including temper tantrums, enuresis, epileptic fits, mental retardation and passivity.

The most accomplished caretakers appear to be warm and open people, with steady relationships and stable work records, not easily threatened by references to the family of origin. They were mostly in their late thirties and forties at placement, often having children of their own or at least one other foster child, and both spouses were active in parenting the children.

The ten children who perceived their fostering as mostly negative and who were currently coping rather poorly, did not differ at placement from the other children in the sample. Six had been placed when aged three or under, and the remaining four when aged between six and nine. Explanations for this outcome have to be sought mostly in the types of interaction that occurred between the children concerned and the foster parents, rather than in the children's background as such. The earlier placed children were similar in all characteristics to the children brought up in the foster homes with a more successful outcome. The only exception was three children placed when aged between six and nine who had a common characteristic: all three had experienced an earlier lengthy fostering arrangement which collapsed, leaving them with strong feelings of rejection and bitterness. These children never settled properly in their new foster homes. Perhaps better preparation and a more tolerant foster family would have helped them to overcome their intense feelings of rejection. Clarke and Clarke, [11] commenting on Rutter's [12] statement that the child, to some extent, also causes his own learning experiences, add that there is the 'possibility that early experiences may produce particular effects which, acting upon later environments, result in reinforcing feedback, thus prolonging early learning effects.' They quote the examples of the disturbed institutional child who, when placed in foster care, may elicit from the foster mother antagonistic responses which strengthen the child's instability.

Foster parents in the unsuccessful group, though similar in most characteristics to those in the rest of the sample, were functioning under greater pressure compared with the rest. Relationship problems, low levels of tolerance, accommodation and financial difficulties produced tensions not found in the rest of the sample. In the eyes of the former foster children, the homes lacked warmth and consistency, and the majority did not regard the foster family as their family.

In the early stages of placement children appear to retain their attachments to their natural families, but with the lapse of time, and particularly where parental visiting becomes too infrequent or ceases altogether, the children begin to transfer their loyalties to the people who care for them. A slow process of psychological bonding seems to develop that gradually cements itself to the point that the foster child becomes indistinguishable from other members of the caretaking family. Knowledge by the child about his family of origin and the circumstances of his fostering contributes to feelings of well-being and to better adjustment. Information and explanation about the family of origin helps the child to integrate it into his developing personality and base his identity on the concept of two families. Furthermore, it helps him to acknowledge feelings of loss and rejection surrounding the original parents, so that he can find his own peace.

The use of the terms 'exclusive' and 'inclusive' fostering put forward by Holman[7/8] provides a very useful concept from which to examine fostering. This, however, is only one aspect and must be considered along with others, such as the quality of relationships and the emotional climate prevailing in the foster home. In spite of the readiness of many foster parents to be open and inclusive, the young adults were generally hazy about their families of origin, including names, place of birth, or current whereabouts. Social workers failed in many instances to provide the children with enough background and other genealogical information to enable them to develop a clear sense of themselves in relation to their natural family. They also need to ensure that the children's history is appropriately recorded and not obliterated.

The majority of young adults in the study greatly valued the quality and continuity of care they received, and many would have liked to be adopted by their foster parents. Similarly, many foster parents would also have liked to adopt the children. At least twelve of the forty foster parents were very serious about adopting the children in their care. Adoption was not pursued, mostly because of local authority objections relating to the foster parents' age, uncertainty about parental consents, or fears concerning the child's background. It was not uncommon for such fears to be raised by the caring authorities rather than the foster parents. The former foster children were both surprised and disturbed to hear that their tenure in the foster home was not as secure as they thought. The rather uncertain tenure of foster care compared with adoption had its impact on some of the young people, but not on all. There were those who felt that it made no difference to their acceptance and sense of belonging.

The study showed that as the children grow up they become more like their foster parents and their foster parents' own children than their families of origin in terms of outlook, management and ambitions. A process of socialisation and absorption into the foster home takes place, and becomes stronger with the lapse of time. Given certain conditions, this process could have been more effective. Instead, both foster parents and social workers seemed to have low expectations and aspirations for the children, and the children had few aspirations for themselves. Setting low sights and expectations appears to be endemic to foster child placement, in contrast with adoption. In cases of long-term fostering, such as the ones featured in this study, there seems to be no logical explanation why foster parents should not be recruited from a much wider range of families. Though the majority of the former foster children were coping fairly well with current life situations, there was also a fair amount of precariousness in their lives. This was mainly because of the kind of jobs they held, their limited education and absence of skills.

The study also points to the need for greater discrimination in the use of foster care resources. Additional studies are obviously needed to yield more detailed information about other forms of fostering besides long-term. Long-term fostering of the type described here makes different demands compared with other forms. Similarly, the needs of these children are different from those where there are realistic chances of rehabilitation with their own families. The finding, for instance, that professional group foster homes have serious drawbacks in the eyes of those who experience them, suggests that this form of fostering may suit some but not all children, particularly not those in long-term fostering. The study also suggests that it is inappropriate to mix short-, medium- and long-term fostering to a degree that it threatens the stability of the long-term child. Another point needing further consideration is the relationship between foster care breakdowns and pressures on foster parents to take on more children than they ideally feel able to cope with. Some of the breakdowns the study came across were not unrelated to this factor.

It could be claimed that the type of long-term fostering described here is indistinguishable from *de facto* adoption, and that with better planning it should arise much less frequently in future. This is partly true, and it serves to remind us that the aim of foster care is to be used as a resource for a definable period of time for hard-pressed families, and not as a form of *de facto* adoption. But with adoption itself now developing into a child care service, the boundaries are becoming increasingly blurred. There is a strong case for adoption being pursued early on for children in foster care whose parents lose interest in them, but adoption cannot be the answer to all the dilemmas facing long-term fostering. Long-term fostering will still occur in situations where the parents of some children placed in short or intermediate forms of fostering again lose interest in them and perhaps disappear; but if the child has formed meaningful bonds with the foster parents and the latter are prepared to look after it indefinitely there should be no reason why the child should not stay on to avoid a new disruption. If this happens, the foster parents may have to give up or limit other forms of fostering in the interests of the long-term ones. Where no meaningful attachments have been formed, it may be preferable to plan for a new family for an indefinite period of time.

Long-term fostering will also be appropriate for children whose own families continue to be interested in them but cannot have them back or do not wish to release them for adoption. In both circumstances, however, both the foster parents and the child will need security and the guarantee of permanence. Finally, there is need not only for greater discrimination in the use of fostering as a resource, but also of more purposeful planning of social workers' visits, with continuity of workers who can take the time and trouble to get to know the children in their care.

Note

I am grateful to the Social Science Research Council for the award of a grant which enabled me to carry out this study. A larger study is under way which is attempting to contrast the growing-up experiences and current circumstances of young people who were adopted after being viewed as 'hard to place', with those who grew up in foster homes and residential units.

References

1 T. Ferguson, *Children in Care – and After*, Oxford University Press, London, 1966

2 S. Theis, *How Foster Children Turn Out*, Publication no. 165, New York: State Charities Aid Association, 1924.

3 E. G. Meier, 'Former Foster Children as Adult Citizens' in A. Kadushin (ed.), *Child Welfare Services – A Sourcebook*, Collier-McMillan, London, 1970.

4 R. Salo, Quoted by Meier in 'Former Foster Children as Adult Citizens'; thesis submitted to Columbia University for a DSW in 1962.

5 A. D. B. Clarke, 'Learning and Human Development', *British Journal of Psychiatry*, 114, 1966, pp. 1061-77.

6 R. Holman, 'The Place of Fostering in Social Work', *British Journal of Social Work*, Spring 1975. See Chapter 5 in this book.

7 E. Weinstein, *The Self Image of the Foster Child*, Russell Sage Foundation, 1960.

8 V. George, *Foster Care: Theory and Practice*, Routledge & Kegan Paul, London, 1970.

9 J. Aldgate, See Chapter 2 in this book.

10 K. W. Watson, 'Long Term Foster Care: Default or Design? The Voluntary Agency Responsibility', *Child Welfare*, vol. 47, no. 1, June 1968, p.332.

11 A. M. Clarke and A. D. B. Clarke, 'The Formative Years?' in A. M.-Clarke and A. D. B. Clarke (eds), *Early Experiences, Myth and Evidence*, Open Books, London, 1976.

12 M. Rutter, H. G. Birch, A. Thomas and S. Chess, 'Temperamental Characteristics in Infancy and the Later Development of Behaviour Disorders', *British Journal of Psychiatry*, 110, 1964, pp.651-61.

Phillida Sawbridge

10 Seeking new parents: a decade of development

In 1965 the case committee of a voluntary agency was considering applications to adopt from three couples. The first couple, an accountant and his wife in their late twenties, were discussed for a considerable length of time, because their infertility tests had shown no obvious reason why they had not produced children. It was finally decided to accept them, but to keep them on the waiting-list for at least a year in case the wife conceived in the meantime. If they could have their own children they would not be considered eligible to adopt. The second couple was quickly accepted because a child had already been placed with them by the same agency, and it was believed another could be found for them. The third couple was rejected because the husband, now thirty-two, had been divorced following a nine-month marriage contracted when he was nineteen, and the wife suffered from *petit mal.*

The committee then moved on to consider four babies it had been asked to accept for placement. Two were immediately accepted and waiting couples selected for them, but two were refused, and the moral welfare worker advised to turn to the local authority Children's Department for advice. One baby's medical report said 'Not fit for adoption' on account of a heart murmur and a club foot, and the other was an infant of mixed race. The committee thought it unlikely that among their approved couples anyone would be found willing to take such children.

In 1977 the case committee of another voluntary agency met to consider three children for placement and the three familes being proposed for them. Two of the children were mentally handicapped: both had Down's syndrome, one a baby of nine months, the other a three and a half year old. The third child was an eleven-year-old boy with a hearing loss. The couples wanting these children had not needed infertility tests, since all had children already. One had had a Down's syndrome child born to them and wanted a second, feeling their lives were geared to this; the other had three healthy, normal children and wanted to share their lives with a less fortunate child. The couple wanting the eleven-year-old had one younger child.

These descriptions illustrate how, over the last decade, a slow but very steady change has become apparent in the field of substitute family care, and not least in the field of adoption. Whereas in the early 1960s adoptive parents were still in fairly short supply, and adoption was by and large considered only for healthy white babies who could be pronounced 'Fit for adoption', by the late 1970s would-be adopters of pre-school-age children frequently had little hope of finding a child, and adoption was increasingly being considered a solution for any child under eighteen who needed parenting.

Perhaps the most fundamental change is the gradual move - still nowhere near completed - from parents' rights being paramount to children's interests being of prime importance, as decreed in the 1975 Children Act. All too often the adult's right to a child has been the deciding factor in planning for the child: either in keeping him in institutional care indefinitely because a parent might eventually want him back, or in precluding him from adoption because an adoptive parent had a 'right' to a 'perfect' child and he had a health problem. Now the new legislation recognises that a child should be 'freed for adoption' if he needs parents and the ones he has cannot fulfil their obligations; and adopters are no longer the chief beneficiaries of adoption placements. In fact, there is the beginning of a recognition that every parentless child could potentially be adopted, and the greater his handicap perhaps the greater his need for adoption.

This examination of these developments is made from the standpoint of a social worker who was active in a placing agency for non-white babies in the late 1960s (the British Adoption Project), moved on to the more administrative side in an inter-agency co-ordinating body (the Adoption Resource Exchange), and then returned to the field in a new agency set up to find familes for 'hard-to-place' children (Parents for Children).

The middle period, spent with the Adoption Resource Exchange, provided an incomparable bird's-eye view of what was happening in the field, since the Exchange becomes closely involved not only in the organisation of inter-agency placements but also in the structure and administration of adoption services. The discussion that follows is based on the variety of experiences offered by these three posts.

The first question to be asked is: why do children need new parents anyway, whether foster or adoptive?

Nobody would dispute that the ideal family for any child is the one he is born into and in which he is wanted, loved, nurtured and raised towards independence. What is often overlooked is that some children are born to people who either cannot or do not want to provide this love and nurture. It is a fact we do not want to believe, because it goes against our most deep-seated beliefs in the one-ness of families, the role of motherhood, and even the sanctity of human life. But we do a great disservice to many children by clinging to a blind belief that everybody can be and wants to be a parent to his offspring. We accept perhaps somewhat more readily that a man may see and feel little relationship between the pleasure of a sexual relationship with a woman and a wrinkled infant presented to him nine months later. We are less ready to accept that a woman also on occasions may not feel or want any real responsibility for the product of that relationship. She has had to carry it for nine months and cope with all the feelings that go with that, but those feelings may have been dominated by fear, resentment, anger or frustration, and she may be no better fitted to be a real parent to this new person that the man who fathered him. Equally, she may long to be a good parent, but without a husband's support may feel unequal to the task.

In denying this we also do a disservice to parenthood because we appear to say that the act of reproduction fits anyone to be a good parent and that fertility is all one needs. In fact we know the two things are barely connected and that infertile couples can make first-rate adoptive or foster parents, while many fertile people have no clue about how to nurture and raise a child. Good parenting is a difficult task which is often under-valued.

This is not to deny that there are many people who want to be good parents but whose circumstances or natural endowments are such that they cannot achieve it. It is a scandal that poor housing, for example, can lead to the break-up of families, and that a child may lose his own parents as a result. Urgent attention must be paid to the causes for family break-up if social provision is ever to be adequate and relevant, but that is not the sphere of this paper. We have to accept that, until we make better provision, some parents will be overcome by the unequal struggle.

In such cases, it is difficult to separate the needs of those parents from the needs of the child; but once the child has had to be parted from them, and certainly once he has remained away from them for more than six months, there is clear evidence[1] that he is unlikely to return, and plans for his future need to be made urgently. If sufficient help can be given to enable him to return home, obviously this is the plan of preference; but if he is to be kept 'on ice' indefinitely while attempts to rehabilitate the parents are pursued, then his needs have been lost sight of in favour of those of the adults. Social work is full of painful and difficult decisions; and the one most often shirked is the one which requires acceptance of the fact that, if a parent cannot offer a child what he needs soon enough to be useful, then the child needs to be found alternative parents who can. This may not involve losing contact with the first parents, but a child needs daily loving consistent care, preferably in a small unit where he knows he belongs, can stay and is important and of value. He needs too the opportunity to experience good parental and good family relationships, on which he can later model himself and his own family. An occasional visit or a birthday card in no way provide this, although they may go alongside. One can argue that a children's Home can provide all these requirements, and many do, but one can never avoid two facts about children's Homes: that the staff are employed and therefore go on and off duty, and also may change jobs; and that the provision is time-limited and so a child is out on his own from age eighteen with no family backing.

However much adolescents may reject their parents, at least they are there to reject, and most people work through to an adult relationship which has value and meaning. Few young people of eighteen are entirely independent of their parents, either financially or emotionally, and certainly the parental home is usually available to go to, or to get married from. Where does the girl who grew up in care get married from? How does it feel to the boy who returns 'home' to find another child sleeping in the bed that was his and nobody around whom he knows? Who reminds them what they were like as children, or shares incidents from their past, or tells them their child is just like they were at that age? Little things, perhaps, but they all go to make up the sense of continuity and identity which everybody needs.

Who are the children?

In the *Children Who Wait*[1] study, three out of five of the children were found to be boys, half of the children were illegitimate, and more than half had brothers or sisters living with them. Nearly two-thirds were of school age, and about a quarter were black or of mixed race. Merely stating these facts shows up one of the root problems in relation to finding new parents for these children: most parents begin their task with one comparatively immobile, unformed and very dependent infant with whom they grow into their role as he develops and matures. The children we are talking about often come in twos and threes, are mostly already at school and have come through all kinds of unknown experiences which certainly include varying degrees of deprivation. To take over the position of a parent to them requires skills and insight of a high order, and people having that to offer do not walk into Social Service Departments every day. That is factor number one.

Where are the children?

The large majority are in institutional care, and this in itself can militate against family placement. To begin with, they are safe, well looked after, clothed and fed, and above all are not an 'emergency'. They therefore receive a low priority among the many groups of people social workers try to serve, most of whom are involved in a crisis of some sort. The facts that a child needs new parents and needs help in accepting his loss of his first ones are crises of a different order and often not even recognised as such.

Besides that, institutional care may well be self-perpetuating. Once the bricks and mortar are there and the staff is employed it may be not only easier but also a matter of policy to use the Homes rather than spend additional resources on family-finding, and risk making staff and buildings redundant. Fundamental to that is the whole philosophy of child care, and in particular the question of who makes the decisions regarding children in care and on what grounds. As regards the philosophy, many social workers do not believe in adoption, least of all for older children; and some do not have much faith in the viability of fostering, particularly when studies like George's *Foster Care: Theory and Practice* [2] show a failure rate of 78 per cent of children aged five years or more at the time of placement. Many social workers have chosen residential care as their area of operation; and although there may be a variety of reasons for this, it must demonstrate a commitment to that form of care in principle. It is hurtful, indeed, to have to say to those colleagues that by and large one does not believe they are offering the best provision for most children. There is and always will be a place for residential care. Some children need specialised treatment, some need an interim placement, for some there are other reasons why it may be the plan of choice. But residential workers themselves are the first to resent their Homes being used as a dumping-ground, and often rightly urge that a child be moved who is not appropriately placed with them.

The other side of this coin is the difficulty for residential staff of being asked to care daily for a child and yet to be prepared to release him to new parents when they come along, and to help him to go. Naturally they become fond of him as they care for him, and yet all too often their feelings in the matter are neglected and surprise is expressed that they may seem reluctant to part from the child, or even may undermine the new relationship by not loosening their own ties. Some are particularly good at preparing a child for new parents and at helping him to adjust to the move, and more study is needed of what makes this possible for them and how they go about it.

But more important than all this is the question of the child's best interests and the need to plan according to these; too often plans are made for the wrong reasons, on the basis of expediency or by default; too often it is the problems of the adults involved rather than those of the child which prevent an appropriate placement. For example, of the first twenty children referred to Parents for Children, nine were referred because the Home in which they were living was closing down; all too often placements are delayed by the failure of social workers to do the preliminary work necessary to refer a child to the Adoption Resource Exchange or another agency, even when a specific family may be waiting.

One of the key questions in discussing planning for children in care is, 'Who makes the plans?' This brings one immediately up against the even more fundamental question of how a local authority can be a parent. Tom Hart, in *A Walk with Alan,* [3] relates how a boy in a children's Home was asked: 'Have you got a mother and father?' and he replied: 'No, I ain't - I got the LCC.' This is the position of thousands of children, but too little thought has been given to what it means in practice and to how a county council exercises its rights and obligations. Working in a voluntary agency in collaboration with a local authority one realises the disadvantages of not having one identifiable person who is the parent. How much more the children are aware of it is poignantly revealed in *Who Cares?* [4] the report of a working party of young people in care. In every authority the system appears to be different. In some the field worker carries a great deal of responsibility for the child, so that when he or she leaves it is almost like losing a parent all over again; and the new worker may have quite different ideas which are then pursued. In other authorities every decision has to be made or at least confirmed by a committee, no member of which knows the child, and quick decisions become impossible. In others again, the responsibility is divided: a child may be technically in the care of one authority but cared for by another or by a voluntary agency; it can then happen that each thinks the other is taking certain responsibilities and the parental task is in fact not carried out at all. If a fundamental component of good parenting is consistency, then a body and especially a changing body of people can never really be a parent. For that reason too, a child should have family care wherever possible, so that day-to-day decisions affecting him are made in the home, as is normal.

Philip, aged fourteen, had been proposed for fostering because his children's Home was closing. He was also awaiting an operation about which he was scared and anxious. It was hard for him to think ahead to life with a new family while the operation loomed on the horizon, and his future seemed to him nothing but uncertainty and frightening new experiences. His social worker in the local authority saw him very infrequently, assuming that the voluntary agency in whose Home he was living were giving him the necessary support. The Home's staff appeared not to see this as their role, and nobody talked to Philip about what to expect in hospital, about his fears, or about the possibility of moving to his new foster parents first and having the operation in their locality. In fact nobody pursued the medical recommendations at all, to find out how soon Philip might expect to go into hospital, how long he might be in, or the implications afterwards, as any normal parent would. Philip's anxieties led him to reject the whole idea of fostering, and it was only because the prospective foster parents, having met him and become committed to him, were able to assume the parenting role, and patiently demonstrate their support and concern, that Philip eventually was helped both to face hospitalisation and then to become a member of their family.

A further factor which may militate against placing the 'children who wait' is the whole approach to finding and working with new families. In the past adoption has been primarily a service for childless couples, and unhealthy babies or older children were not considered adoptable. Fostering has more readily been considered for such children, but often the foster parents have been seen as clients rather than colleagues, and have been offered neither the parental responsibility nor the supports which would have made the job more possible. Now at last we are coming to realise that parents for these children with special needs must be sought out, prepared, supported and trusted, and those four elements figure largely in the recent developments and experiments in the field of home-finding which we will now move on to examine.

1 The British Adoption Project

In the mid-1960s it was still considered a major challenge to find adoptive homes for mixed race or black babies. Many mothers who wanted to have such children adopted were told it was not possible to find parents for them. To disprove this, and also to harness the widespread goodwill which had been demonstrated towards children of other races by a short-lived Hong Kong adoption project, International Social Service and Bedford College (University of London) set up a four-year programme for the placement of healthy black or mixed race children under two. Bedford's involvement was on the research side, studying the programme as it got under way and initiating the first round of a longitudinal follow-up study. The results were described by Lois Raynor in *Adoption of Non-White Children*,[5] and the second round of the follow-up study has been written up by Barbara Jackson in two pamphlets: 'Adopting a Black Child' and 'Inter-Racial Adoption'.

The British Adoption Project was one of the first initiatives in pushing back the boundaries of adoption. In fact there was little difficulty in finding familes for the fifty-two babies concerned; and now, of course, the situation has so far changed that babies of any race or colour are widely sought after. The first child to be placed through the BAP was an Anglo-Asian baby girl. It seems unimaginable now that there was ever a time when there was not a queue of people wanting such a child. The change has perhaps been gradual over ten or twelve years, but is a very fundamental one in terms not only of adoption practice but also of social attitudes.

2 The Adoption Resource Exchange

One of the major achievements of the British Adoption Project was to highlight the need for greater co-ordination in the field of home-finding for children. Inquiries from would-be adopters were received from all over the country, as were requests for help in placing children, and the BAP realised the need for some sort of clearing-house to link the two. After one abortive attempt to set up an informal liaison system, the idea of an exchange based on agency – membership was mooted, and in fact took shape in the BAP offices. The first eight children were placed on an inter-agency basis in 1968 by the first twenty member agencies; the membership and the placements grew steadily thereafter, and in 1978 had reached eighty-five members and 829 placements. The interesting fact about the placements is that whereas in 1968 and 1969 they were confined to mixed race or black babies, the boundaries were again gradually pushed further and further back, so that by 1977-8 thirty-six of the 105 children placed were over five, and children of any race were being referred, including those with a variety of handicaps.

The aim of the Adoption Resource Exchange was not simply to achieve the family placement of children who otherwise were being kept waiting, but also to improve standards of practice by enabling agencies to work together, to trust each other, and to learn from each other. One method used was to make membership dependent on an examination of the agency structure and policies, ensuring a sound basis for good practice. This would help members to have confidence in each other, knowing they were all working along the same lines. Such inter-agency trust is not easy to achieve where planning for children is concerned, and it is a measure of the commitment to the task of all concerned that out of 829 placements arranged through the Exchange only thirty-one have not worked out.

One of the ways in which the Adoption Resource Exchange has tried to help to improve the possibility of family placement for children has been through encouraging and initiating publicity. It was early on recognised that parents will not be found if the public does not know of the need, and the only way to make the need known is by using the news media. Television programmes featuring children needing families have now become fairly widely accepted in spite of the furore the first one caused in the press, although there is still a minority of authorities who will not consent to this method of recruitment being used for children in their care. The use of photographs in newspaper publicity is becoming more usual, and again the shift in opinion over the last ten years is most marked when one thinks back to the early days of the Exchange.

3 'Soul Kids' campaign

One of the specific attempts to recruit parents for waiting children was a campaign aimed at West Indians in London in 1975-6. A rather high proportion of children referred to the Exchange, particularly from London and Birmingham, were partly or fully of West Indian origin, and a minority of black foster or adoptive parents were coming forward. It was felt that part of the reason was the lack of knowledge among West Indians about the need for homes, and also perhaps the resistance to formalities and bureaucracy felt by many people but especially by West Indians. A working party of social workers of both British and West Indian origin met over a period of time to discuss how these obstacles could be overcome, and the result was a one-year campaign sponsored by nine London boroughs which would have the dual aim of publicising the need for foster and adoptive parents, and of educating both the black community and the social workers about each other's attitudes.[6] This was done partly by seminars and regular monthly meetings for the social workers involved, and partly by newspaper articles, radio broadcasts, leaflets, speakers at meetings, personal contacts, and any other methods the group could devise for reaching the West Indian community. Ideas far outran the time or resources available for putting them into action. The outcome, although good, was not startling in terms of numbers (sixteen new approved homes by the end of the year with sixteen more applications in the pipeline), but those involved felt a useful start had been made on improving understanding among a section of the public and also among a small group of social workers.

One of the lessons the steering group of the campaign felt it had learned was that a specific group in the community – in this case West Indians – would respond to publicity aimed directly at them. The number of enquiries received as a result of the campaign far exceeded the normal number received from West Indians and showed how much interest was potentially present. Linked to that was a clear demonstration of the importance of understanding the expectations and pre-conceived ideas of the inquirers. In this instance that involved a knowledge of the cultural background from which they had come as well as of their present circumstances and concerns, and a recognition of their likely attitudes to caring for other people's children and to authority. There is room for a greater awareness of these factors in all recruitment of foster and adoptive parents, of course, and the lessons learned from this campaign could be fruitfully transferred to general social work practice.

4 Parents for children

The concentration of referrals to the Adoption Resource Exchange of not only black children but also of older children or those with handicaps led indirectly to another new project being started. It became increasingly clear that the children being left behind all the time were those well into school age, family groups together, and children with mental handicaps or physical problems. Some were finding homes through the Exchange, but by and large these are the children who need special recruitment on their behalf, because people do not think of walking into an agency saying, 'I want to be a parent to a deaf black ten-year-old'. Few of the social services departments in whose care these children are have the resources to devote to a full-time search for a solution, but that is what is needed. Accompanying that must be a belief that families do exist in the community who can and will take on such children, and this belief has been most strongly found among the very people who should know: the groups of adoptive and foster parents which have come into being with increasing strength in the last five or six years. It was representatives of the Parent-to-Parent Information on Adoption Service who suggested that a specialist agency could perhaps be set up to try to find homes for the children who needed most time devoted to them. A working party of interested organisations and individuals was set up: it drew up plans for such an agency and then started the search for funds. By the spring of 1976 a DHSS grant had been promised, together with funds from the Hilden, Sainsbury and Rowntree Trusts, and in October 1976 Parents for Children came into being.

The new agency had as its remit the seeking of parents for older or handicapped children whom no other agency had yet been able to place. The object was to test out new methods of family-finding, to offer preparation rather than 'investigation' to anyone who felt he had something to offer, to offer long-term support to families taking a child, and to demonstrate not only that most children can be found parents, even if it may not be the conventional childless couples of traditional adoptions, but also what is needed to make such placements work.

A year later, although still in its infancy, Parents for Children had learned some valuable lessons, with much more learning still to come. What quickly became clear was the immense demand on time made by this type of home-finding, and how difficult it must be for social workers with other responsibilities to undertake such work. Fourteen children, five of them mentally handicapped, had been placed in new families by the end of 1977; and for some of them, particularly the older ones, weeks of work had been required both for the preparation of the child and for finding and working with their new parents.

Parents for Children had decided from the beginning to experiment with a new approach to the recruitment of families. One basic commitment was to the finding of parents for each child individually, rather than building up a 'bank' of approved adopters and then slotting in the children. Interested couples or individuals are worked with only for as long as is needed to establish whether they could consider parenting one of the currently waiting children, and if not they are left in abeyance, still receiving the newsletters which describe the children until there is a child they wish to discuss further. This means that time is not wasted on working with families who, however much they have to offer, cannot immediately be 'used', while a child who needs a family waits even longer. Families are not 'approved' in the abstract; the placement of a specific child with specific parents is what the case committee approves.

The agency takes the view that most people who offer can probably parent some child, but Parents for Children needs to find a limited number of specific parents for the particular children it takes on. It does not therefore start from a premise of restrictive requirements: age limits, church affiliation, pre-determined health standards, etc., but rather asks anybody who feels he can offer something to a child to come and discuss it in the light of the children on referral. The emphasis initially is on information-giving and preparation rather than information-taking, so no questionnaires are handed out in the early stages, and a minimum of questions is asked. Open meetings, group discussions, contacts with experienced adoptive and foster parents, and interviews which clarify the aims and methods of the agency and describe the children on referral are the substance of the first contacts. Many people weed themselves out if they find it is not for them, and those who continue at least understand fairly clearly the kind of parenting being sought, and can themselves be involved in the decision as to whether they are capable of doing it. By the time information is needed from them, with discussion of themselves and their attributes, the reason for such self-assessment is apparent and therefore considerably more acceptable than if it had been the very first stage of the process.

Alongside the self-assessment goes a process of education, and certainly once an individual child is in question this must be so. If the child is handicapped the prospective parents need to know all they can about his condition, his education, local facilities, and the prognosis; they also need the opportunity to meet parents of other children like him, and wherever possible Parents for Children tries to ensure this, either through the association related to the particular disability (Down's children's society, Association for Spina Bifida and Hydrocephalus, etc.), or by introducing another family, or suggesting a link through the school or through the medical consultant.

It is not only the prospective parents who need preparation - the children do too. Often a child who has spent some time in care may be very confused as to what originally happened to put him there, and he may still cling to a hope that his parents will come back for him. In one case it was only when a teenager was referred for adoption and efforts made to trace her birth parents that it was discovered her mother had in fact died. Before being able to make new close relationships children need to face, understand and round off the old, or at least to know how they fit in with the new ones.

A child also needs help in developing a realistic expectation of family life. Children who grow up in children's Homes often miss out on experiences which are taken for granted in families, and find adjusting to a new daily routine very difficult. For example, children from a large Home may never participate in the preparation or the clearing away of a meal, and may resent being expected to help wash up - or, like one six-year-old, be horrified at the sight of raw meat. Alternatively, a child may think that rules exist only in institutions, and expect to be allowed to go to bed when he likes, watch all the TV he wants, and think that parents are there only to indulge him. The fact that family life is not centred entirely on the child, as life in a children's Home is, may take some children by surprise; and their adaptation to Daddy's routine rather than the staff's to his may require an unexpected adjustment. This can be made easier if it has been discussed first, and if his conception of family life has been examined with him, along with his perception of parental or sibling relationships. Often a child who has not grown up in a family has no understanding of family relationships such as aunts, uncles, or cousins; and help can be given in understanding what these mean, too. None of the time spent on helping a child think himself into his new environment is ever likely to be wasted.

Another very time-consuming aspect of the way Parents for Children works is the follow-up service offered to families. In the belief that virtually every family is likely to encounter problems of some sort in taking an older or handicapped child, that placing agencies need to know more about what does happen later on, and that the legalisation of the adoption may be only the beginning, not the end, of the real story, the agency offers an open-ended time commitment to every family. Because at the time of writing only three adoptions have been legalised it is too soon to know the full implications of this, but it is expected that demand will go in waves, and that it is a viable offer only because not all families will be wanting service at the same time. Certainly the work does not slacken off immediately following placement, and some families make full use of the constant availability of the team as such, even if their own worker is not there. This has demonstrated the very real advantage of a team approach to working, whereby all the families are known to some extent to every worker, if only on paper and through decision-making discussions, and every family knows at least two workers personally.

Finally, in looking at what takes the time, there are all the other people who throughout the process have to be involved, in the referring departments, the children's Homes, the schools, the medical services and so on; and there are often innumerable administrative or legal problems to sort out. Again it is clear that none of the time spent on this aspect of the preparatory work is wasted. Alongside all that is the need for close and constant support for the social workers doing this very demanding work, so that the weekly team meetings and group consultation are essential. In statistical terms, there is much 'wastage'. Many people are seen and talked to who decide this kind of adoption is not for them. All publicity requires planning and preparation, and little direct response may be received. Yet none of this can really be considered wasted effort, since public education must precede or at least go alongside the actual findings of families. Each individual who learns something about the need for homes is helping the process; and so little is yet known about who or where potential adoptive parents are that no efforts can be spared in talking to anyone and everyone at every possible opportunity. This being so, it is small wonder that generic social workers in busy departments so often find the home-finding task on behalf of older children such a frustrating and daunting experience, since they are not able to give their total time and commitment to it - and it requires nothing less.

Perhaps one of the most significant changes in adoption practice is the swing towards seeking specific parents for certain groups of children or for the individual child, such as more West Indian parents through the 'Soul Kids' campaign, or a specific person or couple to parent a handicapped child for Parents for Children. This means that the attitude of the social workers must change, since no longer are they choosing between a number of competing claimants, but instead they are asking for a service and must offer preparation for the task they want people to do and support in doing it. As the 'Soul Kids' campaign found, there is room for more community work skills in the adoption field, not only in finding families, but also in learning how to mobilise community supports and resources and in becoming more then ever an intermediary and an enabler rather than a 'doer' of all things for all men.

Another lesson of the past decade is the need to pool and share resources. Geographical boundaries should have no place in planning for children, who should not be deprived of a family because they live the wrong side of a line on a map. The Adoption Resource Exchange has shown that distance need not be a barrier to the children being linked with new parents, and that authorities can share their resources amicably, trustingly and with advantage to all concerned. There are other signs of this kind of co-operation developing, as in the all-London 'Mums and Dads' fostering campaign in 1976, when for the first time all the London boroughs worked together to develop a pool of homes. It can only be hoped that such joint ventures will continue, with the needs of the child as their focus rather than administrative conveniences or the concerns of the adults.

References

1 J. Rowe and L. Lambert, *Children Who Wait,* ABAFA, 1973.
2 V. George, *Foster Care: Theory and Practice,* Routledge & Kegan Paul, 1970.
3 T. Hart, *A Walk With Alan,* Quartet Books, 1973.
4 R. Page and G. A. Clarke, *Who Cares?* National Children's Bureau, 1977.
5 L. Raynor, *Adoption of Non-White Children,* Allen & Unwin, 1970.
6 For a detailed discussion of the project, see 'Soul Kids Working Party: The Soul Kids Campaign', ABAFA, 1977

Mary James

11 Home-finding for children with special needs

The Independent Adoption Society (IAS) is a voluntary agency, which was established in 1964. Growing out of the needs of those times, when most adoption work was undertaken by church-based adoption agencies, it was first known as the Agnostics Adoption Society. From the outset IAS aimed to have an open approach to prospective adopters irrespective of their race, religion and creed, and to find homes for all children in need. In the mid-1960s, when it was often difficult to find a home for a healthy mixed race baby, IAS became a founder member of the Adoption Resource Exchange and consequently has a tradition of finding homes for children from differing racial backgrounds. From 1972 the Society adopted an active policy to seek families for children with all kinds of special needs, such as those identified by the research study *Children Who Wait.*[1] Since such children were in the care of local Social Service Departments, it was recognised that the Society must attempt to develop close working relationships with these departments. Additional staff were then employed and were encouraged to move into what was then a fairly uncharted area of adoption work.

Work with one local authority

IAS is based in what is probably a fairly typical Inner London borough with all that this entails in terms of social problems, housing difficulties, mobile population and a high demand for social services in general. In 1973 this borough had approximately 1,600 children in care, most of whom were cared for in residential provision often situated outside the borough. At that date the borough did not have any special fostering unit and never operated as an adoption agency. There was a fairly high turnover in staff at all levels. It was a local authority aware of its difficulties and shortcomings and very much wanting to improve services for all client groups. Its senior staff were interested in considering ways in which IAS and the local authority could work together to provide a much needed additional service for children in care.

The first job was to identify children in care who needed placement with long-term or permanent substitute families. To tackle this a small working group was formed, which consisted of representatives from two area teams, a local children's Home, the embryonic Fostering Unit, the child care consultant and IAS staff. A survey carried out by this group identified a number of children needing either long-term fostering or adoption. Having identified the children, the next step was to consider them individually in more detail and to make individual plans.

An independent, small, specialist agency and a large local authority Social Service Department do not work together without tensions and difficulties. The focus, philosophies and priorities of two such agencies are often quite different, their decision-making procedures vary, their time scales and use of resources may also produce conflicts. In adoption, vital decisions have to be made concerning natural parents and their capacity to care for their children, the needs of the children themselves, the potential of prospective adopters and the progress of subsequent placements. These decisions are always difficult to reach but must be based upon genuine agreement if the plans are to be carried through successfully.

As well as professional trust, collaborative work between two agencies requires the co-ordination of differing policies and procedures. It is essential that all concerned are clear where the authority to make decisions lies, and what is required administratively and procedurally by each agency. All information, decisions, plans and actions have to be recorded and understood. A child in care is usually at the centre of a complex network of adults and so tasks must be clearly defined and allocated, time limits agreed upon, responsibilities delegated and jobs done. We also learned that any collaborative working relationships must be constantly reviewed. Working with a Social Service Department with a high turnover of staff makes it important to allow time to gain the interest of new members of staff as well as to keep the enthusiasm of the old. Practice will need adaptation in the light of experience, and the agencies must always be alert to meet new needs. As time goes by the cases referred for placement are likely to become more complex in relation to the children's individual needs and overall situations, and equally the approach of work must adapt to reflect this.

Adoptive families

Finding them

Agencies engaged in finding families for children with special needs have to develop an approach which enables not precludes, and sets aside fixed ideas and rigid rules. It may not be the people social workers think should adopt who do so, or the people who live like they do, or the people with whom they feel comfortable that will necessarily offer homes or even make the best parents. Families who are satisfied with their own lives are perhaps less likely to consider the needs of others; maybe the very things which lead families to offer their services make them suspect to social workers. For example, the family who already have a handicapped member and offer a home to a handicapped child, or the family where a child has died, or the family who say they do not wish to have children of their own. Developing an open door approach may not be easy for the case committee or the workers in agencies who have previously worked hard to find excluding criteria such as age and family composition and number of years after marriage, in order to keep people away. What has to be sought is an approach which helps as many people as possible to consider whether they can be parents to children now needing families.

For agencies already offering an adoption service the first place to look for families will be among the people who already come to them. Mostly these will be childless couples who are hoping to adopt the baby they were unable to have themselves. Not all of these prospective parents will be able to consider a different kind of parenthood; but experience has shown that there are a number of couples amongst this group who are eager, willing and very capable of making this step, and find happiness and satisfaction from doing so.

Reaching out to people who have not traditionally had contact with adoption agencies will be another task, and all the usual methods of recruitment need to be considered: the use of advertisements and articles in papers and magazines, posters, talks to groups, special campaigns, and now the use of radio and television are all possible. The social workers will need to be prepared to deal with the response that these methods evoke, not only numerically but also the kind of people who may come forward and offer their services.

> One of the very first TV Adoption Programmes brought IAS in contact with Mr and Mrs H, a family who in the past would have been excluded from adoption agency consideration. They were both in their early fifties, Mrs H excessively overweight; they had an adult mongol daughter, were known to the local authority as occasional private foster parents, lived in small and rather overcrowded conditions, and did not have an easy manner or comfortable way with social workers. This family offered a home to a young mentally handicapped child. They eventually had placed with them a twelve-year-old severely mentally handicapped girl who had lived most of her life in a mental subnormality hospital and whose legal situation as far as adoption was concerned was unclear. Lily has now been with them for nearly two years and it is hoped that she will be adopted within the next twelve months. It has not been easy working with Mr and Mrs H. When they first applied, there were anxieties about the family and how it operated which presented problems not only for the adoption social worker but also for the local authority and for the Society's medical adviser. The work following the placement has also presented challenges, since Mr and Mrs H are not people who easily work alongside professionals; they have their own ways of dealing with life and their own expectations from schools, doctors and society in general. They have, however, taken into their family a child whom they love and cherish, whom they accept with all her handicaps, and whose only other alternative would have been permanent care in an institution. Lily will never make great progress but she now copes with ordinary family life, goes to special school, and no longer needs the assistance of drugs.

Individual adoption agencies may have needs specific to them which will have to be taken into account in recruitment strategies. IAS is currently undertaking a community recruitment project focusing on black children and trying to recruit foster and adoptive parents of similar ethnic origins. The approach has been twofold: to use a staff member to work in the community to discover interested individuals and groups who may offer homes or provide links to other potential parents; and to use someone already active in the community to act as a link into the adoption agency. This development has made the Society become far more community-based and has increased its awareness of important issues in race relations such as the general social and political atmosphere, the cultural background and present life styles of various ethnic groups, all of which are essential to any organisation providing social services in a multi-racial society. As far as finding families is concerned, progress is slow; but even with only one part-time worker during a period of six months twelve families offered a home to a child, which is a small but positive beginning.

Working together from the beginning

Having worked hard to locate interested families it is important to remember that they are potentially a priceless resource which needs to be nurtured and cherished. The job is to work together so that the family learns about children and adoption and the agency gets to know the family. This should be a real experience, with the emphasis on learning and sharing rather than scrutinising, and with the social worker remembering that caring for children may often be a practical rather than an intellectual task. The social worker and the adoption agency do not hold all the information and expertise which prospective parents need to consider. Adopters and foster parents in their various consumer groups and other organisations can all contribute through their individual members, their publications and their activities, as can residential staff or any one with personal experience of children.

A logical and comfortable beginning point for anyone considering adoptive parenthood is ordinary family life, thinking about being a parent, considering children and their needs and development. Everyone has some views and expertise on these matters, since everyone has at least been a child. Opportunities to visit adoptive families or children's Homes can all add to the picture. Discussion groups with other prospective or actual adopters can also be a good way of providing real information and a forum for the exchange of ideas and common concerns. IAS experience has been that groups aiming at selection and self-selection may not always be successful, since they can inhibit people and make them anxious. Meetings which focus on and explore specific shared interests can, however, be a satisfying and helpful experience for all concerned, as well as providing the opportunity for future links and friendships. A group of white families contemplating the adoption of a child from a different race can explore various aspects of community relations and inter-racial living; they can have the opportunity to hear at first hand personal views on a very complex subject, and learn about the attitudes and pressures which black people experience in everyday life.

To establish the kinds of close relationship needed by the social worker and members of a family, which will be an important factor in future work together, individual and personal contacts with the family are important; stylised and formal interviews may not be the best way of achieving the aim. Sharing ordinary family activities and experiences can be a very good way of getting to know a family and understanding their relationships and life style and generally developing a feeling of the family as a whole. Spending a day with a family, having a meal together, taking the children on some kind of trip or excursion: these may all be more natural ways for people to learn about one another. The social worker, like the family, will also need to be prepared to give of herself, her views and feelings for this exercise to be successful.

Since successful placements depend on those involved being as prepared as possible for likely eventualities, it will be helpful for the social worker and the family to consider together in advance various aspects of family functioning and relationships which are likely to be important. These may include how the parents handle their children, how they talk to them, discipline them, show affection, see them as individuals and in relation to each other. How do families resolve differences, between the children or between the adults and the children? How have family members coped at times of change, perhaps when another child is born or when someone dear is lost? Giving and sharing is important, sharing people and possessions like toys or food. How do the family see themselves in relation to outsiders, friends, neighbours, schools? One member of the family may be more vulnerable than others; this may be particularly important to recognise when considering the kind of child they could best help.

> William, aged seven, was placed in the middle of five children, the next in age being Richard, two years younger. William seemed to be one of nature's survivors, the kind of child who was noisy, noticeable, fairly competent and used to demanding adult attention and affection. Richard was seemingly quite secure in his family, much loved, an affectionate but rather gentle boy; he had never needed to fight for attention. The advent of William had a considerable effect on him. For a while he became a very sad-looking little boy, weepy, not coping at school, and reverting to bed-wetting. Concern for Richard made his parents and social worker think more about him carefully and realise that he had always been a fairly quiet gentle boy who easily gave up in difficult situations. Richard had also been the one most affected when

> his brother was killed in an accident. Retrospectively, it was clear that had we all thought a little more about Richard before William came, we could have been better prepared for his reaction and given him more support and help at an earlier stage.

The adoption worker will also be working with couples who have not yet experienced parenthood for themselves. It is important to remember that they may have a lot to commend them and are much needed, since often it is to these couples that agencies look for the parents of sibling groups; but they will need to consider the realities of parenthood. Childless couples will not have expectations of children based upon the experience of their own children, which can be a freeing and positive factor in their favour. They will not be faced with some of the divided loyalties faced by existing parents in reaching a balance which meets the needs of their new child and their expectations of their existing family. They may, however, have an idealised view of children and too high expectations of themselves as parents. The adoption social worker may then need to encourage childless couples either to become more actively involved with children they already know or to find ways of spending time with children. Baby-sitting for friends and relatives, helping at a local play group, generally noticing children in everyday situations can all help. Similarly helpful is the provision of opportunities to meet adoptive families, to visit community Homes, and generally to become more involved with children in all kinds of situation.

From the experience of four years' working with children and their new families a number of factors have emerged which may indicate something about adoptive parents. They are not startlingly new or unexpected but nevertheless perhaps worth recording. Among the most successful adoptive parents seem to be people who have experienced some trauma and difficulty themselves, which may have to do with loss and separation, but who have demonstrated an ability to cope with painful past experiences, learned from them and grown through them. One aspect of this is perhaps demonstrated in another important feature, their ability to put themselves into a child's shoes, to think how a child may be feeling, and consequently react to this rather than to their feelings. It is also fairly vital for special-need parents to be good communicators, with an ability to talk about feelings, about good and bad experiences, and to be without taboo subjects. They need a good degree of self-confidence, which is exhibited in their ability to know what they think, to make decisions, and to offer clear guidance to their children. Such people usually have a reasonably good self-image and consequently can face criticism from outsiders. They are people who have found some fulfilment in their lives despite the fact that there have been problems and disappointments. They do not expect life to be easy, but have some optimism that difficulties can be overcome even if there may not be a total or perfect solution. A sense of humour is also important; sometimes being able to see the funny side of a problem enables people to keep going.

The children

Working with children can be a stressful and difficult task, but is essential in many areas of social work, including adoption and fostering. Children needing new families are likely to be confused about their past, insecure in the present and anxious about the future. One hopes that such children will be surrounded by adults who can all help them to sort out the vital questions, 'Who am I? Why am I here? and What is going to happen next?' (DHSS, *Guide to Fostering Practice*).[2] Adoption social workers are involved in helping children to take important steps into the future; this task is likely to require talking about and remembering sad and painful experiences from the past, which may cause both the child and adults distress. Talking to children is not likely to be enough in itself. It is primarily an adult way of communication; and often a much more imaginative approach to children will be required which can take into account their feelings, their age and their ability to understand. Play can be used in various ways, such as imaginative games, pretend, drawing or painting; as can other shared activities such as walks to the park and visits to the zoo. The social worker will always need to be sensitive to what the child is doing as well as saying, trying at the same time to understand what it feels like when faced with change and insecurity.

Knowing and understanding the past is important for everyone's sense of identity, and this is especially so for children whose lives and relationships have been disrupted. A life-story book is often used as a way of piecing together the past and providing a pictorial memory for the child which can accompany him into his new family, and to which he can refer and add in the future.

It had been decided that Danny should be placed for adoption when

> he was six-and-a-half years old. He had lived in his own family until he was three, when he was admitted to care, grossly neglected. It seemed that Danny had been emotionally rejected by his mother from birth. Between the ages of three and six-and-a-half Danny had had four foster homes, eventually being placed with professional foster parents. He had no physical or personal links with his past, knew very little of where he had been, what had happened to him, or who or what was a mother or father. His social worker and foster parents together gathered information for Danny's life-story book; they obtained photos and mementos; his mother actually had the hospital label from the time he was born. Danny helped to stick in the pictures and write the story. He was very proud of his book, he recognised everyone in it, knew who they were, where they had lived, and seemed to understand their relationship to him. It was during the time that Danny was being introduced to his new family that an incident occurred which highlighted the importance of communication and its pitfalls. Talking to his future adoptive cousin, Danny was overheard to ask her when she had gone to live with her Mummy and Daddy. Talking to Danny later, it emerged that although he seemed to understand what had happened to him some vital pieces of information had either been overlooked or not understood, and these were to do with his birth and conception. Danny's life experiences had consequently led him to surmise that everyone first came to their parents through the intervention of a social worker.

It is sometimes sad to see how children in care have labels attached to them which would not be used for children in their own families; and also important to remember that a child in care is subject to many extraordinary stresses. Perhaps the aggressive, acting out, hyperactive child may have a better chance of surviving because he is still continuing to struggle with life, but equally he runs the risk of being labelled maladjusted or disturbed. This form of labelling can in turn prevent him from having the opportunity of a normal life with a family. Knowing a child well is essential, not only in finding the best possible family for him and helping that family to prepare, but also in supporting the child himself.

> One child who at the age of nine years had lived in eight different families, including one failed adoptive placement where he had been for over a year, where he had really begun to feel part of the family and had grown particularly attached to the adoptive mother, understandably found considerable difficulty in trusting people, especially mothers. This was apparent when he was being introduced to another family. He attempted to spend all his time with his new father, hardly ever speaking to his adoptive mother when father was present. To exclude his new mother he would always try to sit in the front seat of

> the car, next to his father on the settee, accompany him to the garage, garden shed, in fact anywhere.

Such behaviour can be very disconcerting and distressing. It is particularly painful and rejecting to someone who is very much wanting to be a mother and trying to establish herself in that role. To know that this is likely to happen is helpful if the new parents are prepared for how they may feel, and can think about ways of handling this behaviour and their feelings in advance.

Learning to live together

Before a child joins his new family there will be a period when introductions, visits and stay-overs take place, during which the child and his new family begin to get to know each other and learn about their respective ways of life. This introductory period is very important, and provides at least some general indication of whether this is likely to be the right family for the individual child, and what may be involved in future adjustments. It does nevertheless provide only a limited indication of what it will really be like living together, since that cannot begin until the child joins the family as a full member, not as a visitor or a guest. Learning to live together takes time, everyone is involved and will need to adjust and change, since the end result will be a different family. Learning to become a member of the family is probably hardest for those children who have spent long periods in institutional care.

> Mark had lived in children's Homes for all his seven years. He understood such organisational arrangements as staff duty rotas and was conversant with the hierarchical structure in the nursery. He tried to relate to his new home, enquiring who was in charge and who was on duty. He found it strange to discover two adults who appeared to be equals, and he tried various ways of confirming the status of his new parents, their relationship with each other and how he fitted in. This involved what appeared to be a haphazard switching of his affections from one parent to the other and definite attempts to cause friction between his parents. Mark took a great interest in his parent's relationship with each other. He was surprised at first and then very interested in the way they showed physical affection to each other, worried and anxious when they disagreed or quarrelled. He was catching up on a great deal of lost experience which a child in an ordinary family gathers gradually in early childhood.

There are practical considerations to take into account when a child is learning to cope with new situations and relationships. Sometimes the difficulties may just be part of his adaptation from one life style to another: perhaps his days had always been clearly organised with set times and routines for meals, getting up, performing ordinary daily tasks, and play. Sometimes expected and appropriate behaviour in one setting seems strange in another. In the early stages of any placement, before the new parents have learned to communicate fully, difficulties can arise from simple misunderstandings and misinterpretation of the child's signals. Parents and children will need time to tune into non-verbal communication. For a while everyone is learning and working out what is allowed, each is testing the limits of the other's toleration. Social workers talk a great deal about testing-out behaviour, which can take many forms depending upon a child's past experiences and self-image as well as upon the parents' confidence and expectations. One mother was prepared to expect testing-out behaviour but the child's ingratifying behaviour was both unexpected and difficult for her to tolerate.

> Charlie joined his family when he was five, having been emotionally rejected by his mother and cared for in a number of unsatisfactory private foster homes as well as in the care of three local authorities. He tested out his family in various ways: he was disruptive and difficult to settle at bedtime and during the night, sometimes also waking his younger sister, preventing her from sleeping; there were periods when he stole both at home and at school, times when he was very defiant and refused to co-operate with his parents in any simple daily tasks such as cleaning his teeth; like many other children in similar circumstances he went through periods of constantly saying he wished to return to the nursery and always seemed able to find some way of undermining his position in the family and bringing his new parents to the point of despair about helping him to face the future. Understanding Charlie's need to test out new relationships to the limit of endurance and beyond did not make it any easier to love him and live with him on a daily basis. His parents needed to be emotionally and physically very strong to withstand his onslaughts; they needed understanding and support from their social worker, friends and family and other adopters, as well as simple practical assistance with baby-sitting so that they could get some respite by having an evening out together.

Experience shows that it can take a long time before the family feel 'right' together. Some families talk of achieving this feeling only after eighteen months or two years. The importance of the first four to six months in any placement also needs to be stressed. The child has so much to learn during this time, not only about personal relationships but also his physical environment, his new neighbourhood and general location. He will be meeting many new people, his new family and all their relatives, friends, neighbours and other social contacts. He will encounter new experiences, perhaps a new school, and new social activities, and will be facing many anxieties since he has a great deal at stake. The parents are also having to make major adjustments and changes in their life. For a childless couple there is the adjustment from an adult-centred unit to a family including a child or children. There will be a loss of privacy coupled with new emotional and physical demands. It is a time of heightened sensitivity and concern for them as they first accept parental responsibility and learn to recognise and meet the everyday needs of their child. Just as the parents of a newly born baby are vulnerable and extra-sensitive, so are the parents of an older child.

Many decisions about the child which are later taken instinctively may be subject to major consideration and uncertainty. Decisions about allowing the child to go out on his own, about bedtime, meals, what to eat, what to allow. All of this is emotionally and physically exhausting for the new parents. During the beginning stages of any placement there is a danger of making life too exciting, too stimulating and too extraordinary. New parents are often eager to do the kind of things they would enjoy doing with a child and which no doubt would also be fun for the child. It may be wiser to hold back and try first of all to establish a more ordinary family routine rather than embark upon a series of outings and treats which, while seeming to help the placement along, in reality may be creating unrealistic expectations and not promoting a natural rapport and communication between the child and his parents.

For parents who already have children of their own, the first stages of placement may present a different set of obstacles. During this time they are likely to encounter rivalries and jealousies between the children and they will be trying to decide if, when or how to intervene. It is not uncommon for these parents to experience conflicts of loyalty, to be worried that perhaps they do not or cannot love the new child as much as they love their own children, and to be anxious if the advent of the newcomer seems to be having a detrimental effect on other children in the family. The children of the family will also be coping with the newcomer, and like their parents will be having some mixed feelings. A new brother and sister will perhaps be expected to bring some gains such as someone to play with and to have fun, but to begin with the losses will seem more apparent, toys may be broken and mother's attention taken. Rivalry between the children will be natural; they will need time to learn how to share both possessions and people and to cope with the disagreements and sort out differences. It will fall to family children to explain to friends and schoolmates who the newcomer is, how and why he or she has become part of their family. This task is not always easy and can disrupt or impose strains on existing relationships.

When parents who are either in the process of adopting or who have adopted older children meet together to discuss their experiences areas of common experience and feeling emerge. Such parents have usually recognised the special needs of the children to whom they offer themselves and consequently feel disappointed when they, the adults, have negative, angry, hostile and sometimes rejecting feelings about the children. They are equally amazed and disappointed when their negative feelings result not from major behaviour difficulties but from small day-to-day incidents, habits and problems which they feel should be taken in their stride, but which seem to have a cumulative and seemingly disproportionate effect. A number of issues are mentioned as illustrations. Food is often the focus of conflict for various reasons: children being demanding about food, children rejecting food, children eating compulsively, children's habits at mealtimes. Other minor social or personal habits can develop into major irritations and become the focus of conflict and difficulty. One adoptive mother described how on a wet camping holiday she was nearly driven to a murderous outburst when her adopted son spent long periods totally absorbed in picking his nose. As learning to love another person takes time and love grows in different ways and at differing speeds, it is not unknown for parents to discover that they are feeling differently about their new child. This realisation may be shocking as well as disappointing, difficult to comprehend and talk about, not only with each other but also with their social worker. The parents may need help with their feelings and reassurance that it is better to express negative feelings rather than keep them to oneself.

Adoptive families can feel particularly vulnerable to the opinions and views of other people, whether family members, friends or acquaintances. Taking any outsider into a family is rather unusual, and taking an older child, a group of children or a 'problem' child may be judged by the outside world as quite extraordinary, by some people as altruistic, by others as foolishness verging on madness. Consequently families may not always find the support and understanding they need to cope with their different family. Comments of 'I told you so' can add to feelings of guilt or failure.

The social workers

Working with children, natural parents, adoptive families and colleagues in other agencies during the past four years has been an exciting experience for the workers at IAS. During that time the boundaries of possibility have shifted, as can be seen from the children currently on referral, among whom are Gay (aged fourteen); Robbie (aged thirteen) of mixed racial parentage; Mike (aged four), also of mixed racial parentage, who is partially sighted and intellectually retarded; Nicky (aged two months) and Jon (aged twelve years), both Down's syndrome children; and Jackie (ten), Jane (six) and Elsa (eight), an Anglo-Nigerian sibling group. Many things have been learned about the children, the families who adopt, and ourselves during this period.

Social workers who choose this area of work need a real personal commitment, a belief in the work, considerable professional expertise, and support, as well as emotional and physical stamina. The agency needs to recognise that the work is time-consuming and demanding and to allow for this in its staffing. Perhaps this is more easily achieved in a small specialist and voluntary organisation such as IAS. While the work is satisfying and sometimes has quite spectacular successes, mostly social workers are engaged in helping children and families at crucial times when much is at stake and feelings are high. It is essential for the families to have social workers with whom they can share the real concerns and the problems they are bound to encounter from time to time. The workers need to be able to listen with sensitivity and understanding and not to react impulsively or impetuously, since even in times of crisis there may not be immediate answers or solutions. What will be important is that the families and workers together attempt to find ways of coping with immediate issues as well as pursuing long-term objectives.

The social workers will also need advice and support, since they are sharing the burdens of a number of families and children all of whom have similar but individual and particular needs. The support of colleagues is of great value and may be available informally as well as through formal supervision arrangements. There is also much to be gained from group support through general staff discussions; these can enable the concerns of the individual social worker to become the concerns of the agency as a whole, enable combined experience to be shared, and provide a good learning opportunity for all staff members. There will be times when workers will need access and special advice from people outside the agency, like child psychiatrists or other experts with experience and knowledge in such areas as education, handicap, and child abuse. Specialists may be able to help to interpret the facts pertaining to an individual case and advise the social worker on her own involvement in the situation and the management of the case. Despite everyone's best endeavours some placements will not succeed. There will be difficult decisions about supporting or ending a placement to be made by the social worker and the agency. The social worker's close personal involvement and commitment to a placement may add to the difficulties in trying to reach the best decision; and when this is so the help of outside expert opinion can be valuable and help to clarify the various relevant issues and factors to be taken into account.

Breakdown

Despite everyone's best endeavours, some placements will not work out. The fact that a child and a family are not right for each other will, it is hoped, become clear during the introductory pre-placement period, when various things may emerge showing that a placement cannot proceed. Sometimes the child may not have been sufficiently prepared, and consequently may find it impossible to move into a new situation. Not enough may be known about the child as an individual, which can mean that the wrong family has been selected for the individual child. Faced with a real child, prospective parents may discover feelings which prevent them parenting either someone else's child or this particular child; such feelings may be related to their own childlessness or may be to do with existing family relationships and dynamics. Confused roles and ambivalent feelings among the adults involved in helping the child through the insecurities, fears and losses involved in a move can also negate plans.

The fact that an individual placement is not 'right' may emerge only gradually as the child and his new family begin to live together. Despite most careful preparative work and introductions this is bound to happen from time to time, since the realities and feelings involved in living together can only be fully experienced when a child joins his new family as a full member. In the past four years three IAS placements involving four children have eventually ended in the children being removed from their new families. The children concerned were Dickie, aged six, who joined a couple with a boy of their own three years his senior; Stuart and Sue, aged seven and five, who were placed with a couple and their adopted son, aged nine; and Julie, aged six, who was placed with a childless couple. Dickie lived with his family for fourteen months, Stuart and Sue for eight months, and Julie for six months. Dickie has since been successfully adopted by a childless couple, Stuart and Sue have now been placed with a family without children, and a new family is currently being sought for Julie.

> Dickie's confused and disrupted childhood had left him with a strong desire to feel he belonged and a great wish to be loved and mothered. The strength of his feelings and the force with which he expressed them in his new family through his behaviour and his demands created a considerable strain on all family relationships. There was considerable rivalry between Dickie and his new brother, but it really seemed that a fourth member of the family seemed to put considerable strain on all family relationships and had an effect on long-established patterns of family functioning which could not be absorbed. In retrospect, another crucial factor in the failure of this placement seemed to be communication. The existing family members communicated mainly by indirect means, but Dickie's advent meant that this was no longer enough. With him more direct and verbal communication was required, certainly until he had an opportunity to learn the signals and indirect communications within the family group.

When a placement does fail it will be traumatic, distressing and demoralising for everyone concerned. At such times it is easy to try to apportion blame, to be wise with the knowledge of hindsight, or to allow negative feelings to spill over and immobilise not only the worker concerned but other colleagues. This is all very natural but to no purpose. It is more helpful to try to learn from mistakes by recognising the negative factors which contributed to the failure, while not overlooking any positive features which can contribute to the future for the individuals concerned as well as help work with other children and parents. A cohesive, supportive and astute staff group will help to provide support and encouragement for the individual worker undertaking what is likely to be a most painful piece of work.

Legal implications

During the past four years a wide range of children with varying needs have been found homes, and each year the limits seem to stretch a little farther. Ten out of the 1977 placements, which represented twelve children, were complicated because of legal difficulties. These were children whose care authorities had assessed that adoption would be in their best long-term interests, even though parental agreement to the plan was not certain. The Society is asked to help with an increasing number of children in this latter group, which has important implications for social work practice and also means that legal advice and help must be available.

It is a comparatively recent development for adoption to be considered for the children described here. Fortunately, there is now a greater willingness on the part of social workers to see children as having individual rights, to face up to some of the more difficult and painful issues involved in planning for such children, and to embark upon more imaginative and legally hazardous placements in order to secure their future. The general climate of public opinion and attitudes of the courts is also more sympathetic to such placements, although some of the legally hazardous adoption placements have yet to be tested in court.

Professional decisions which override the rights of individuals must always be taken with care. All available facts, feelings and views must be considered and carefully balanced. The knowledge and expertise of other professionals and colleagues such as doctors and teachers also must be taken into account. Access to good legal advice is essential at the very onset in order to provide an assessment of the legal problems and a prognosis of eventual outcome. The legal rights of everyone involved must be identified and carefully balanced. The care authority, the children, the parents, the adopters and the social workers will all need to know what may be required of them if a plan is agreed and implemented. Lawyers are able to evaluate available evidence, advise on the keeping of records for future use, identify essential witnesses, and advise on the gathering of additional evidence. Social workers will be responsible for explaining the plan and the reasoning behind it to all concerned.

Natural parents must know what has been decided and be made aware of their rights, and have every opportunity to express their views. Potential adopters will need to be clear what is likely to be involved for them if they become parents to a child whose original family is not in agreement with adoption. Many crucial questions may need to be explained to them personally by the placing agency's legal adviser. While having to accept that the outcome of any adoption can never be totally certain, adopters will need some reassurance that the care authority is committed to any agreed plan and will not be changed or swayed by minor issues or accidents such as a change in social work staff. Litigation is a costly business; so an important issue to be explored and agreed upon at the very beginning of a placement is whether the placing agency will be prepared to assist with the legal costs incurred in carrying out their plan.

Conclusion

It is now clear that children previously considered unadoptable can be adopted, that there are people willing to be parents to such children and prepared to work hard to build a family in this different way. To help this process home-finding agencies and their workers have to be prepared to expend considerable effort in time, personal commitment, professional expertise; and sometimes to take what may appear to be a calculated risk. Adoption workers are primarily engaged in a collaborative exercise with parents and children, helping them to discover a way of family life which meets their needs and which, as in every other family, will include some problems, some pleasures, some good times and some bad.

References

1 J. Rowe, and L. Lambert, *Children Who Wait,* ABAFA, 1973.

2 Department of Health and Social Security, *Guide to Fostering Practice,* London, HMSO, 1976.

Carol Lindsay Smith

12 The New Families Project

This chapter sets out to describe the setting up of a special project to find families for hard-to-place children in the west of Scotland. It also discusses the practice issues the staff had to consider in the process of finding families and placing children.

In November 1976 Barnardo's New Families Project came into existence, to find permanent homes for children growing up in residential care who had no realistic chance of returning to their natural parents. It was widely believed that the quality of life could be vastly improved by adoption for many children in care in the west of Scotland, an area acknowledged to have social problems probably beyond comparison in western Europe. At that time there was no other adoption agency in Scotland really attacking the backlog of children waiting in institutions, and Barnardo's agreed to sponsor this scheme because they were convinced that a concentrated search would yield many useful homes.

Against a background of hostility to voluntary intervention, Barnardo's set up a small project, hoping to demonstrate that limited specialised resources focused on just one area of need could bring about quick results. The belief was that children otherwise destined for residential care throughout their childhood could instead be found families in the community.

From spring until autumn 1976 formal discussion took place between Strathclyde Social Work Department and Barnardo's, culminating in a practical working agreement. The home-finding unit, which became the New Families Project, would seek and prepare families, and Strathclyde would formally refer children for placement. The management and financing of the Project would be Barnardo's responsibility; but representatives from Strathclyde would become part of the mechanism for developing and running the Project, through membership of its policy advisory and case committees. Although protracted and difficult, these negotiations produced the essential ground rules before the Project began work.

Financing the project

By November 1977 the staff included two full-time and three part-time social workers and two clerical staff. Expenditure was estimated in the region of £40,000. Barnardo's has footed the bill, except for a once-only grant (£5,000) from the Scottish Office towards the capital and other expenses of setting up the office. Job creation funds for salaries totalled £4,764 for the first six months. Other income included fees charged to the local authority for each placed child, currently at £750. It would be possible for the Project to place children in care of English and Welsh authorities and charge the much higher fee of £1,530 agreed by their Association of Directors. The cost-effectiveness of the Project is beyond dispute. To keep a child in residential care costs a minimum of £3,000 per year at today's prices. Taking the first sixteen children to be placed by the Project, who ranged in age from one to fifteen years, had they all remained in care until the age of eighteen they would have clocked up between them 169 child care years. If we calculate each child care year at £3,000 the accumulated saving would eventually be more than half a million pounds. The Project has demonstrated how a small investment for the right purpose can save a vast amount of money and capital costs, apart from probably improving the quality of life for many children.

The project staff

At the outset we agreed to abandon conventional ideas about who is and who is not suitable to adopt, along with the usual social worker-client relationships. Families applying to the Project would not be clients. They would be offering us a service without which we could not exist and must be nurtured accordingly. Because the Project had no statutory obligation to shoulder excessive amounts of work, there would be no excuse for delays, evading decisions, or leaving work half done. Placing children for adoption would involve the social worker in making harsh decisions: to override the needs of pitiful natural parents, to split siblings, to take risks on behalf of children already damaged by too many moves. We decided, therefore, to seek staff who displayed resourcefulness, independence, persistence, a feel for atmosphere, a willingness to do slow detailed work and the courage to get off the fence, rather than staff with long experience of conventional adoption work. By working intensively, sharing a belief in positive planning for children and being unencumbered by other duties, we quickly learned the trade. We were also aware that children remain in care not because of lack of experts but because the system does not allow the time nor encourage the initiative to do this work.

Committee structure

The policy advisory committee has three representatives from Barnardo's and three from Strathclyde Social Work Department, and four neutral members representing social work training, the law and the consumer. It does not control the Project but certainly influences its direction and remains the main channel of communication between the Project and the Department.

There is a case committee whose members have relevant professional skills. Besides accepting or refusing applications and recommending placements the case committee are increasingly asked to give advice on doubtful applications. Where appropriate, committee members have undertaken direct work with applicants and children. From our experience, involvement of the committee in this way provides far more support for social workers, reduces the amount of wasted work with unsuitable applicants, and enables the latter to withdraw without the humiliation of a refusal. Because of their close involvement in the work the committee can frequently agree on a placement plan the day an application is accepted. Where a child is to be placed on a fostering basis (for legal or financial reasons) the plan must be further discussed with the relevant Strathclyde Fostering Panel, who will, usually after six months, have responsibility for supervising the child. The child's local authority social worker and residential worker and other relevant adults are always included in placement discussions. Case committee members include a doctor with experience of psycho-sexual counselling, a psychiatrist who is also a paediatrician, an educational psychologist, two residential workers, a psychiatric social worker, and a social work teacher. Project social workers participate in all discussions.

Which children?

Every social worker and residential unit in the target areas has received information about the Project and how to refer children. Planning meetings for referred children are held in their units, enabling full involvement of all levels of residential staff. Staff and children are frequent visitors to our office. Social workers from the target areas are seconded to the Project for six months. We also ask area teams to refer on to us families they cannot quickly use themselves. These efforts to work together have produced an atmosphere of trust and recognition of one another's pressures. It is becoming clear that children who get placed are not always the most urgent cases, but those whose social workers know them well and who are determined to give the time and effort to make it happen.

The Project took up to twenty-five children on referral. From their case histories we found that most of them could have been placed years earlier as relatively straightforward pre-schoolers. Because of this we set up a small survey to identify younger rather than older children needing family placements. The results suggest that there are many young children, probably less damaged and easier to place, who will languish in children's Homes unless special efforts are made within the local authority to identify and place them quickly.

In our experience families are most urgently needed for teenage boys, for groups of siblings who wish to stay together, and for younger hyperactive, low-intelligence boys who have been labelled 'brain damaged'. Typically they have all had erratic moves and numerous social workers. At the time of writing twenty-four children have been placed, and a further ten are at different stages of introduction to new families. They range from young mentally or physically handicapped children to disruptive teenagers (including a fifteen-year-old girl whose testing-out subsided with the comment 'If they want me after all that, they really must mean it').

More than half the children have been placed with one or more siblings, but fourteen children have been split from siblings with whom they had been in recent contact. Children who are old enough are always involved in the decision to separate family members, and usually outstrip the professionals in accepting that this is the only realistic way to achieve family life. (More 'split' children remain in touch, adopters fully understanding the importance of maintaining what few contacts the child has.)

Six teenagers have joined couples aged around thirty years, in most cases with very young children already in the family. The presence of toddlers seems to break the ice and enable the incomer to revert to babyish behaviour, rough and tumble, playing with woolly toys, and opportunities for physical contact are provided with less embarrassment in a home where little children are being cuddled and comforted.

Twenty-two of the children have been linked to families with existing children, in fourteen cases being older than all or some of the existing children. In several instances natural children have created more havoc than the incomer, such as when an older, only child has longed for a brother or sister and been less than thrilled by the reality. We aim to avoid placing children close in age to existing ones but in the four instances where we have 'sandwiched' them there has been no undue disturbance.

The children placed by the Project are distinguished from the 'children who wait' not so much by the degree of their problems as by the happy accident of allocation to a local authority worker who is spirited enough to push through legal, medical and attitudinal obstacles towards placement.

Which families?

We are looking for families to fit children referred to us – and not the reverse. Families are assessed for any of the categories of children we know are waiting and usually, by the end of the assessment, it is clear which child should join the family.

We set off with no rigid criteria. We try to consider couples or single people on their merits, older people, younger ones wanting teenagers, rejects from other agencies, divorcees, childless. There is no religious bar. Removing the rules puts strain on the social workers because we let in the non-conformers. As a result a high percentage of couples accepted by the Project had previously been refused or deterred by other agencies or had assumed themselves automatically disqualified. Others have weathered serious problems and this 'crisis factor' provides us with a measure of how they deal with stress and an indication of how they may cope with the rough patches of an adoption placement. A survey of families accepted in the first year shows that many are independent, enterprising, highly mobile people with strong religious or moral convictions and on the whole not much concerned with what the neighbours think. This is in some contrast to our expectations of well-adjusted problem-free, semi-rural couples, well supported by generations of family and friends.

Arrangements which appear to be thriving include a seven-year-old boy (previous placement disrupted) placed with a couple who had been refused by four other agencies; a teenage girl with a couple in their sixties; an obstreperous fifteen-year-old with a couple not yet thirty; a family of four (placed in stages) with a childless couple; and brothers with serious medical and developmental problems placed with one of a number of self-sufficient families who have come to us spontaneously from the Highlands and Islands. A persistent and courageous single man has worked through our system, but placement with him must be delayed until we find a local authority brave enough to co-operate. An overall impression is that relatively young, energetic couples do well with difficult teenagers. Applicants with strong religious beliefs are undoubtedly helped by their faith to cope with crises and are often well supported by ministers or church contacts in the absence of close family. Most applicants derive support and inspiration from other project families, through groups or individually. Some couples, after seeing other unexceptional couples cope, decide to take older and more complex children than they first intended.

Assessment procedure

Potential adopters are lit up with excitement at the thought of helping a waiting child, and we try to react quickly and efficiently to make the most of this enthusiasm and goodwill. Enquirers get an immediate response: written information about the Project, a list of children currently waiting for placement, and an invitation to an open information meeting (held on the first Tuesday of every month throughout the year).

The meeting allows them to test the atmosphere of the Project, size up the staff, and explore older child adoption a little further without being trapped by questionnaires. The 'baby' adopters can withdraw quietly, or they can adjust their sights. (Besides prospective adopters, open meetings are attended by social workers, students and curious members of the public.) Those who wish to proceed are seen by the Project leader within two weeks. Enquirers too far from Glasgow are seen at home. The initial interview is used to screen out clearly unsuitable candidates and those already pursuing an application elsewhere. The Project's purpose – to find parents to fit existing children – is hammered home and couples are reminded bluntly of the kind of children available, although they are not expected at this stage to specify the child they want.

Applicants who appear suitable and eager to proceed are given an application form, and by returning it they signify a serious intention to proceed (those not returning the form are not contacted again). Assessments take approximately four months, culminating in a case committee decision to accept or refuse the application. There is an appeals procedure which has not so far been used. Applicants are seen individually and together. Referees and significant relatives and neighbours are visited, and 'own' children are included in discussions. Additional interviews may be offered with the Project's psychiatrist, medical or other consultants. All applicants are seen by at least two members of staff. They are encouraged, but not compelled, to attend group meetings – which inevitably combine assessment with information sharing. There is no set number of interviews, and with long-distance families assessments may be compressed into a few days with the worker moving in for the duration, for an intensive impression of their life style and personalities.

During their assessment families will see pictures and hear about waiting children. Some will begin to focus on specific children. Most applicants prepare scrapbooks about their own family life aimed at the sort of child they have in mind. Although they are not promised a specific child in advance (and children are not told about families in the pipeline who may be suitable for them), it is nevertheless possible in most cases for the committee to accept an application and recommend a placement plan at the same meeting. Project staff feel the pressure to keep up the pace because applicants have responded to publicity on 'the urgent needs of children', and it makes no sense to keep them waiting.

The Project's groupwork programme

We were enabled to develop groupwork with applicants from the outset, and more recently with children, because of the support and skill of a university teacher who had the essential experience which the Project staff lacked. Her approach has been meticulous and calm, and has helped us to avoid the embarrassing and unconstructive sessions which too often await adoption applicants. Adult groups are in three phases. Phase I consists of a series of four meetings at weekly intervals for four or five couples with two leaders. Participants share ideas about adopting and fostering, why children wait, legal process, behaviour problems and ways of coping. Various 'experts' have been introduced: residential workers, adopters of older children, and couples who have already been through our application process. Phase II groups are for families just starting an introduction or placement. The intention is to increase the participants' depth of understanding of what is happening to all concerned when a child joins the family, to share ways of coping and to give mutual support. In Phase III families with a child may offer encouragement to others where a child is creating havoc, or the natural children in the family are reacting outrageously. We hope that Phase III groups will become self-help and self-perpetuating, with a nucleus of 'old' adopters providing the service for the next generation.

Phase III group members have begun to help us to organise study days in Glasgow for the out-of-town families, so that they can make contact with other couples and share the advantage of mutual support. Additional strength has come through including senior staff from other agencies and from the Social Work Department as group leaders. Applicants to other agencies have been included in the Project groups, and we believe that we have all gained by this cross-fertilisation of ideas.

Groupwork with children is in process of development. A series of eight meetings held in a local authority Home, and attended by a mixture of children, showed that even the most inarticulate children could grasp ideas about adoption and family life. They became intensely involved and concerned about their future. It was alarming to see some of them made aware of the abyss of leaving care at sixteen with nowhere to go. Many of the children presented themselves in a new light, and several were without social workers with whom this important information could be shared. The group leaders found the direct work with the children was the least of it. They had raised expectations and stimulated ideas which had to be followed through, involving extra sessions with children and their caretakers. The revelations of the children's group have shown us that it is futile to concentrate on families while we leave the children unprepared. However desperate the needs of non-referred children may be, we intend to confine our efforts to referred children. At least we can guarantee them some individual social work support and the likelihood of family placement.

Referral and preparation of children

The Project does not guarantee placement for referred children, although every known method including direct advertising will be tried. We concentrate on children who are free for adoption either because the parents are dead or have given voluntary consent. (We have found many natural parents consenting after years of guilty absence, particularly if they are included in the planning for their children. They can often be helped to see that agreeing to adoption is the one generous gesture they can make for the child.) We also accept children for whom the Social Work Department holds parental rights, so long as the Department makes a firm commitment to the plan for the child. We ask for this undertaking in writing, because a change of philosophy in the Department or a change in the natural parents' circumstances could lead to plans being reversed and a child being uprooted at the crucial moment.

Social workers contact the Project direct to discuss family placements for individual children, but firm referrals are routed through the adoption advisers to make sure all available resources within the Department have been tapped. Children referred to the Project are involved in planning their own futures. They come to the office to see pictures of other children; and if they agree their picture goes up too, often with their own description of their hopes and fears.

To help us to understand what the child needs, we hold a planning meeting in the children's Home, attended by all levels of residential staff who know the child. We require ABAFA Form E, large coloured photographs, and background reports on any area of his development which is unusual. A Project worker takes responsibility for co-ordinating placement plans; and now that we have more staff we undertake direct work with the child to help to prepare him for a return to family life. This is likely to include going through the child's file, pulling together significant information from social workers and former caretakers who may be scattered across the country, and helping to make a scrapbook of his life so far. It is stunning to discover how little information and how few mementos of the past exist for many of them. Children have discovered through this process their own second Christian names, the simplest information about their natural parents, details of brothers and sisters in care elsewhere and, most importantly, the reasons for coming into care. One seven-year-old thought he did not have parents, and so he could not have been born like other children. Most scrapbook work takes place in the children's Home, and we have found residential staff excited by what can be achieved and avid to embark on similar work with other children in their care. They see the reason to hang on to every detail, photographs of mum, the first baby tooth to come out, birthday cards, swimming certificates, anything which helps to jog the memory and makes sense of the past for a child who will almost certainly change hands several times during a career in care.

So far, in our experience, children who have been the subject of publicity have not been damaged by the experience. On the contrary, they have enjoyed the fleeting notoriety and the reassurance that the adults are at least trying to find a family. A child whose picture is going in the paper is always told that he will represent a group of children, that a home may not be found for him but indirectly he may help someone else. He is assured that we shall not just pick any family in desperation. We have found children infinitely more realistic and courageous than adults in these matters. They know very well what their circumstances are, that their parents do not exist in any meaningful way, that time is running out; and even children who have clung to fading memories of mum and dad have suddenly shown interest in adoption when flesh-and-blood options have been offered.

Young children can be helped to carry the burden of disloyalty to natural parents if their adopters understand the reasons for the original family breakdown and avoid denouncing the first parents. In many cases, children need not cut off all links with the past; and Project families are prepared for the possibility of continued contact with siblings, caretakers, relatives, even natural parents, either direct or by letters and photographs via the social worker. We have found natural parents relinquishing children more readily if they are promised progress reports; equally children move more comfortably if their original family is not being denied. Older children, anyway, can lift the 'phone and keep in touch with anyone they choose, and it is better for them to do this openly than on the sly. We have seen adopters handle natural parents with sympathy and generosity, and only once has the contact been of a threatening nature.

Placement

Before first seeing the child the new family is given detailed social, medical and psychiatric information about him, meets his caretakers and, sometimes, the natural parents. Wherever possible, blind viewings are arranged, a precaution which saves families being catapulted into relationships which they feel from first impressions will not work. Most families, however, wish to proceed; and for properly prepared children, who know about adoption and plans for the future, the actual meeting is part of a logical sequence. The speed of introduction must be governed by the child's ability to latch on, the family's willingness to be patient, geographical considerations and circumstances in the residential unit. Occasionally children are moved quickly to avoid them being torn apart by adults who cannot let go. In every case care staff need to be properly briefed if they are to co-operate in a smooth transfer to the new family. We have learned the hard way that, to avoid misunderstandings and manipulations, plans must be written down, and we now prepare a timetable of visits, with copies for care staff, new family and child.

The average length of introduction is two months, with the child making several overnight stays before the final move. Introductions for several families from the north of Scotland have been speeded up by their moving into the children's Home for a few days and by the child being accompanied to their home and settled in by a member of the care staff. Several establishments have co-operated magnificently in this way. Eventually we hope to extend this system, not just for reasons of distance, but because it is clearly easier for the child, particularly where the new parents are competent to explain changing relationships.

With older children, the first meeting and subsequent visits to the new family are planned openly from the outset. They know how desperately they need to be settled, and we hope pre-placement work will have given them some awareness of the need for give and take in family life. In return for this cosiness and individual care they will have to make efforts to respond, to co-operate, to finish a conversation and to join in family life. Family life may feel positively claustrophobic to children more used to the surface relationships of life in care. One child being introduced to a family took three weeks out in the wilderness to work out by himself whether or not he could bear the intensity of family life. He took the plunge, but still, when the pressure builds up, he slides off for a few hours back in the wilderness.

We beg families to refrain from giving the children a diet of undiluted treats. Children need to taste the monotony, routine and chores of family life as well as the high spots. We have learned that the beginning of the summer holidays is the worst time to place moody, bored teenagers who will have few local contacts.

Supervision and support

The Project's top priority is to support families once children have been placed. Other arrangements must go by the board if a family is in difficulties and needs moral or practical support. The Project takes responsibility for the supervision of placements, but always in co-operation with the local authority social worker. Joint visits often continue for months. There has been no conflict because we specify in writing each person's role. Supervision includes regular visiting, an opportunity for both child and family to moan privately about each other, with frequent 'phone calls in between. The telephone is invaluable, and all families have access to a social worker on a twenty-four hour basis. Some families say that 'a 'phone call now is more help than a visit next week'. For families under stress we can offer a range of services: direct work with the child to try to modify behaviour; consultation with a range of experts, many from our case committee who will already be familiar with the situation; practical help with baby-sitting, and Phase III group support and individual support from adopters who have faced similar problems. In the near future we hope to employ bridge families (see later), who would take a disruptive child into their own home for a few days to give the new family a break.

We cannot predict when trouble will come. Some children settle down and are no trouble at all. Others erupt or react in an unexpectedly negative fashion. In a few cases where we have been preoccupied with legal or specific medical problems the child's general behaviour has given no cause for concern. It would be premature to call any of the placements a success, but we have seen children change dramatically, in their physical, emotional and intellectual development. We have seen uncherished children gain weight and firm-up to the touch. Children previously lacking initiative have developed independence and with it sometimes cheeky or mildly delinquent behaviour. We have also seen unco-ordinated children learning to ride bikes, and gruff uncuddly teenagers unashamedly asking to be tucked up in bed.

This improvement in the children is often at great cost to the families. I don't think we have yet come near to preparing them adequately for the emotional upheaval and often erratic reactions of their existing children, and we cannot overstate the battering to confidence and stamina some of them take. A number have reported unusual (for them) medical symptoms and periods of depression, something akin to post-natal depression. Nearly all express real doubt about continuing with the placement at some stage. We live with the constant anxiety that precarious placements will collapse, with frightening repercussions for the child, the family, the social workers and residential staff. Many of these people will have their worst fears confirmed. For the moment the mostly optimistic results encourage us to persevere and to continue taking calculated risks.

Legal aspects of the work

Because the Project offers continuing support for families and children to use as they want it, we see no advantage in delaying the adoption order. Most families notify the local authorities of their intention to adopt when the child moves in. We believe legal adoption will reinforce the child's sense of security and the parents' confidence, commitment and ability to make decisions on that child's behalf. The changed legal status encourages the new family to act as a parent, and the child to feel he is a real child of the family.

We have no enforceable contract with the local authority, but a senior member of its staff is required to agree to our terms of working in relation to each child referred for placement. The essential condition is that the authority will continue to support the placement plan for the child, despite changes of staff or policies, so long as the plan remains in the best interest of the child. Thus children who are not legally free for adoption, or where the family cannot forgo foster fees, can nevertheless be placed on a permanent basis, and families can be reassured that the plans will not be reversed. We have made a number of unconventional placements and now must await the outcome of the courts. We feel we need a channel of communication to the judges so that placements with few precedents, at least in Scotland, could be informally discussed: such as teenagers joining young couples not old enough to be their parents and unrelated children placed with single men.

Breakdowns and bridge families

Inevitably some placements will not stick. Spalding,[1] for children in the USA, estimates that at least 10 per cent of placements will disrupt. This is a no-go area for discussion and it is difficult to plan ahead. Barnardo's has agreed to the appointment of bridge families, high-calibre foster parents who would take a child at the time of breakdowns, attempt to salvage something from the turmoil, and hold the child until new plans are made. Returning the child to the unit he left, probably in a blaze of glory, could be humiliating and, if his bed is filled, impossible.

Currently we have the choice of placing breakdown children in Barnardo's establishments for handicapped or maladjusted children, or using the best available vacancies in local authority establishments. Eventually we hope to replace children with alternative families without always needing an interim arrangement. With close supervision, it should be possible to anticipate breakdowns in most cases, and to have some control over the timing and way in which the child and family part.

At the time of writing one Project child has been returned: an eight-year-old mentally handicapped boy who lived in a subnormality hospital before placement. On top of his hyperactivity, incessant questioning and slow social progress, problems developed unrelated to the child. The family felt unable to continue, but worked with the Project towards moving the child in a planned way to a well-staffed children's Home. They sincerely tried to explain this crisis to him. The Project worker continues weekly visits to the child with the hope of bringing his feelings to the surface and preparing for another try.

The Project staff were shocked and demoralised by this breakdown; and only the team's solidarity enabled the key worker to keep going and make constructive plans for the future. We learned that extricating the child takes as much time and planning as supporting a placement. Also, that besides the child – the centre of the crisis – the breakdown family, the disillusioned local authority and the new children's Home all need detailed explanations, reassurances and support.

Advertising and publicity

The Project is publicity-conscious, and approximately one third of all enquiries have come through radio, TV and newspaper publicity. We have found journalists sympathetic and reliable in their handling of information about children needing families. It is astounding how many enquirers say, 'We've been thinking of helping a child for years but we didn't know how until we read it in the paper'. An increasing number of journalists are now experienced in talking sensitively to children and perhaps we should involve them in pre-publicity preparations with children and staff alike.

In November 1977 we took responsibility for preparing several of the fourteen children featured in Strathclyde's first large-scale publicity campaign. The children were helped to anticipate reporters' questions, to decide what to reveal about themselves. They were also warned of the inevitable delay between publicity and a family being found, including the real possibility that NO family would be found. The children were confident and realistic about the outcome, glad that adults were making real efforts to sort out their futures, and relishing the moment of fame. The results confirm that appropriate families can be attracted by straightforward descriptions of children. Obviously a vast number of unproductive enquiries are also generated, approximately ten for every positive response. For a number of reasons in future we would not agree to join in a large-scale campaign, but would rather focus on one or two children featured in a pre-selected paper.

Conclusion

In spite of gloomy predictions and administrative complications, the Project had demonstrated a number of things. First, that when dealing with 'hard-to-place' children needing families a specific and separate programme, with specially assigned staff, can respond quickly and effectively. Second, that, contrary to earlier assumptions, there are families in the country who are not prejudiced or rigid in their requirements and who actually *want* to offer their homes to older, handicapped or coloured children. But many professionals and administrators have yet to be convinced that these methods work. Obviously there are many risks in this kind of work which need to be faced rather than avoided, and the safest thing for professionals is to leave the children in warehousing conditions. Finally, it is important to find families not only for children already in care, but also to ensure that newcomers into the system do not experience lengthy and unnecessary stays in institutions. Families are easier to find at an earlier stage; and early placement is also in the children's best interests.

Reference

1 Figures quoted by Kay Donley of Spalding at a conference in Edinburgh in September 1978.

Wendy Cann

13 Maintaining the placement

This chapter examines some of the implications that follow from the placement of older children with new families, and how the placement can be supported.

Placing children in new families

When arranging the placement of children in new families I try to bear in mind the concept of the family as a 'mobile', first postulated by Satir, [1] the idea that relationships, power, alignments and splits shift and change when a member leaves or a new one joins. The process of family formation is highly charged. Members may want things from others but the others may not respond, or response may create envy or rivalry.

The arrival of a new member in the family, in this case of a child, imposes a change in the family's general pattern of interaction. The new forms of interaction may be appropriate to the new situation, thus helping to incorporate the new member; or the family or some family members may carry on as if nothing new has happened, excluding the new member from much-needed access either to parental figures or to sibling relationships. To reach a harmonious balance, adaptations in role and other forms of functioning will obviously be necessary. Resultant changes in role, power and influence are tied to love and affection. The worker needs to look at the impact of the new arrival on the total family as well as upon each individual. The achievement of a balance may depend on the kind of preparation that has gone on before the new child's arrival, and particularly the opportunity offered to all the members of the existing unit to share in the decisions. Difficulties can arise, not so much from a reluctance of family members to adapt to new situations, but from a failure to share information and involve all those concerned in considering the implications for each one of them. It is also very easy to concentrate upon the child who has joined the family and neglect its impact on the whole family functioning.

Increasingly social workers are involved in the placement of older children who already carry memories of previous experiences, and these may have a bearing on the outcome of the placement. It is well known, for instance, that older children (and particularly disturbed ones) attempt to recreate past relationships and conflicts or have an ability to arouse primitive responses in their new carers. Social workers, by becoming aware of each individual child's pattern of responses before and after joining his new home, can help the family to accept and understand them too. The child joining a new family has the formidable task of entering the family's history that has been going on for many years. Equally the family will need to enter the child's history and experiences. Beginnings can be very threatening and anxiety-provoking for all concerned. Some of the issues may present themselves in the following ways during the post-placement period.

The impact on the marital relationship

Often the child will form a closer relationship more quickly with one new parent than with the other. This means that the parent left out has to be helped to see that his time will come and that it is not a reflection of his parenting, but more the particular need of that child at that time to make one special relationship. It may well be that the child is unable to form a relationship with two new people at once. Occasionally this relationship may have very understandable reasons. For example, Mary, who had spent most of her life in a children's Home until placed with her new parents at the age of seven, had always been cared for by female staff and was fascinated by her adoptive father. She rushed to the end of the road as soon as it was time for him to return from work and then sat upon his lap, stroking his moustache, until tea was ready. It is important in such circumstances to understand how the mother might feel.

Despite similar past experiences, Doreen showed her interest in her new father in a very different way. She found his Achilles heel and tested out his patience. She refused to eat her food, and picked at it so much that mealtimes became a dreadful experience. She would push the food around her plate until her new father lost his temper. Worse, the father was beginning to feel that his wife was not supporting him in his handling of Doreen. The worker needed to accept and understand his anger and explore with him and his wife how this was affecting the whole family. Eventually both decided to ignore Doreen's behaviour and to back each other up in this.

In the case of Caroline, who was eight years old at placement, things did not work out so happily. Her easier relationship with the adoptive father created considerable insecurity in the mother, who demonstrated inability to tolerate a threesome relationship. The placement eventually collapsed.

A similar situation arose where a childless couple took a child and the husband was so overjoyed by his advent that he was quite unable to discipline him. The wife's arguments that discipline gave a child a sense of security only served to make the husband tense and anxious whenever the child misbehaved. This anxiety was conveyed to the child, and both father and child succumbed to asthma whenever the child made attempts to control his behaviour. This in turn reinforced the father's feelings that discipline was bad for the child. The worker's role was to support the wife in her efforts to impose some limits on the child's behaviour, whilst also helping the adults to examine their relationship more and find some common ground upon which they could agree.

Some very needy children appear so adept at wrecking apparently stable marriages that they can only cope in a one-parent family. They seem to have great difficulty in coping with relationships generally. The 1975 Children Act has recognised the valuable role single people can play as substitute parents, and has made it easier for a single person to adopt a child.

Other children in the family

The child has to learn to make relationships, not only with the new parents, but also with the other children, and these children have to accommodate a new member. Parker [2] has suggested that it is better to absorb into a family a child not too near the ages of the existing children, and that, ideally, the new child should be the youngest. This is not always possible. The social worker can help parents and children to look at relationships and apparent disruptive behaviour as a family. The worker has the chance to observe and comment on the interaction. Often there will be several different ways in which a child, particularly a toddler, will show his feelings about his new family. These may or may not be acceptable to the other children in the family; and it is important that in helping one child to find security, another child does not feel pushed out. A child coming into the middle of a family group may be less of a threat, since both the oldest and youngest retain their special positions. The worker tries to understand the dynamics of the whole family and the effect of the new child upon each individual member and on the total family. The reactions of each person can often be explained, either by reference to past incidents, or to current forms of interaction and the feelings they stir.

Sometimes the new child gangs up with the other children in the family, who take advantage of his position to get at the parents. The other children know that some behaviour might be forgiven the new child, because he has not yet learned the rules of the family. The new child may well go along with these suggestions in the hope of obtaining the love and acceptance of his new brothers and sisters. The adults in the situation need to show they are aware of what is happening, and to find ways of distracting the children from one form of behaviour, so that more constructive play can be enjoyed. However, the worker must be understanding of the parents' dilemma and the need to discipline all children in the family. It is so easy to suggest that they be indulgent to the new child as he is settling in; but part of that settling in means learning what is and is not allowed within the family.

It is equally important that introductory visits and getting to know each other before placement should be based on the reality of what life is to be like within the new family, both for the new child and for existing children. One child first met his new parents within his own surroundings and saw them on several occasions alone. One day they arrived with their other children and he was shattered to find that he must share his new and much wanted parents with several other children. One family sensibly felt that the new child should get to know his new family a few members at a time, and the new mother and one daughter spent much time with him before being joined by the very boisterous son and father. However, he knew about these family members early in the introduction, as he saw photographs of the whole family.

An incident which often causes much distress to children is the breaking or damaging of some precious toy or object by the new family member. It is little comfort to tell the child who owns the toy that 'John didn't understand' or 'You should have kept it out of his way'. One needs to acknowledge the hurt that has resulted and help John to appreciate the worth of possessions by allowing him to have some of his own. It is still common among children in Homes not to have toys, books, etc. which are individual to one; however, if other children in the family have seen the children's Home and learned something of the way it is run they will be able to initiate John into the new system of individual ownership. Jealousies may equally be stirred among existing children of the family when the new arrival claims their parents as 'mum' and 'dad'.

Other relatives

A family consists not only of parents and children but also of aunts, uncles, grannies, cousins, etc. Sometimes these relatives may not fully understand the advent of a new family member not born to the parents, and there may be resentment on all sides. If at all possible, members of the extended family should be involved in the preparation before placement; but they should certainly be helped to understand that their place in the family remains secure, and that the new child may well enjoy having a new granny and grandpa as much as having new parents. One child became so possessive of her new grandparents that she refused to accept that they might have any connection with other members of the family, least of all with her new parents.

If a grandparent or other close relative is resentful of the arrival of the new child, this matter needs to be explored with the adoptive or foster parents. They may feel hurt or angry that their decision to have another child has not been accepted; and they may be apprehensive of telling the social worker, for fear that the child will be removed or that the worker will upset the 'offending' relative. Perhaps ways may be found for the child and relative to do something together which will be mutually satisfying. Granny may enjoy being asked to knit a new jumper for Johnny, or Johnny may like showing granny photographs of his former home and family.

Role of social workers — especially where more than one is involved

Frequently there may be more than one social worker involved in each placement; if so, it is important that each worker knows what is expected of him or her by the child, family and the other worker. It is not unusual for the child and family to know different social workers prior to the placement; wherever possible, this contact should be maintained for a while at least, as it is often easier to talk about feelings to the person whom one has already come to know and trust.

The involvement of several workers in each placement is particularly common when two different agencies have been put in touch with each other through a resource centre, e.g., Adoption Resource Exchange. In these circumstances there will be not only the social worker who knows the child and the one who knows the family, but also the linking person and possibly senior workers or co-ordinators within each practice agency. Ideally there needs to be good planning and a clearly defined role for each person at each stage.

The child may have strong feelings about contact with the former social worker, and could need reassurance that the person still cares about him and is concerned for his welfare. This person could be the child's one link with all that has happened in the past, and with whom he can discuss the significance of various episodes in his life. Although one hopes that adequate preparation has been done, so that the child is ready to make new relationships, this does not mean that relationships from the past no longer have any significance, and sometimes incidents and people fall into place when one is embarking on a new experience. A child can become very confused if he thinks of his new family as yet another temporary place or even 'just a holiday to see how you like it'. By the time the placement happens, the child must understand that this is intended as a permanent new family, and the confidence of the social worker can do much to help the child understand this. The continuing contact with the social worker could therefore help the child to make the adjustment necessary. Alternatively, some children become anxious when their former social worker retains contact, as they associate this person with moving from place to place.

It is not often easy to combine the social worker's duty to ensure the well-being of the child with the equally important function of providing support to the family as a whole. The family should feel they can discuss freely with their social worker what the placement has meant to them all, and can expect support and guidance. A balance needs to be found between acknowledging that there may be problems of adjustment and conveying the belief that the placement will be successful. This latter is very important, since families under stress need to know that someone believes in them and believes that all will be well in the end.

I have found it helpful to have joint visits of the two social workers involved. Part of the time can be spent in a full family discussion, preferably in an informal setting (e.g., whilst having a meal), since it is necessary to understand how the advent of a new member is affecting the family as a whole. After this, the child's worker can give him an opportunity of talking away from the rest of the family, if necessary, by taking him out for a walk, being shown his new room, etc., leaving the family's worker to discuss the reaction of other members of the family. There may also be times when the roles are reversed, since the child's social worker may be the best person with whom to share difficulties or behaviour problems, because she can often relate them to past incidents or put them into context for the new parents. A joint visit not only allows these changing roles to occur, but also shows the whole family that both workers are aiming at a common goal.

Contact with other professionals

There will be many other persons who, in their professional capacity, contribute towards the successful outcome of the placement. The general practitioner might be a vital person in giving help and support to the adoptive family and to the new arrival, especially if the new child suffers from any handicap or medical problem. It is essential that he is kept fully informed of progress and is put in touch with doctors who previously cared for the child.

Teachers spend a large part of each day with children; so, once again, early contact with the school can add greatly to success. The adoptive family may already have a good relationship with the school, and are able to build on this when the new child arrives. However, if the child has to attend a different or a special school, the social worker may need to help the family to establish contact. It can be helpful to have direct contact between new and former education establishments, thus ensuring a smooth transfer of school and the placing of the child in a class suited to his abilities.

One does not want to convey the impression that there will be difficulties and perhaps make the school look for problems which do not exist. Equally, to give no information about a child's past experience and academic achievement can make the task of the teacher doubly difficult. There are some details which the child himself will want to keep secret, and discussion with him about what to reveal and what to withhold could be appropriate.

Confirming permanency of the new relationship

This must be a joint decision of all concerned: child, family, and both social workers. The granting of an adoption order or custody order should not mean that 'the case is closed'. It may be several years before the family no longer feel the need of some support from the social worker, but the fact of legal recognition can have a bonding effect upon the new unit. Parents and children can be reassured that all is going well and that they are trusted, by putting into legal terms something which they all feel. It is possible that the greater success of placement for adoption of older children, as opposed to placement for fostering of such children, is mainly due to the fact that everyone concerned acknowledges the permanency of the new relationship, by agreeing to the adoption. If a family have been made to feel that they can seek help and advice, despite the fact that an adoption order or custody order has been granted, they may readily do so when they need it.

There are various ways of offering help and support, apart from home visiting. Informal discussion groups of substitute parents, perhaps with other discussions for adolescents, can give mutual support. Sometimes other members of the group can offer help and advice which seems specially relevant, as the individuals concerned may have faced similar issues. These shared experiences can also be valuable to social workers, since this is a way in which they obtain feedback and increase their experience. Such discussion groups can also provide an 'early warning' system of problems ahead.

The assimilation of an older child into his new family will inevitably be slower than that of a baby. There is a danger in pushing people into relationships for which they are not yet ready, but each case must be looked at individually. There should be no set rules that a period of fostering must always precede a notification of intention to adopt, and the plan could be that the probationary period is extended rather than preceded by boarding-out. Each step has great significance to the family and is an indication to them that initial intentions are being carried through. When families are ready to proceed to the next stage, this should happen quickly and not be delayed by administrative procedures.

It is, however, important that all members of the family are ready to acknowledge the changing relationships. One twelve-year-old boy, very used to sharing his parents with short-stay foster children, was not at all keen on acknowledging that one child could become a permanent new member of the family. A family faces a risk to itself and its existing relationships whenever it admits a permanent new member, and especially when the new member does not arrive as a baby but has defined likes, dislikes and a will of his own.

Handling the question of names

The changing of a child's name can be a very significant factor in placement. Foster children often suffer from dilemmas in these situations; and I know of one child at a residential school who saw his name changing each time he crossed the suspension bridge on the car journey between home and school. Whilst at home, he sensed his foster parents' wish that he be known by their name, showing that he was an integral part of the family, but at school he was always referred to by his original name. Similarly, a child and his new family may regard the change of surname as indicative of the acceptance by all that the child is now a full member of his new family. If a child has a special attachment to his old surname, he may wish to retain this in some way, perhaps by keeping it as a middle name.

First names can equally be changed upon adoption. Although most children will probably want to retain that name by which they are usually known, they may wish to keep or change other names. The child himself should be consulted, as well as his new parents.

If a child is old enough to comprehend, it is important that he be agreeable to the changes and involved in the discussions. No new name should be forced upon the child just to please the parents, since they must accept the child 'warts and all', even if one of the warts is a name they do not like.

With younger children, changes of name have been achieved over a period of time. One couple preceded the child's old name by the new one they had chosen, and soon the two-year-old responded to his new name, without any apparent upset at losing the old one. Another couple wanted to reverse the order of the first names and again achieved this by using both for a while, then slowly dropping the less favoured.

Contact with former caretakers or family members

Some children wish and need to retain contact with former caretakers or members of the extended family; and adoption does not preclude this contact. One adoptive family commented that they would love to have another granny around and could fully understand why this continuing contact was important to the child concerned. In this case granny became a regular visitor to the new family home. In other cases it may be better for contact to take place in some neutral situation, the local park, a visit to the zoo, or even the social worker's office if this possesses the informal surroundings which will make all feel at ease. The fact of adoption may help the new family to continue such contact, since they no longer view the relatives' interest as a threat to remove the child at a later date.

Contact with former caretakers may be equally important. This could be the first time that the child has been able to go back to his former home. He may find security in knowing that everything has not disappeared because he has left a place; and he can tell them about his experiences. Equally the former caretakers and other children can be reassured that all is going well for the child with his new family; and this reassurance conveys itself to the child and family, who continue to strengthen the new relationship.

There may be occasions when this contact should be at the new home. The former caretakers and the child might find visits to the children's Home or foster home too painful or disruptive because of the presence of other children. The child may want to show off his new family and home, and the houseparents can more easily see him as part of his new family in his new surroundings. One child of eight put it very clearly when on a visit to the children's Home where she formerly lived, saying, 'It's been very nice to see you all again and I'll probably write to you, but now I've got a new bed you can use my old one!'

It is important that former caretakers are not only involved fully in the planning stages, but also in the successful outcome of those plans. Letter and telephone contact may need to replace face-to-face meetings, especially if long distances are involved, but we should not underestimate the value to all concerned of such contacts. There are times when only the former caretakers can help the new parents to understand the behaviour patterns or remarks of a child, since they relate to a joint experience, unknown to the social workers concerned. However, one can have too much contact with the former home; I can think of one situation where the placement failed, possibly because the frequent and regular contact led everyone to believe that the new situation need not be a permanent one.

The way in which a child views his former home can tell us a great deal about his feelings for his new family. One little boy of three years talked first about returning to see his former foster parents, but as he became more settled, he talked of their coming to see him, thus indicating that he saw his new placement as permanent.

Talking of past experiences

There are many questions surrounding this area, and once again there cannot be set patterns. Sometimes a child does not want to talk of the past whilst he is trying to make a future by concentrating on present relationships. It could be easier for the child to think about former relationships when he is really sure about the present ones, e.g., after legalisation. Similarly, the adoptive parents may be able to cope with such discussions when they know their new child really belongs to them. Mary's adoptive mother said, 'I knew she really trusted me and was one of us when she started to talk of the unhappy time she had when she left her foster home. She never mentioned it for the first three months, yet I knew she was thinking about it sometimes.'

Although the child's social worker needs to give the new parents information about his past, so that they can help him to put experiences into place, we must not forget the child's right to confidentiality. Equally, he may want to be the first person to tell his new parents what occurred before he came to them. The social worker should, wherever possible, discuss with the child what he wants his new parents to know before placement. The use of scrapbooks, photograph albums, etc. can be an important asset to this. One child wanted his baby photographs to go into the new family's photo album with the ones of other children in the family. He was trying hard to show that he was part of his new family, and this was agreed to. Another child wanted to keep his scrapbook intact, and copies were made to allow him to show his links with both families.

Another way in which the former history can be put into context was described by a mother, in a discussion group for prospective adopters, who said, 'If you keep in touch with his granny she can help him fit the jigsaw together, that's a definite advantage of keeping up old contacts.' This may also be a reason for keeping some contact with a former social worker. Another useful asset is writing down information which the child and his new family might otherwise forget. This has important implications for the way we keep our records. The most precious possession of one child in care was the photograph of his dead mother, as it unlocked all sorts of doors to talk about his future as well as his past.

Conclusion

The placement of children in substitute families is not an easy task, and imposes stress upon social workers to ensure that sufficient care goes into the preparation and continuing support for placements to be successful. It does seem that the most success is achieved when the whole family is prepared to face and adjust to change. The social worker's role in the placement of older children is very much an enabling one. The real work is done by the new family, which has to make the necessary adaptations to include a new member. Some adjustments take longer, and like a 'mobile' a family is never static. It faces challenges for change and adaptation all the time. The perception of time varies greatly with age, and sometimes children adjust before the adults.

References

1 V. Satir, *Conjoint Family Therapy*, Science and Behaviour Books, Cupertino, Calif., 1967

2 R. Parker, *Decision in Child Care*, Allen & Unwin, London, 1966.

John Triseliotis

14 Counselling adoptees

The 1975 Children Act (Section 26), which came into effect in January 1977, enables persons who have been adopted in England and Wales (at least eighteen years old) to apply, if they wish, to the Registrar General for information from the original record of their birth. Those adopted before the Act was passed in 1975, now wishing for access to their original birth records, are required by the Act to have a meeting with a counsellor before such information is made available. For those adopted after November 1975 counselling is optional.

In Scotland, adopted people for many years had the right, on attaining the age of seventeen, to obtain a copy of their original birth record by applying to the Registrar General. They also had the right of access to the court records of their adoption proceedings, on application to the court who made the adoption order. The 1975 Children Act has not changed this. The Act provides for counselling being made available to adopted people in Scotland; but because there is no retrospection, counselling is not compulsory. The adoptee may seek counselling either retrospectively or prospectively, if he so wishes. The Scottish provision, which was in the first Adoption Act 1929, had nothing to do with the adopted person's possible psychological needs. It was merely a way of facilitating issues concerned with inheritance.

The compulsory nature of the English provision was devised to calm the anxieties of those who felt that some adoptees might misuse the information made available, perhaps to harass unaware natural parents, the implication being that the counsellor can act both as an enabler but also as a restraining influence on those adoptees who may contemplate vindictive ways of going about the search for the first parents.

Information from the birth records will give the adoptee his original name, when and where born, and the name and address of the mother at the time the birth was registered. The father's name was normally not included on the birth certificate unless the child was born within wedlock. If the mother was married to a man other than the father, his name was sometimes given. It was also not uncommon for the occupation of the natural mother and of the father, where he was included, to be recorded. These records make it theoretically possible for adoptees who so wish to set out to trace the original parent(s). When the adopted person lets the Registrar General know which agency he chooses, the former will send the appropriate information there.

The adopted person can choose to see a counsellor at Register House (for England and Wales), at the nearest local authority Social Service Department, or at the local authority in whose area the court granted the adoption order. Voluntary adoption societies had not yet, at the time of writing, been approved to carry out such counselling duties. The advantage of calling at the agency who arranged the adoption, whether voluntary or local authority, is that it should have fuller background information from its own records, and should be able to share it with the adopted person. This also applies to the local authority where the court who granted the order sat. It should have records taken at the time the application was made. These records are, however, not uniform and sometimes they may be difficult to trace. Some agencies are also known to have destroyed records. The object of a meeting with a counsellor is officially seen as being to help the adopted person to obtain the information he needs, including any further information if it is available, with the minimum of frustration; and also to ensure that the adopted person has considered the possible effect both on himself and on others of any further enquiries he may wish to make.

The compulsory element in the new law raised many issues about the nature of counselling and how useful it can be to 'involuntary' adoptees. This may be so, but on the other hand many of these adopted people had been trying for years to obtain some information about their origins, and they came up against blank walls. They felt despondent, frustrated and often angry. Provided the compulsory aspect of counselling is not abused, the experience could prove beneficial to adoptees. When an adopted person meets with the counsellor, this is an indication that he accepts counselling, and the counsellor has an obligation to pass on the information at his disposal. The counsellor has no right, for instance, to withhold information on account of the adoptee's reluctance to state his motives for the search or share aspects from his personal life. This form of compulsory counselling is based on the belief that the adoptee will use the opportunity not only to obtain the information without red tape, but that he may also reflect, if he so wishes, on his adoptive situation, react to the information, and consider various implications arising from a possible search for reunion with the first parents.

Though the basic role of the counsellor has a legal origin, where necessary it can be widened to encompass needs that go beyond mere information giving. Besides the seeking of information there may be other unexpressed needs surrounding the whole issue of adoption, but the initiative for mentioning these should rest with the adopted person. The decision on the part of the adoptee to use the opportunity for ventilation or reflection will depend on the kind of expectations he has and the kind of pressures or stresses he may be under, as well as on the attitude and person of the counsellor. It would be wrong to assume that all those seeking access to their birth records are also in need of counselling. Experience, however, suggests that many will wish to explore with another person deeply felt needs or views surrounding their adoption and their birth parents. An experienced counsellor could be of considerable help at a time of crisis.

The right to know

In recent years we have seen an upsurge of minority groups insisting on greater equality of rights with majority groups. In the USA there are at least two strong activist groups demanding right of access to their birth records. The changes in English legislation in 1975 were based on our research in Scotland, which demonstrated the value of the Scottish provision. All adopted people want to learn about their parents of origin and to establish continuity between past and present. A tiny minority may also wish to meet their birth parents. Adoptees need to trace their roots, establish their identity, and generally place themselves in relation to their present self and past heritage. The undue secrecy built into successive adoption laws in many countries deprived the adopted persons of true autonomy and independence, and may have contributed towards creating in adoptees feelings of inferiority and second-class citizenship.

It is recognised that some of this secrecy was thought necessary at one time to protect adopted children from the stigma of illegitimacy.

Attitudes towards illegitimacy, at least in the West, have changed considerably over the last ten to twenty years, and greater openness is sought in matters of genealogy, adoption arrangements and agency practices. It is also claimed that some natural parents who gave up children for adoption would like information about them in later years. Obviously the needs and desires of all parties to the adoption should be respected, and information and support offered to adoptee, birth parents and adoptive parents alike.

Though a moral dilemma presents itself in the case of natural and adoptive parents who were assured that the agencies and the law would protect their anonymity, it could also be argued that the adopted child was not a party to the agreement and therefore cannot be bound by these contracts for life. In my own view, the wish to know and have information is a basic natural right that should not be taken away from adopted people. The right to know is further strengthened by the fact that many of those seeking access to their birth records in our Scottish study were doing so because their adoptive parents failed to tell them about their adoption. This was greatly resented by the adoptees. Evidence suggests that however well adoptive parents are prepared and however many promises they make, when it comes to the crunch a tiny minority will fail to tell the children of their true status. Even in the case of some children who were recently adopted when aged between two and four and who could be expected to retain memories, their adoptive parents had not told them of their true status by the age of eight. Equally to blame were, in the past, adoption agencies which withheld or distorted the information given to adopters in the misguided view that they were protecting the interests of all the parties involved.

My own research with adopted people seeking access to their birth records in Scotland has convinced me of how important and necessary it is for adopted people to know about their heritage and to have as much meaningful information as possible about their genealogical background. All adopted people have a deep psychological need to know about their families of origin and this need must be satisfied by the adoptive family. This information is of vital importance to enable the adopted person from early on to build his developing identity on the concept of two sets of families. In addition, adopted people want to know the circumstances of their adoption and why they were given up. This type of information, sensitively shared, can help the adoptee to come to terms with feelings of loss and rejection by the biological family. Where these psychological needs are not satisfied, there is an increased probability that the adopted person will try to find out for himself and even seek out the first parents. For most adoptees the search for information for the first parents is an emotionally draining experience and it is not entered upon lightly. We have similarly found that the adoptive parents' fear of losing the adopted child is unfounded. The adoptive parents are the only real psychological parents to the adopted person. Furthermore, the search by the adopted person often helps to cement the relationship with the adoptive parents, which is now accepted from a perspective more meaningful to them.

Motivation for the search

The Scottish study identified two main groups of adoptees who gained access to their original birth records. To begin with the largest group (60 per cent) were searching for background information but were also hoping that the information would enable them to locate their first parents. A reunion with the first parents was desired by most of these adoptees. The second group (40 per cent) were only interested in background information about their parentage and genealogy because none or very little had been made available before. (There were also a couple of adoptees who needed the information in connection with medical issues where possible hereditary factors were suspected.) Experience so far suggests that broadly similar reasons are prevalent amongst adopted people seeking access to their birth records from the Registrar General's office in England.

Adopted people in general share an obvious curiosity about their origins and roots. It is the kind of curiosity that stays with them until the end. However, the intensity of this varies considerably, and it is not always translated into a search. In fact the final search seems to be a minority response. The Scottish study found that only about two per thousand of adopted adults got in touch with Register House prior to 1972. The considerable publicity that surrounded Section 26 of the 1975 Children Act dramatically increased these figures from around 60 in the late 1960s to 144 in 1975, and 254 in 1977. Following the introduction of Section 26 in England and Wales in January 1977, there was a flood of applications at the beginning, but these dropped considerably within the next six months. When the Scottish study took place, the number of those enquiring and their motives had not yet been influenced and perhaps distorted by the considerable publicity of the mid-1970s. The assumption is that those enquiring before the early 1970s were mostly motivated by some intense psychological need. The increased figures suggest that either adopted people in the past did not know how to obtain access to information, or that under the flare of considerable publicity some adoptees came to feel 'different' if they too did not set out on a quest. Among those enquiring in 1977 in both England and Scotland, two out of every three were women, though in general more males are adopted than females. Similarly, approximately two out of every three of those enquiring were aged between twenty-five and thirty-nine. Only just under 5 per cent were aged eighteen to twenty.

All adoptees appear to have a deep psychological need to know about their origins and heritage. They also retain a certain amount of curiosity about their birth parents. The wish to search, however, is usually associated with the adopted person's self-image, the quality of relationships in the adoptive home, the timing of telling, the amount and type of genealogical information made available, and with the impact of recent events or personal crises, e.g., bereavement, loss, separation, pregnancies. Adoptees who have a positive self-image, who have experienced a happy home life and to whom information about their parentage and the circumstances of their adoption has been made available by the adoptive parents, and who have not experienced a recent intense crisis, are less likely to feel the need to seek reunions.

Though the Scottish study found that a great number of those searching at the time were under some personal or social pressure, it would be wrong to assume that those who set out on such a quest are necessarily under stress. Sheer curiosity can sometimes act as a spur for some adoptees, particularly when considerable publicity is being given to the subject. Among some married couples, a fair amount of the curiosity and insistence to search was fanned by the other non-adopted spouse who wanted to satisfy his or her curiosity.

The search, for most adoptees, represents an attempt to establish their roots and their genealogy and thus to 'complete' themselves. They feel that some part of their identity and self is missing, and they wish to collect and piece together information that could help them to understand themselves better. Some will not be satisfied with just additional information and their desire will be for a reunion with one or both of the first parents. In meetings and reunions they may be looking for a relationship, for 'love' or for 'comfort', or simply to see what the people who gave birth to them 'look like'. The available evidence suggests that the more unsettled the adoptee the more likely it is that he will be looking for reunion, but that not all those seeking reunions are necessarily unsettled. Sometimes an adoptee who starts with a wish to find more information decides to take the next step and search for the original parents. A smaller number who initially set out to meet one or both of the original parents drop their plans because of disappointment at what they found so far.

Many of those enquiring in Scotland grew up in families where there was a deliberate effort to hide from them the fact of their adoption. There was an equal reluctance to share any available information about the family of origin. The secrecy and evasiveness of adoptive parents only served to make the adoptees more determined to establish the 'truth'. The evasiveness and deception referred to here were usually, but not exclusively, associated with unhappy and unsatisfactory relationships between the adoptee and his adoptive family. The quality of relationships was, in fact, more important than the fact of telling and the amount of information being revealed. (The assumption by some writers that it is only childless couples who have problems in telling because of their feelings about infertility was not borne out by this study.) Yet the search in the end was usually triggered off by a recent crisis in the adoptee's life, such as death in the family, serious illness, separation, or the happier event of pregnancy or birth of a child. Because of the retrospective nature of the English legislation, it is apparent that many of those who for years were frustrated because they could not obtain information may try to do so now, even where the original crisis may have faded away.

Some of the adoptees who set out on the search may wish to share feelings surrounding their adoption and reflect on their situation. They may have never talked to anyone else before about their adoption. A frequent question they ask is 'Why was I put up for adoption?'. This question hides a further one, namely 'Was I wanted before I was given up?'. The wish to know if he was wanted and loved before being given up is of fundamental importance to the adopted person. To be given up when wanted seems to feel less distressing than the knowledge of being abandoned or rejected. The knowledge of being wanted or loved seems to enhance a positive self-image. Other possible questions will include 'Who am I?'.

> I often look into the mirror and ask myself, 'Who am I? Who were my first parents? What were they like?' I feel as though something is missing from me.

The concept of a whole person is made up of many bits of experience, knowledge and influences, including the history of one's genealogy and the myths and culture of one's country.

> It is like a jigsaw puzzle – not knowing about the stock I come from is like a missing piece from the puzzle.

Other adoptees will want to speculate on how life would have been for them had they stayed with their first parents. 'I wonder where I would be now? Meeting my mother or father would help me understand.' This does not mean that adoptees have no feelings for their adoptive parents. Far from it. Even in situations of very poor relationships within the adoptive family we found that most adoptees' first loyalty was to the people who brought them up, and not to an imaginary set of natural parents. It is for this reason that often adoptees leave the search until after the death of one or both adoptive parents; or if the adoptive parents are still alive they want to make sure the latter will not be upset by knowledge of the search.

> The parents who matter are the people who bring you up. Not those who gave birth to you. I only want to find out what sort of people my birth parents were, but I wouldn't like my adoptive parents to know because they might be upset.

Obviously, where relationships become too sour or where the adoptive parents are dead, the hope of a new nurturing relationship is always around: 'We might be able to do something for each other. . . start a relationship or something.'

The kind of ventilation and reflection described above sometimes helps to clarify feelings and to dispel distortions. It can free adoptees to look at their situations in a new way or with new understanding. Some will react to the information given by the counsellor, ponder over it or wish to rehash it. Every piece of information will have some special meaning, especially if it is the first time they came across it. The clarification of feelings surrounding adoption and the opportunity sometimes to vent angry feelings towards the 'parents who gave you up' can make those seeking reunions become more understanding of their birth parents. They may then continue the search in a more positive frame of mind.

The presentation of information

The counsellor's aim should be to clarify the kind of information the adoptee is interested in and to pass it on, if it is at his disposal. Though it is preferable to share the information within the space of a single interview, the pace of doing this will have to vary to take account of the adopted person's reactions. Some information is likely to cause considerable upset to some, and it would be inappropriate to press on more facts without giving the person time to reflect. Adoptees who happen to share in advance their expectations and hopes from the search offer the counsellor the opportunity to listen and sometimes to prepare them for possibly 'painful' facts.

Some adopted people become very disappointed when they hear that their natural mother was, for instance, a maid or a shoe-shop assistant and not the titled or professional person they imagined her to be. They may feel embarrassed and 'shamed' before their spouses and in-laws. There are those who are upset to discover they were born illegitimate. Some may have never before connected their adoption with illegitimacy. Much time can be spent ventilating feelings surrounding illegitimacy and fears about its possible 'transmission' to offspring.

Some adoptees may react to the knowledge that they were legitimate. Those born within wedlock may ponder and find it difficult to understand how married couples can ever part with their children. The suspicion that enters their mind is that they were not wanted or loved. The counsellor can play a very positive role by being able to put across how circumstances can at times make some parents take decisions or act in ways that it is difficult for others to understand. Even in the case of the mother who deserted her children or the father who went to prison it is difficult to understand the circumstances at the time that prompted them to act in ways that had distressing effects on their children. It helps many adoptees to hear that, with few exceptions, parents who give up their children also love them, and parting is a harrowing experience. Even the simple fact of explaining to some that, contrary to what they thought, illegitimacy is not something that 'runs in the blood' can be very reassuring to them. The counsellor can sometimes enlighten, put across a view or reassurance, which offers the adoptee the opportunity to reflect on his situation from another perspective.

There can be many distressing moments during the counselling period. The counsellor's response is to try to understand, to listen patiently and to share sensitively what further information he has at his disposal. To withhold information on the assumption that the adoptee must come back again, and perhaps again, would amount to a sort of 'means test' and face the adoptee with a repetition of the type of evasiveness that he came up against all his life. Many adoptive parents withhold either the fact of adoption or information surrounding the circumstances of adoption under the misguided view that it is the best way to protect the child and avoid hurting it. Yet all the adoptees we interviewed emphatically said that they wanted to know the truth, however hurtful it was.

> You come to terms with the truth eventually, but evasiveness only fosters fantasy and suspicion.

The postponement of sharing information may exceptionally be justified in the case of an adoptee who is so distressed that he cannot take any more and asks to come again. Otherwise it should be entirely left to the adoptee to decide whether to take up the offer for further discussions or not. Experience, both from the Scottish system and the operation of the English one so far, indicates that quite a number of adopted people eagerly accept the offer of one or more meetings to take stock of everything that has been said. Others will return after they start a search for reunions, and will want to keep the counsellor informed and even ask for 'advice' about possible courses of action. The counsellor can help them to look at their situation in different ways, clarify emotions that cloud judgment and perceptions, and offer the possibility of wider choices. Some of the adopted people will want to use the opportunity to review an important aspect of their lives, and generally try to understand their situation and themselves better with someone they have come to trust. Once information is obtained, an almost lifelong effort comes to an end and some adoptees are left with feelings of 'emptiness'. They can be at breakdown point. The search in their case served as a purpose in life, and once over it has to be replaced either by contentment or something else. When adoptees appear to be under too much stress, the counsellor may have to urge them to obtain further help.

Satisfactions and dissatisfactions from the search

Information about the birth-place, including the original parents' most permanent address, fills many adoptees with tremendous satisfaction and expectations: 'At least I can now say where I come from and where I was born.' 'Where I work people often say "I come from Lancashire, or Devon", and then, "Where do you come from?" Now I can tell them.' Whilst some adoptees use the address of the natural parent as a means of placing themselves in terms of their origins, others will want to use it to pursue reunions.

Many of those seeking information about their adoption and their genealogy will express disappointment at the dearth of available facts from Register House. They will want to know more, and they will ask how they can find out. For many it is the detail about their 'family tree' and first parents that matters most, not simply names and addresses: information, such as about the sort of people the birth parents were, their physical characteristics, their interests; e.g., she was a good ice skater, or he liked playing the flute, or she liked dressmaking. Detailed information brings people to life, and it is then easier to accommodate the information within oneself. Such information is not available in the birth records, nor perhaps in any records held by courts or placing agencies. Adoptees will want to hear from the counsellor where and how they can obtain more information. Sometimes it is the absence of meaningful information about their heritage that drives them further towards reunions. The counsellor needs to respond as an enabler and use his knowledge and experience to link the adopted persons to sources where additional information may be available. Alternatively, he could try to obtain it for them, to avoid sending the adoptees to different agencies. The counsellor's bargaining power in cutting through administrative procedures could be greater than that of the adopted person.

There are two sources where some additional information may be found. The first is the agency that arranged the adoption. Depending on what the agency's practice was twenty to fifty years ago, there may be considerable, little or no information, provided the files are still being kept. The counsellor can refer the adoptee to the original agency, but it is still not certain how adoption agencies will receive such referrals. The hope is that agencies will follow the example of the law and become more open and willing to share information from their files without applying unnecessary controls. Where appropriate it should be possible for them to send the information to the counsellor who started the process, to avoid long journeys and unnecessary transfers.

The second source of additional information is, of course, the court where the adoption order was made. Depending on how thorough the reports of the supervising agency and of the curator were, there may again be considerable, little or no substantive information. (In Scotland, until recently, it was exceptional for the supervising agency to submit a report to the court. Similarly, most curators' reports were found to be stereotyped and with little or no individualised information.) Permission to open the sealed records has to be obtained from the court, to which the adoptee must apply. No clear pattern has so far emerged concerning the courts' attitude to such requests. The kind of information to be shared from the court records is usually left to the discretion of the judge or magistrate.

Those seeking reunions will use the names of the parent(s) and the original address to search for them. They will want to ask the counsellor how they can go about locating their first parent(s). The counsellor's role again is to give all possible facilitating information, whilst also engaging the adoptee in discussion about how he proposes to go about the search. They can then jointly examine possibilities and implications. The fostering of some foresight through exploration and discussion can help towards safeguarding the feelings of all those involved in the adoption situation, i.e., the first parents, the adoptive parents and the adopted person. Again it is not the counsellor's job to put off people from searching, but to look into the various implications and possible distress that may be caused, something that adoptees usually want to examine.

The Scottish study, confirmed by the recent English experience, found that almost all adoptees who were seeking reunions were very concerned not to go about it in a way that would cause pain to any parent. Even adoptees who had nobody else in life to fall back on wanted to approach their first parent(s) through the help of a third person who might be able to establish some initial contact. We came across no evidence of blackmail or vindictiveness, and no such accounts have appeared in any of the national newspapers. (The portrayal of 'adopted' children as 'vindictive' and 'ungrateful' in some British literature of the nineteenth and early twentieth centuries, particularly in the novels of Thomas Hardy, such as *Desperate Remedies, The Laodicean* and *Tess,* is not confirmed by actual experience and facts.) The official leaflet (*Notes for Counsellors*) describes situations in which a counsellor may act as mediator in making contact with natural parents. Even better placed to arrange such contacts is a counsellor attached to the agency that made the original placement.

If the natural parent is no longer living at the address given on the birth certificate, the adoptee is likely to go into all kinds of efforts to locate him/her. Telephone directories, electoral rolls, street directories, death registers, the engagement of a private detective, and other similar routes are being pursued in the quest. (For a remarkable American experience describing one person's search, readers are referred to Anne Fisher's account of her attempts to locate her parents in *The Search for Anne Fisher*.) In Britain the following agencies are willing to receive letters from natural parents and from adopted people in the hope of linking them up. *Contact:* 93 Rudston Avenue, Wolnston Court Estate, Billingham, Cleveland TS22 5BLO. *Link-up*: 6 Roseland Crescent, Truro. The Society of Genealogists at 37 Harrington Gardens, London SW7, may exceptionally be of assistance to some.

A more dignified way of pursuing reunions might be devised in future to take account of the feelings of both the adoptees and of the natural parent(s). The present desperate efforts of some adoptees to establish contact with natural parents are certainly not enjoyed by the adoptees. With a minimum of expense and red tape it should be possible to set up an official register in which both the original parent(s) and the adoptee, if they desired reunion, could enter their names. When both sides entered their names and addresses, then the registrar would inform the parties concerned. The parties should be free to up-date the entry; that is, if an adoptee entered his name in the register, thus indicating his desire for reunion, he could always ask for the entry to be erased at a later stage. This type of approach could also serve to resolve some of the moral dilemmas inherent in the present process, mainly that it is unfair to the natural parent, who has not got a similar right for access to adoption records.

Evidence about reunions so far suggests that in their vast majority they do not work out, and few permanent relationships are formed as a result. In fact, for some adoptees a new set of complications are raised. But adoptees who have been successful in contacting one or both natural parents claim that the meeting(s) helped them to understand themselves better, and to come to terms with their situation.

> At least I know where I stand now.
>
> I have no regrets about it. I hope my first mother also feels like this . . .

Further contacts wouldn't work, we were like two strangers meeting.

One of the values of reunions is that they offer the adopted person the opportunity to re-examine his feelings of rejection and anger towards the first parent(s), and perhaps to 'forgive' them. In return the natural parents may feel glad for the opportunity to deal with possible feelings of guilt and self-blame.

Conclusion

Agencies and practitioners should not come to view this form of counselling as relevant only at the time adoptees embark on a search for their origins. Much could be done by providing counselling opportunities at an earlier stage. There is no apparent reason why voluntary or statutory agencies should not provide this service to any adoptee who wishes to discuss issues about his adoption or his first parents. This may be especially helpful when such questions arise in adolescence. The adopted person alone, or with his adoptive parents, should be able to visit the adoption agency, preferably the one that arranged the placement, and ask to discuss his adoption with a counsellor from the agency. Agency records could be made available and non-identifiable information shared without undue secrecy or reservations. Openness and sensitive handling at this stage could make unnecessary later searches, as a lot of the curiosity, confusion and uncertainty will have already been tackled and clarified. It is also hoped that agencies will offer a similar service to natural parents who may wish to have information about the children they surrendered years earlier. Natural parents should have an equal right of access to information as the adopted adult.

Note

This chapter draws from research which appeared in *'In Search of Origins'*, by John Triseliotis (Routledge & Kegan Paul, 1973); and from discussions the writer had with adopted adults in countries outside Britain. Reference is also made to the DHSS circular LA(76)21 of 3 November 1976. I am also indebted to Cyril Day, Counsellor at Register House, London, for his observations and comments on my paper.

Select bibliography

Adamson, G., *The Caretakers,* Bookstall Publications, Bristol, 1973.

Association of British Adoption and Fostering Agencies, *Child Adoption,* 1977.

Berry, J., *Social Work with Children,* Routledge & Kegan Paul, London, 1972.

Charnley, J., *The Art of Child Placement,* University of Minneapolis Press, 1955.

Cornish, D. B. and Clarke, R. V. G., *Residential Treatment and its Effects on Delinquents,* HMSO, London, 1975.

Department of Health and Social Security, *Guide to Fostering Practice,* HMSO, London, 1976.

Dinnage, R. and Kellmer-Pringle, M. L., *Foster Home Care: Facts and Fallacies,* Longmans, London, 1967.

George, V., *Foster Care: Theory and Practice,* Routledge & Kegan Paul, London, 1970.

Heywood, J., *Children in Care,* Routledge & Kegan Paul, London, 3rd edition, 1978.

Holman, R., *Trading in Children,* Routledge & Kegan Paul, London, 1973.

Jenkins, S. and Norman, E., *Filial Deprivation and Foster Care,* Columbia University Press, New York, 1973.

Jones, M., Neuman, R. and Shyne, A., *A Second Chance for Families,* Child Welfare League of America, 1976.

Kadushin, A. *Adopting Older Children,* Columbia University Press, New York, 1970.

Kellmer-Pringle, M. L., *Deprivation and Education,* Longmans, London, 1965.

Kline, D. and Overstreet, H. M. F., *Foster Care of Children – Nurture and Treatment*, Columbia University Press, New York, 1972.

Packman, J., *The Child's Generation,* Blackwell, Oxford, 1975.

Page, R. and Clark, G. A., *Who Cares?* National Children's Bureau, 1977.

Parker, R., *Decision in Child Care,* Allen & Unwin, London, 1966.

Raynor, L., *Adoption of Non-White Children,* Allen & Unwin, London, 1970.

Rowe, J. and Lambert, L., *Children Who Wait,* ABAFA, 1973.

Seglow, J., Kellmer-Pringle, M. L. and Wedge, P., *Growing Up Adopted,* National Foundation for Educational Research in England and Wales, 1972.

Sherman, E., Neuman, R. and Shyne, A., *Children Adrift in Foster Care: A Study of Alternative Approaches, Child Welfare League of America, 1973.*

Timms, N., The Receiving End, Routledge and Kegan Paul, London, 1973.

Tizard, B., *Adoption – a Second Chance,* Open Books, London, 1977.

Trasler, G., *In Place of Parents,* Routledge & Kegan Paul, London, 1960.

Triseliotis, J., *In Search of Origins,* Routledge & Kegan Paul, London, 1973.

Weinstein, E., *The Self Image of the Foster Child,* Russell Sage Foundation, 1960.

West, D. J. and Farrington, D. P., *The Delinquent Way of Life,* Heinemann, London, 1977.

Winnicott, C., *Child Care and Social Work,* Bookstall Publications, 1970.

Index